COMMUNITY DEVELOPMENT
IN ACTION
Putting Freire into practice

Margaret Ledwith

P

First published in Great Britain in 2016 by

Policy Press   North American office:
University of Bristol   Policy Press
1-9 Old Park Hill   c/o The University of Chicago Press
Bristol BS2 8BB   1427 East 60th Street
UK   Chicago, IL 60637, USA
t: +44 (0)117 954 5940   t: +1 773 702 7700
e: pp-info@bristol.ac.uk   f: +1 773-702-9756
www.policypress.co.uk   e:sales@press.uchicago.edu
                                       www.press.uchicago.edu

© Policy Press 2016

Reprinted 2016

British Library Cataloguing in Publication Data
A catalogue record for this book is available from the British Library.

Library of Congress Cataloging-in-Publication Data
A catalog record for this book has been requested.

ISBN 978-1-84742-875-2 paperback
ISBN 978-1-84742-876-9 hardcover
ISBN 978-1-4473-1224-6 ePub
ISBN 978-1-4473-1225-3 Mobi

Cover design by Andrew Corbett
Front cover: image kindly supplied by istock
Printed and bound by CPI Group (UK) Ltd, Croydon, CR0 4YY
Policy Press uses environmentally responsible print partners

For my family

Grace, Steve, Duncan, Gavin

and Sebastian

Other books by Margaret Ledwith

(2011) *Community development: A critical approach* (2nd edn), Bristol: Policy Press.

(2010) *Participatory practice: Community-based action for transformative change*, Bristol: Policy Press.

(1997) *Participating in transformation: Towards a working model of community empowerment*, Birmingham: Venture Press.

Contents

List of figures

Foreword

I could not pass up the opportunity to write this foreword for Margaret Ledwith's book, *Community development in action: Putting Freire into practice*. It is a joy to see that, through her work over the years and now this book in particular, my husband Paulo Freire, is again being studied and used as a reference point for those who think, desire and act in the struggle towards the UTOPIA of a better, fairer and truly peaceful world.

As modern capitalism reveals itself to be a system leading the world to chaos, it has become obvious that the wealthy countries and individuals become wealthier, and the poorer countries become poorer, generating unprecedented injustices of all kinds. One can no longer hide from the fact that the inequalities between countries and peoples today are more dramatic than ever before.

This new infrastructure and superstructure, this new manner of social organisation, has shown itself to be equally cruel to the other beings of nature. What I mean is that to obtain these distortions, the 'holders of power' have been mercilessly and unscrupulously destroying Planet Earth for their own enrichment. This has led to widespread suffering from lack of food and water, the propagation of disease, malnutrition, desperation, hopelessness and the death of millions, especially in Africa and Latin America; in short, inflicting suffering and bitterness of absolutely subhuman levels.

Fortunately, those who have compassion and concern for all the earth's inhabitants focus their reflections on the everyday nature of this violence, which I stress is triggered and generated at the core of and because of neoliberalism and the globalisation of the economy. The organised counter-hegemonic society has, in truth, grasped the need for a deeper reflection about this cruel reality, which affects everybody indiscriminately if they belong not to the elite, but to the more socially underprivileged strata.

A question has hovered among these minds thirsty for freedom and justice. One such mind, for sure, is that of Margaret Ledwith, who asked: who will come to underpin the *theoretical thinking and practical tasks* that throw light onto the humanist option of LIFE? Where can we turn for ideas to inform action against this everyday violence?

Margaret has found the answers to these questions in the voice of my husband, who sought to return the *humanity stolen* from men and women.

In this book, Margaret encourages us to re-engage with Paulo's work in theory and praxis, reflecting on this work in order to rebel against the devious and overbearing discourse of those who think only of themselves and their equals. Using his most radically humanist substantive theory, this book is designed to assist, not to 'assistencialise'*, the militants of the 'communities in action'.

Margaret believes in Freire's hope and in the possibility of a better world that annihilates the wrongs caused by those who do not love, do not think of others as human beings as such, who are incapable of acts of generosity and solidarity of any kind, under any circumstances. Drawing on his work, Margaret shows that with Freire we are able to build a world that can develop through a sustainable environment and social justice. A world that brings joy and cordiality among one another and peace in social relations, even accounting for the contradictions inherent in the human condition. By means of cartoons, photographs and local stories, Margaret shows us how we can apply Paulo's work in practice, *raising awareness* of injustice and paving the way to a dignified and dignifying society.

Margaret believes in empowering the community (never empowering the individual, as this would only reproduce the vertical relationship of command that Freire always condemned), and through her work she shows us how to create critical awareness in people to inspire the fight for the transformation of an unjust, lawless and discriminatory society that today rules all over the world, certainly more than ever before.

Margaret knows that social justice is compassion, tolerance, respect for the human being, for the human existence that carries within it, as its ontological essence, equality in difference, a celebration of diversity that counters the fragmentation of the wholeness of LIFE.

She knows that, through day-to-day action, we are able to change the world and build a new, eminently human, course of history. As Freire so often repeated, 'change is difficult, but it is possible'. That is why Margaret wrote this book, which makes it possible to change people in the way they act in the community, paving the way for the transformation of society.

These are good reasons to read this book. I therefore invite its readers to do so attentively, carefully, with lovingness and with the intention to recreate your militancy, wherever or whenever it may be, *with* Margaret Ledwith and *with* Paulo Freire.

São Paulo, 1 July 2015.

Nita
Ana Maria Araújo Freire
Doctor in Education at the Pontifícia Universidade Católica de São Paulo
(PUC/SP), widow and legal successor of the work of Paulo Freire

★ **Assistencialise:** to treat people as passive Objects worthy only of benevolent gestures, rather than active Subjects capable of transforming their world.

Acknowledgements

This book has been growing organically over the last few years, as a work of praxis should. My ideas and experience have engaged with the experience of many activists and practitioners along the way, and this process has, in turn, intertwined with new theories that have taken practice to more critical levels of analysis. I am happy to have this chance to thank all those who played their part in stimulating my ideas with such inspiring enthusiasm, and hope that this book plays its part in encouraging all those involved in social justice to aim high!

It is important to acknowledge, in addition, that my life is a work of praxis and as such the many players in my own story continue to be the foundation for evolving analyses that continue over the years. Many are acknowledged personally in the text: all of them stay in my mind's eye, a panorama of life stories shared from the heart.

I have been lucky enough to grow through the movement of Black and White feminists, those who have changed the world forever by theorising power from experience and acting for social justice for a better world and a common good. In this regard, I celebrate the life of Paula Asgill, whose friendship baptised me (and many others) into the raw nature of Black women's oppression in ways that no abstract theory could ever grasp.

Many years ago, when I was grappling with the political nature of power, Paulo Freire captured my critical imagination with his extraordinary insight into the essence of critical consciousness and its fundamental role in transforming the world. My grateful thanks go to Nita Freire, Paulo Freire's widow, for her inspiring Foreword to this book, and her succinct critical comment. It is a privilege to have her endorsement.

I would also like to thank those who have kept me on track at Policy Press, most particularly: Isobel Bainton for her profound caring and commitment throughout the process; Jo Morton for levels of dedication over and above the call of duty, and for impeccable attention to detail in the final stages of the editing process; and Dave Worth for his skilled work on the quality of the illustrations.

Finally, my gratitude goes to Steve Casstles for unfailingly being there when needed, nurturing me through the exhaustion, raising my dampened spirits and turning his hand to anything asked of him!

Glossary

These are important terms. Each is emphasised in **bold** the first time it is mentioned in the book.

Abjection: a social process that portrays certain groups of people as worthless scroungers, dehumanising them in the eyes of society at large in order to maintain power over them.

Alienation: a state of being socially fragmented and disconnected from a whole.

Animateurs: popular educators who create the context for critical learning and social change with community groups.

Annunciation: Freire used this term in dialectical relation to 'denunciation': a process of denouncing dehumanisation in order to create humanisation, transformed ways of being in the world based on equality, mutuality and reciprocity.

Authentic praxis: a stage when theory and practice become so integrated that they cannot be detached from one another; practice becomes a process of generating theory in action and generating action from that theory. Freire saw critical reflection on lived reality as the key to authentic praxis, otherwise, action for social justice becomes 'pure activism' and theory becomes 'armchair revolution' (Freire, 1972).

Banking education: a system of teaching which is top-down; the teacher 'deposits' pre-determined knowledge into the minds of the learners without any two-way dialogue or any discussion of different ways of 'knowing'.

Codification: a medium used to capture everyday experiences of the community – drawings, photographs, drama, video, story, music – to take the familiar out of context for a community group to see it with fresh eyes.

Coercion: force exerted on people to act in ways that are contrary to their own interests. Gramsci used this term to identify state control through the law, the police and the armed forces.

Collective action: the stage of community development that builds on critical consciousness as the basis of people acting together to bring about change for social justice.

Collective lie: a term coined by Martin-Baró, Jesuit priest and intellectual activist, to capture the importance of challenging the 'collective lie' that persuades us to accept a way of life based on maintaining the interests of the privileged.

Common good: a society that aims to benefit everyone equally.

Conscientisation (Portuguese: *Conscientização*): a process of critical consciousness that starts with creating the context for people to question their everyday experience in order to recognise oppression as a political injustice rather than a personal failing. Freire's definition gave fresh insight into the political nature of popular education, with the beginning of transformative change as simply seeing the world with all its contradictions.

Consent: Gramsci saw 'consent' as a significant dimension of power operating in parallel with 'coercion'. People are persuaded to accept the way things are as 'common sense' as a result of insitutionalised cultural values; as a result they unquestioningly consent to the dominant social order.

Counternarratives: these not only counter the dominant narratives that reduce 'little stories' within a single truth, but they also challenge the hegemonic narratives of everyday life that manipulate people to think and behave according to a dominant set of cultural beliefs (Giroux et al, 1996). Gramsci talked about 'rearticulation' as the dismantling of hegemonic stories in order to create counternarratives that capture new possibilities for a more just and equal future.

Critical consciousness: Freire's third level of consciousness (after 'magical' and 'naïve') indicating a level of insight at which people recognise oppression as a structural problem rather than an individual failing. Critical consciousness is reached when life situations are connected with socio-economic contradictions, such as seeing poor children in a rich society as a political contradiction rather than a personal pathology.

Critical dialogue: 'Only dialogue which requires critical thinking, is also capable of generating critical thinking. Without dialogue there is no communication, and without communication there can be no true education' (Freire, 1972, p 65).

Critical dissent dialogue: engaging in questioning lived reality in order to understand the contradictions that are taken-for-granted.

Critical pedagogy: a form of popular education based on people's life experience. Critical pedagogy begins by simply questioning everyday life's taken-for-grantedness to see the contradictions we live by more clearly in order to act for change.

Cultural invasion: the colonisation of one social group by another. The 'invaded' abandon their own culture because the dominant culture of the privileged imposes values that come to be internalised as superior and desirable.

Culture circle: a community group with a common cultural connection which comes together with the purpose of engaging in the process of conscientisation.

Culture of silence: the values of dominant social groups are superimposed on subordinated groups, silencing them and denying their culture. Internalising dominant cultural attitudes, the reality of oppressed people is seen as inferior and their knowledge as insignificant. The dominant culture is elevated as desirable, and subordinated people are encouraged to feel ignorant and unimportant.

Decontextualisation: to see something out of its social and political context.

Dehumanisation: to rob people of their right to be fully human in the world.

Denunciation: exposing structures of discrimination that exploit some social groups in order to privilege others.

Dialectic: the juxtaposition or interaction of conflicting ideas or forces.

Dialogue: purposeful, respectful communication between people in mutual inquiry.

Disempowerment: to rob people of their freedom by asserting power over them.

Domesticating education: teaching people to absorb facts without questioning the source of the knowledge or the cultural basis of its relevance.

Dominant ideology: the cultural beliefs of a privileged social group that asserts power over subordinated groups.

Dominant narratives: the stories that project powerful messages of the inferiority of subordinate groups and the superiority of dominant groups. These help to maintain the power of the privileged.

Dominant truth: a truth that is asserted so powerfully by a dominant group that it is accepted as 'common sense' without question.

Domination: the way that power interests in society maintain control over subordinated groups.

Education is never neutral: Freire saw education as either liberating (acting in the interests of a common good) or as domesticating (oppressing people to serve the interests of the privileged).

Empowerment: a process of collective liberation from oppression by becoming critical.

Epistemology: a theory of knowledge about the way we make sense of the world.

Equality: ensuring that people have fair and equal treatment in comparison with others, not influenced by social difference, such as 'race', gender, 'dis'ability, religion, ethnicity, sexual orientation or age.

False consciousness: the way that subordinated groups are persuaded to accept inequalities by pathologising their subordination.

False generosity: a term coined by Engels which influenced Freire's thinking about the way that tokenistic gestures give the appearance of equality without changing the underlying structural conditions that are causing inequalities.

Generative themes: the common concerns that emerge from people's stories about everyday life are called 'generative' by Freire because their relevance generates passion and releases energy for action.

Hegemony: the ways in which a dominant group asserts control over other social groups.

Historic bloc: Gramsci's concept of a new balance of political, social and economic forces operating in favour of maintaining the status quo, constructed in response to crisis.

Horizontal violence: Freire's concept for the way in which people who need to be acting in solidarity turn on each other to become oppressors, modelling the top-down power relations that have subordinated them to create a divide-and-rule effect.

Humanisation (or **re-humanisation**): is a process of restoring the right to become more fully human.

Ideological persuasion: Gramsci identified a subtle process of power that persuades people to consent to the dominant social order by reinforcing dominant attitudes and values through schools, the family, the media, religious organisations, etc, selling this view of the world as 'common sense'.

Inferiority: discrimination in society subordinates people in order to dominate them, a process that robs people of their dignity, confidence and self-belief because they see privileged people as superior.

Liberating education: Freire used this concept to emphasise the connections between knowledge and power. Dominant ideology is based on the social construction of knowledge that is sold to society as 'common sense', a way of accepting the dominant order of things according to values that serve the interests of the most powerful rather than the least powerful. Becoming critical involves exposing the assumptions that create this reality. Teaching people to question everyday life begins the process of liberating education, seeing the world in new ways changes the way we act in the world, and this leads to collective action for social justice.

Liberation: a process of achieving freedom from oppression.

Listening from the heart: involves engaging with empathy, connection and compassion to equalise power relations between people as part of the process of empowerment.

Magical consciousness: Freire's concept of the first level of consciousness at which people have a passive acceptance of life circumstances, often explained away as fate without questioning social injustices or making connections with socio-economic contradictions.

More fully human: Freire described the process of 'dehumanisation', the consequence of oppression, as a crime against humanity, a violation of human rights. His commitment to liberation was to unlock a counter process in which the oppressed *and* the oppressors who have stolen their humanity become more fully human.

Mutuality: is a basic Freirean value indicating equal relations between people, rather than power relations.

Naïve consciousness: Freire's concept of the second level of consciousness: an awareness of individual problems, but seeing them as personal failures rather than disadvantages due to structural discrimination.

Narratives of the people: for Freire, the stories people tell about their everyday life experiences hold the key to the theory and practice of social justice.

Neoliberal globalisation: neoliberalism's global project has been to assert an ideology of individualism, an elevation of greed and self-gratification over a common good. This has resulted in destruction, alienation and fragmentation, a world in which the disconnected parts take no responsibility for their impact on the whole.

Neoliberalism: an ideology that prioritises a free market principle that elevates profit above human or planetary wellbeing. This justifies policies that exploit people and planet, increasing social inequalities and threatening environmental sustainability, trends that need to be understood in a global context, and the emergence of a global super-rich.

Ontology: a theory of being about the way we see ourselves in relation to the world around us, helping to make sense of why we live life as we do.

Organic intellectuals: Gramsci's term for those who emerge from a social class to take a key role in the process of change. Their significance is that they are likely to stay committed to their own class.

Pathologising: persuading people to accept their poverty as a consequence of their own inadequacies rather than a consequence of power relations and structural discrimination, at the same time as convincing the rest of society that their poverty is a result of personal irresponsibility.

Placatory practice: tackles the symptoms of discrimination to make life a little bit better around the edges, but fails to go deep enough to tackle the root sources of discrimination that continue to produce social inequalities.

Popular education: 'popular' here means related to poor and marginalised communities, a form of informal education that is committed to creating a more fair and equal society. It is based on the idea that education that does not focus on the disadvantaged is inevitably going to privilege the privileged, maintaining the unjust structures of society that discriminate against the least powerful.

Praxis: a unity of action and reflection, so that practice (or doing) and our thinking about what we do (theory) are bound together in one process, applying theory in action and developing theory from that action.

Problematising: a process of capturing the taken-for-granted contradictions of everyday life as codifications (photographs, drama, etc) to present them to a community group in order to see the situation with fresh eyes.

Pure activism: Freire's term for uncritical action, practice that is not part of a process of critical reflection.

Rearticulation: Gramsci talked about the dismantling of hegemonic stories in order to expose what is going on as the basis of creating counternarratives that capture new possibilities for a better future.

Reciprocity: one of the founding values of Freire's approach, capturing the mutual, horizontal, equal nature of the process of empowerment.

Reflection: Freire saw critical reflection on everyday life as the basis of authentic praxis because it leads to informed action capable of social change. Without this he saw action as pure activism.

Reflexivity: we could see this as the process of reflecting on our reflections in order to go deeper into the unconscious attitudes and assumptions that we have internalised. This enables us to 'see' the world more critically, and act more critically in practice.

Safe spaces: a term used by Patricia Hill Collins to denote critical spaces where people can be free to explore life experience without fear of recrimination.

Status quo: the existing state of affairs relating to social and political structures and the values that underpin them.

Structural discrimination: oppression as experienced in everyday lives is not random and personal, but systematically structured into society in relations of 'domination' and 'subordination'.

Subordination: to be dominated by the authority and control of those who assume superiority.

Taken-for-granted: extraordinary contradictions that get lived out in the ordinariness of everyday life with such familiarity that they are not noticed as injustices and people accept the unacceptable.

Tokenism: the strategy of making a hollow gesture towards the inclusion of members of minority groups without changing the structures that continue to embed discrimination in society.

Traditional intellectuals: Gramsci's term for those who, despite their privilege, ally themselves with oppressed groups with a commitment to ending social injustice. Gramsci saw this role as a catalyst in unlocking social change by creating the context for questioning lived reality.

Transformative praxis: praxis is the concept for a unity of action and reflection, binding theory and action together as part of one process. This has transformative potential when people are situated in their political context, identifying and questioning the unjust contradictions of everyday life.

Unity of praxis: a way of becoming more fully critical in the world, in which thinking and doing become inextricably integrated into a way of being.

INTRODUCTION

Some very good reasons for reading this book!

This book is filled to the brim with exciting ideas for busy practitioners whose lives are fraught with competing demands. It captures the complex thinking necessary to become a social justice practitioner in the most straightforward of ways, providing an everyday reference for practice. It has two pivotal intentions: one is that of **praxis**, to introduce theories as stories which make such sense of life that they become effortlessly integrated into everyday practice; and the second is to do that by offering Freire as the bedrock on which to build new ideas and action. The whole amounts to a *critical living praxis* for our times.

In my years as a grassroots practitioner, I was acutely aware of the challenges of keeping theories at the forefront of practice in the action/**reflection** cycle that structures community development. Today, pressures that are put to bear on grassroots workers distract even more from the principles and purpose of community development, obscuring the social justice intention at the heart of practice. In a world in which social divisions are widening, not lessening, in which the poor are getting poorer and the privileged are becoming even more privileged, we need handy tools to analyse the ways in which poverty becomes 'normalised'.

The sad contradiction of our times is that there is a distinctive trend in rich countries for the privileged few to get excessively rich, and for the poor to get even poorer. We are living in political times in which a **common good** has given way to justification for greed. A symptom of this is that wealth is diverted from the poor to the rich, and poor children are reduced to living with hunger in rich countries where there is no need. This trend is being repeated in the new industrialising powers, like China, where the same patterns of excess are making the few ridiculously rich, while the starving millions are abandoned to bare survival. The other pattern that is being repeated is the degradation of the Earth in this process. Carbon emissions and other pollutants are hastening climate change and the destruction of Planet Earth. Neoliberalism's **dominant ideology** continues to tell us a story of inevitability, that we have to aim for more of the same, that the market is a god fed by profit reigning over people and the planet. Now it is time to tell a different story, one that contains a **counternarrative** to competition, one that connects community, compassion and cooperation in a common good for all!

Community development has a role to play in both telling this new story of hope and possibility, and acting collectively to make it a reality. Creating a world that inspires us all to play our part in interrupting the world crises of social justice and environmental sustainability of our times, involves constructing a worldview that has the good of the people and the planet at heart. The time is now, and we must be the change!

Don't stop here! These rather grand aims have very simple and practical everyday solutions. I am merely saying that we need to question and challenge the dominant stories that we are told so forcibly and that have such dire consequences for us all. A new world is possible. This is the challenge I am taking on in this little, practical book of everyday ideas: change your practice, and in doing so, change the world, and change the course of history!

Community development has, for many years, suffered from a dislocation of its theory from its practice. This results in us not only making it up as we go along, but we put ourselves in danger of acting to support a **status quo** that continues to churn out the same inequalities with the same results. As **neoliberal globalisation** escalates, it projects the discriminatory message of 'profit not people' that has become embedded in Western, neoliberal thinking. This carries such a powerful story of the deserving rich and the undeserving poor that it becomes woven into the structures of societies, producing inequalities that justify disadvantage as personal failing on a global level. Community development theory needs to get to grips with understanding the way that power works to target some social groups as disposable in a world measured by profit and excess. Until we have insights into the way that power works against the interests of some people to privilege others, narratives of prejudice will continue to feed into the ongoing story of the powerful that disadvantages the rest. Once we begin, quite easily, to grasp the ways in which this happens, we can truly start to use the concept of **empowerment** as a transformative tool. It is simply about seeing things differently. So prepare yourself for a journey of curiosity, challenge and discovery, one that will delight you with the ease of lifting the blinkers of everyday life contradictions to see critically, and discover the possibilities for an approach to practice with social justice at its heart.

The layout of this book is designed for you to keep it handy in your everyday practice, for reference. Yet within this simple approach, the ideas inside its covers are world-changing. At the end of each chapter, you will find a practical exercise for taking theory into action based on a relevant aspect of the chapter's content, often by extracting a quote from the body of the text to apply to practice in greater detail. I have divided the exercises into four sections: issue, evidence, analysis, and action. These can be used for critical reflection, or can be adapted for use in training workshops, or integrated into everyday practice with local people. The more that you apply theory to social trends, local culture and current policy changes, the more the exercises will be relevant to your practice.

Paulo Freire, the Brazilian popular educator, emphasised that **transformative praxis** (a unity of theory and practice capable of social change) begins in stories of everyday life experience. This idea has always worked in my own practice, and for that reason, I use stories to illustrate theory in action. I find that this makes theory relevant – it brings ideas alive in reality, and you will find that they connect to all the stories you hear in your own practice. In this sense, I am using different ways of knowing that work through story, sometimes with cartoons and photographs to capture complex ideas in simple ways.

The content of this book is based on ideas that I have shared with practitioners in workshops, seminars and **dialogue** groups, and in this sense it is an engagement with the knowledge produced in action from people involved in collective struggles against injustice. I have attempted to include you, the reader, in the conversations, constantly threading critical connections together, emphasising and re-emphasising key points as they become relevant in successive chapters.

A framework for thinking about this book

Co-creating knowledge and action from the ground up

1   Power and knowledge are interrelated: we cannot be agents of change without being agents of knowledge.
2   Changed consciousness is the basis of action for change: dialogue and praxis are the basis of humanisation.
3   'Only dialogue which requires critical thinking, is also capable of generating critical thinking. Without dialogue there is no communication, and without communication there can be no true education' (Freire, 1972, p 65).
4   Knowledge is key to understanding the power relations of domination/subordination.
5   We do this by questioning a *dominant ideology* that is sold as truth as a self-perpetuating system of domination and subordination.
6   We change our understanding of oppression by seeing the world through a changed lens.
7   A politics of empowerment calls for seeing the world through the lens of 'race', class and gender relations as three overriding sources of oppression to help us to identify the complex interlinking, overlapping system of oppressions that embraces sexual preference, age, religion, culture ...
8   Empowerment is about exploring new ways of knowing, a paradigmatic shift that allows us to see our identities and realities within this system of competing oppressions.
9   We cannot do this without contextualising our practice: decontextualisation results in fragmentation of understanding and action.
10 Empowerment demands analyses of power and collective action to change the world to a more fair, just and sustainable place: a mutual, self-sustaining ecosystem linking all humanity and the rest of the natural world in compassionate balance, so changing the course of history.

One of the prime purposes of this book is to provide a ready reference for busy practitioners working in grassroots practice. The challenge has been to present and develop important ideas from the popular *Community development: A critical approach* (Ledwith, 2011), a book that you may wish to explore in due course. Here, I have concentrated on introducing these ideas in ways that are much more immediately accessible. In fact, ideas should leap off the page with little effort! Paulo Freire said, 'Reading is not walking on words; it's grasping the soul of them' (Freire, 1985, p 19). So I have tried to put the soul of the words within your grasp, not densely embedded in academic text, but expressed simply and reinforced by different ways of knowing beyond the written word, using stories, photographs and cartoons, supported by quotes from Paulo Freire and emphasised at key points as the book unfolds. Freire talked about the stories of everyday life containing both theory and practice for a more just and sustainable world. I use stories to bring theories alive, stories that paint a vivid picture of the forces of power that privilege some lives and discriminate against others. In these ways, I build bridges over the theory/practice divide, creating an approach to practice that uses practical theories in action.

Chapter One begins this process by exploring the principles of community development and the context for its social justice practice.

A couple of notes
Throughout the book, I choose to emphasise the socially constructed nature of 'dis'ability and 'race' with the use of inverted commas, and the profoundly political nature of the categories White and Black with the use of initial capitals.

In the cartoons, Freire's heart-shaped speech bubbles are a shorthand for his unwavering emphasis on a pedagogy of love to counter a politics of hatred; love as an act of courage and commitment, 'a politics of love for the world and its people rather than hatred' (Freire, 2005, p 49)! All the quotes displayed in these speech bubbles come from the same source: *Education for critical consciousness* (Freire, 2005).

ONE

Principles of community development

Let's start from basic principles. These should be revisited at least once a month as a reminder! They offer a system of checks and balances for every stage of the process, offering a clear way of explaining our purpose to every stakeholder, from local residents to managers, policy-makers and funders. They also offer a structure for planning and evaluation, ensuring that we are doing what we claim to be doing at any stage of the process. In other words, if community development is predicated on social justice, we need to be able to explain how this fits with what we are doing at any point in our practice. If what we say we do in theory doesn't fit what we are actually doing in practice, this needs challenging!

What is community development?

Community development comprises:

- **Vision**: a just and sustainable world.
- **Principles**: social justice and environmental justice.
- **Values**: an ideology of equality – respect, dignity, trust, mutuality, reciprocity.
- **Process**: critical consciousness threaded through practical projects.
- **Collective action**: from local projects to campaigns/alliances/movements for change.
- **Theories**: power/disempowerment/empowerment.
- **Context**: practice situated in political times.

Community development begins in the everyday reality of people's lives by 'extraordinarily re-experiencing the ordinary' (Shor, 1992, p 122). I always think this notion of seeing the extraordinary in the ordinary perfectly captures the essence of our work, that of questioning the taken-for-grantedness of everyday life. In the stories of everyday life as told on the margins of society lie the theory and practice of community development, beginning in exposing the contradictions that result in discrimination, the power relationships that cleave divisions of superiority/ **inferiority**. For those of you who are new to these ideas, I will unfold them in straightforward ways by following the process through, from vision to action.

Community development is rooted in a vision of a more fair and just world. So let's first explore this vision as it contains the ideas that make us passionate about our practice. We believe that it is possible to create a world in which everyone and everything is encouraged to flourish, a democracy based on participation and collective wellbeing. More than this, this vision challenges us to put an understanding of all life on earth, not just humanity, at the core of our practice.

It took a while for community development to understand that social justice and environmental justice are inextricably linked, and therefore essentially part of the community development agenda. This understanding came about largely through the connection between the poorest and most vulnerable of the world being most immediately affected by environmental degradation. The natural world flourishes as an ecosystem, a sustainable world in dynamic balance that adjusts flexibly to change. This dynamic interaction is a self-righting mechanism, but the more it gets out of kilter, the more dramatic the environmental reaction. This is a reminder that humanity does not sit apart from the environment, but is part of the ecosystem, and therefore needs to see itself as part of this balance. This sense of connection brings with it a responsibility for the wellbeing of people and the planet, a way of healing the **alienation** that has come about as a result of individualism, a self-centred way of seeing the world that led to the destruction of a responsibility for a common good. A divided world does not sustain humanity nor the natural environment of which it is a part. Here I want to emphasise that it is not necessary for us to see a just and sustainable world as utopian and beyond reality, but perhaps as a practical utopia that is founded on knowing that what we have created is simply not fair, not just, and not good enough.

From this point, the process unfolds. If we believe that a better world is possible, we need to understand more fully the principles of social justice and ecological sustainability that will guide the process of change. These are important times for community development: the world is facing crises of social injustice and ecological unsustainability. Divisions between poverty and privilege are growing, both within and between countries, putting excessive wealth in the pockets of the privileged at the same time as poverty is damaging an increasing number of lives, putting children in particular at greatest risk. At this stage, it is important to understand that this pattern of widening social inequalities in rich countries is a stark contradiction, suggesting that poverty is a choice. In other words, increased wealth is not being distributed equally, and anyone working for social justice needs to understand why this is happening.

This places community development in a pivotal spot in times of change and crisis in the world. No wonder we are constantly walking a tightrope of **liberation** on the one hand, and domination on the other: our strong relationships with everyday people in the community make us attractive to target as agents of the state. If we are uncritical, the danger is that we become distracted from our social justice purpose, and end up thoughtlessly delivering top-down policies that act against our principles, increasing injustice rather than acting for change. The evidence is before us: poverty is increasing, leading to crises of social justice, and the escalating divisions between the richest and poorest are making humanity unsustainable.

At the same time, the emphasis on profit that leads to exploitation of not only people, but also the planet, has created ecological crises. This makes it vital for us to understand the forces that set this in motion. I say this because practice cannot be understood without it being contextualised in its political times. This exposes the way that power is structured into the fabric of society to advantage some people and disadvantage others as the basis of empowering practice. We are all making sense of life, all of the time. The difference here is that without a critical, questioning approach, we are likely to unquestioningly absorb stories told by a dominant ideology that intends to reinforce the way things are, the status quo.

The next stage, knowing that we want to bring about change for a better world, is to become familiar with the set of values that in shorthand I call an ideology of equality. These values are based on a celebration of diversity and difference, in a world in which there are divisions of superiority and inferiority that come at a cost to humanity as a whole. There are no winners in a divided world – society as a whole is reduced in potential when vast numbers of people are marginalised and excluded. So when I think of the values that are fundamental to community development, I am thinking from a human rights perspective. Everyone has the right to trust, dignity and respect formed out of experiences that are equal, reciprocal and mutual. This is built into cooperative relationships that work together to connect people in ways that build towards a participatory democracy.

These are the values that define community development: trust, dignity, respect, equality, reciprocity, mutuality. They provide a system of checks and balances that tell us whether we are on track, doing what we say we intend to do at every stage of the process. It is important that all practitioners, whether involved in generic community development, community drama, health approaches to community development, housing associations, campaigns or any other of the diverse approaches to practice, use the values as a framework for planning, evaluation and action in practice at every level. By this, I mean that every encounter has to be evidenced according to the values in order for our practice to maintain integrity. No one should be diminished by the experience, whether we are in roles as managers, policy-makers or in grassroots practice. Community development is a way of life, not just a job, and to practise it calls for us to embrace these values in every aspect of our being. Otherwise, we are in danger of being duplicitous, and our well-intentioned commitments get assigned to empty rhetoric!

Community development as critical pedagogy

These values become embedded in our work through **critical pedagogy**, a form of **popular education** based on people's life experience. It is critical pedagogy that gives community development the potential to bring about change for social justice. The process begins by simply questioning everyday life's taken-for-grantedness to see the contradictions we live by more starkly. This leads us to seeing the world through a new lens – seeing power in action and co-creating new knowledge, a new story of the world that forms the basis of action for change.

Perhaps at this point it is important to introduce Paulo Freire, as community development has been more influenced by him than any other single theorist. I will discuss his work in some detail as we go on, but at this point it is enough to know that he was a Brazilian adult educator who believed that teaching people to question the contradictions of everyday life is the basis of empowerment.

The essence of his thinking lies in education as a process that cannot be understood in isolation from the other processes that construct our reality, particularly political processes (Irwin, 2012). This is a key, defining feature of Freire's approach to life as a **unity of praxis**. Education is both the source of domination and the key to liberation. In others words, by teaching people to question everyday life, we begin the process of **liberating education** – seeing the world in new ways leads to changes in the way we act in the world, and this is the basis of collective action for social justice. It really is as simple as this! A note of caution at this point, however: Freire does not work in a partial way, as his approach calls for an 'indivisible totality based on assumptions and principles which are inter-related and coherent … we cannot take hints from Freire or use bits of Freire; we must embrace the philosophy as an integral whole and attempt to apply it accordingly' (Allman and Wallis, 1997, p 113).

Despite the ongoing popularity and relevance of Freire's work, the only sustained Freirean project in the UK remains the Adult Learning Project (ALP) based at Tollcross Community Centre in Edinburgh. I studied community learning and development with David Alexander at the University of Edinburgh in 1981–82. It was there that I met Gerri Kirkwood, who had recently studied on the same course. She returned to talk about putting a Freirean approach into practice in Gorgie-Dalry, where she was one of the three original developers of the ALP when the Urban Programme funded it in 1979. They started, I remember, simply by knocking on doors and getting to know local people. It is now an internationally recognised Freirean success story rooted in Scottish culture and identity.

Freire's seminal book, *Pedagogy of the oppressed,* translated into English in 1970, had an instant impact on practices ranging from community work to literacy, health promotion, liberation theology and many more around the world. His ideas are very straightforward and emerged from his initial voluntary community work in Recife. Sharing the lives of people in poverty led him to understand the nature of social injustice, and to wonder what it was that led to people giving in to their oppression with apathy rather than anger. This developed into a concept he named the **culture of silence**, capturing the way that political, social and economic domination lead to passive acceptance in those who are marginalised. At the basis of this understanding is the idea that how we see the world has a direct impact on how we engage with the world. So, if the **dominant narrative** is one that promotes the story of the 'welfare scrounger', it is likely that public consciousness will reinforce this idea. The consequence will be that people in work will feel that they are supporting 'undeserving scroungers' so they will be likely to favour policies that reduce benefits and resist redistribution of wealth:

people out of work will lose a sense of their own worth, reducing potential, increasing ill health, lowering expectations and destroying self-belief.

Freire's approach is that by questioning what is happening in everyday life, we expose the contradictions that lead to domination and subordination, divisions cleaved by poverty and privilege. This thinking helped community development change itself into a radical activity committed to action for social justice rather than a **placatory practice** that attempts to make life just a little bit better around the edges! We begin to see the world in different ways when we question what is going on and in whose interests it is happening. This leads to an altered **epistemology**, a changed way of making sense of the world. And as practitioners, all we need to learn is how to teach people to question. As Ira Shor puts it, we teach people to ask thought-provoking questions, 'to question answers rather than answer questions'! (Shor, quoted in McLaren and Leonard, 1993, p 26). This, in turn, changes the way we see ourselves in relation to the world around us, leading to a greater sense of self and the determination to change things, not just for our personal benefit, but for the good of everyone. A divided society is an unhealthy and unhappy society, and we will be exploring the evidence for this as we go, exploring theories of power and discrimination to build a practical toolkit for practice. At this point, it is only necessary to recognise that community development's process involves *critical pedagogy*, a form of *popular education* that begins in the everyday reality of people's lives creating the context for seeing the ordinary as extraordinary.

History of radical, transformative community development

At this point, let us take a brief look at the roots of radical practice. To be clear, when I use the term 'radical practice', I am referring to practice that has a transformative agenda. In other words, rather than a placatory approach, making life a little easier on the surface, radical practice goes under the surface, deeper into the root causes of discrimination embedded in the structures of society that perpetuate social divisions. So think back to what I said about questioning the taken-for-grantedness of everyday life, and you begin to see that this process of becoming critical starts by simply asking why things are the way they are. I hope it is becoming clearer to understand that community development is a contested occupation that sits at the interface of *reactionary practice* and *revolutionary practice*: the first reacts to the symptoms of oppression; the second transforms **structural discrimination** that embeds inequalities in the fabric of society. If we fail to stay critical, constantly re-examining our practice in changing political times, we are likely to err on the side of domination rather than liberation.

In the UK, community work emerged as a distinct occupation with a strong educational component in the 1960s, after the publication of the Younghusband report (1959), which identified community organisation as an approach that supported people to define their own needs and to work together to achieve them. It was the Gulbenkian report (Calouste Gulbenkian Foundation, 1968), based on research into UK community work, that took this a stage further by locating community work at the interface between people and social change by improving service delivery, developing interagency coordination and influencing policy and planning. The proposal was to recognise community work as not only a distinct occupation, but also part of wider professional practice for teachers, social workers, clergy, health workers, architects, planners, administrators and other community-based occupations, despite the fact that the fundamentally political nature of this work was not fully addressed in the report (Craig et al, 1982; Popple, 1995).

Thomas (1983) suggests that it was the drive of the Wilson government (1964–70 and 1974–76) to transform British society that led to community work becoming identified as a strategy to bridge the divide between the state and the working class within the same capitalist social relations, clearly more reformist than revolutionary. Nevertheless, social reforms in education, health, housing, gender equality, price controls, pensions, provisions for people with disabilities and child poverty came about with this Labour government, one of the most significant being Wilson's vision of The Open University, established in 1969, which offered everyone open access to university education without entry qualifications.

For community development, 1968 was a significant political juncture, with 'race' riots, student demonstrations, civil rights marches, anti-Vietnam protests, and the assassinations of Martin Luther King and Robert Kennedy, described by Popple (1995, p 15) as a year of 'revolt, rebellion and reaction'. In response to the social unrest triggered by unemployment and immigration, and inflamed by Enoch Powell's 'rivers of blood' speech, the Labour government set up the Urban Programme in 1968, with the Community Development Project (CDP), the largest government-funded action research project, emerging from it the following year. Twelve local CDP projects were set up in marginalised communities, to make interventions based on the assumptions of Keith Joseph's (Secretary of State for Health, 1972–74) 'cycle of deprivation' theory (Rutter and Madge, 1976, p 3), blaming poor people for being stuck in an underclass of their own making. A key group of CDP workers challenged this from a structural analysis, that is, that discrimination is woven into the structures of society targeting specific social groups. This was a turning point for community development, identifying practice as a political activity based on structural change.

Community development literature emerged from the CDP identifying a contested space between top-down and bottom-up, placing community workers in a paradoxical role that became coined as 'in and against the state'. This marked the birth of community development as a radical alternative to social work, rooted in a political/structural analysis, rather than a personal/pathological analysis of poverty and discrimination. At the same time, the radical ideas of Frantz Fanon, Antonio Gramsci and Paulo Freire became available in English, and profoundly influenced community development theory. We saw ideas and action woven together in projects such as the ALP in Gorgie-Dalry, Edinburgh in 1979, and the Organisation of Women of African and Asian Descent in Moss Side, Manchester in 1975, from which the radical action of the Abasindi Women's Cooperative emerged in 1980.

This marked a critical moment in history, a time of theory in action in which grassroots social movements – women's, anti-racist, disability, gay and lesbian, green, etc – emerged from local action.

Social, economic and environmental justice

> The richest 300 people on earth have as much wealth as the poorest three billion. This is no accident; those in power write the rules. Together, we have the power to change those rules. (InvestmentWatch, 2013)

A socially just society is based on equality and mutual responsibility, one that values human rights and recognises the right to dignity of everyone. In this sense, poverty becomes a human rights issue, peace can only be achieved from a social justice perspective, and social justice cannot be understood without paying attention to economic justice and ecological sustainability. (These points will be explored in the **Theory in action** exercise at the end of this chapter.) Social justice is at the heart of all these processes, and is the reason why practice needs to operate on local, social and global levels. It is the main goal for a fair and sustainable distribution of social, economic and environmental resources. This is the route to a world in which everyone and everything flourishes in mutual, respectful connection.

You begin to see that community development's guiding principles of social justice and ecological sustainability carry a weighty responsibility; far beyond a feel-good factor, we need to understand the implications this carries, and how we put social justice practice into action in the everyday. This calls on us to understand the ways in which structural discrimination is sewn into society, resulting in inequalities that lead to social marginalisation and exclusion. For this reason, we need to have insight into the ways that poverty works to destroy hopes, aspirations and potential, not just at a personal level, or at a local level, but throughout society as a whole, as a mutually reinforcing system on all these levels. Only when we understand how power works in unequal ways can we aspire to a level of practice that contributes to a world in which equal worth, equal rights, opportunities for all and the elimination of the inequalities reinforced by poverty are achieved (Commission on Social Justice, 1994).

> Economic inequality in the UK grew dramatically during the 1980s and 90s and has remained at historically high levels. A cycle linking wealth, education, the labour market and globalisation has created the conditions for inequality to flourish and feed on itself. By examining the policies of more equal countries, we find that inequality is not inevitable and that it can be effectively tackled by addressing its root causes. (Lawlor et al, 2011, p 3)

Figure 1.1: The Occupy movement's slogan

The rich are getting richer the world over. Economic inequality in the UK is at its highest in recorded history. This changed from 1979 onwards, when we had inequality levels similar to the Netherlands, to our current status as one of the most divided countries in the world. This has now reached a level where it is damaging to society as a whole. There is little understanding that inequality has grown so much and that it is harmful for everyone, so it is important that community development contributes to the debate foregrounding inequality as a generally bad thing for all. It is a trend that is evident across the world, and triggered the Occupy movement with its slogan 'We are the 99 per cent', capturing the injustice that income, wealth and power are concentrated in the pockets of the richest 1 per cent, and fuelled further by the belief that those who took the risks that led to a recession are not the ones paying for it.

Inequality encourages economic, social and environmental problems that are complex and interconnected. The New Economics Foundation (NEF; www.neweconomics.org), a leading UK 'think tank' on social, economic and environmental justice, identifies 10 reasons why we need to care about economic inequality in an attempt to make these interconnections easier to understand:

1. **Your pocket:** consumerism creates increasing debt. We want things not because we need them, but because we measure our own status by what we own in order to gain respect, and to have self-respect.

2. **Your talent (and your pocket again):** inequality limits potential. Privilege breeds privilege. If you are born poor, you are likely to stay poor, or at least not make it into the top half of income earners in your lifetime. Initial advantages give privilege: there is a growing divide between those who go to top universities and get highly paid jobs, and those who do not.

3. **The economy (and your pocket for the third time):** (a) Failure to develop individual potential reduces the benefits for society as a whole; and (b) easily available consumer credit encouraged low-income people into debt for home ownership and consumer goods beyond levels they could afford, which, in turn, contributed to the financial crash of 2008.

4. **Your children:** the UK has one of the lowest social mobility levels of all high-income countries. In other words, inequality blocks the realisation of potential, so children in poor families are likely to earn the same as their parents. Countries with high social mobility are likely to be more equal. Resources concentrated at the top of the social ladder are more likely to stay there, and not benefit the whole of society.

5. **Your streets:** large income gaps between rich and poor create segregation and social tension. Rich and poor live in different communities, lives become distanced, and this results in distrust, disconnection and unwillingness to help each other. Crime, violent crime in particular, increases in unequal societies that emphasise competitive achievement. There are acknowledged links to inequality as a violation of human rights, economically wasteful to all society, and a potential detonator of social unrest.

6. **Your health:** links between inequality and health have long been recognised. Poverty lowers life expectancy. It also leads to greater infant mortality and ill health throughout the lifespan. It is now understood to create stress and stress-related illnesses in those lower down the status hierarchy of a divided society, linked to anxiety over low status and feelings of negative judgements. Other links relate to weakening social bonds and high rates of depression. All these have a direct impact on health and efficiency costs to the economy as a whole.

7. **Your happiness:** all the above issues make us unhappy. Research indicates that wellbeing declines as inequalities rise. High levels of consumerism result in a culture of wants, and so wellbeing gets measured in material possessions rather than the things that bring happiness, such as good relationships. Pressure to work more to spend more reduces the time to spend with family and friends. But importantly, perceptions of fairness and the opportunity to realise potential affect our happiness.

8. **Your planet:** the rich are consuming to excess; the rest are over-consuming through debt. We are consuming 50 per cent more than the planet can sustain, and these trends have spread to China and India. Research undertaken by NEF and the Centre for Analysis of Social Exclusion (CASE) at the London School of Economics and Political Science (LSE) (Gough et al, 2011) found that greenhouse gas emissions rise as income rises, most pronounced in emissions for the richest households. Here is a connection that suggests that not only

do excessive incomes cause problems related to inequality, but they also create lifestyles that are not environmentally sustainable.

9. **Your government and policy:** accumulated wealth accumulates power! This can assert political influence on governments to act in the interests of the rich. Take, for instance, the resistance to redistribution of resources necessary to achieve greater equality.

10. **Your sense of justice:** abysmally low social mobility and the ways in which the system favours the rich give the UK a bad reputation, leading to a poor sense of national identity and civic pride.

Ending on a note of optimism, research evidence indicates that people like the idea of a more equal society, suggesting that if managed well, the shift to a more fair and just future could have widespread support (www.neweconomics.org).

Deepening democracy

Community development, as I am sure you are beginning to see, is part of a broader democratic process. Its particular view of democracy is one that is participatory, one in which people act together to demand social justice for all, knowing that a fair, just and equal world is vital for the future of people and the planet. *Critical pedagogy* lies at the heart of this process, beginning in dialogue, questioning the contradictions we live by, and working together to tackle the significant problems that have been created by inequalities. In doing so we can begin to imagine the kind of world that is possible, where everyday folk have a say in the way the world operates, a participatory democracy founded on difference and diversity, on cooperation rather than competition. This begins in the community, building on those core values of trust, respect and dignity, in mutual and reciprocal relations, to create critical consciousness, a new way of seeing the world which leads to altered ways of being – 'A democracy which does not fear the people', in Freire's view, but which is *of* the people (Irwin, 2012, p 97).

The most useful summary of learning for democracy I have come across comes from the Learning for Democracy Group (2008) initiated by Mae Shaw, Ian Martin and Jim Crowther in Edinburgh.

Pause for thought ...

Read the following summary. Reflect on the implications for your role and for community development as an occupation.

Learning for democracy means:

 1. **Taking sides:** educational workers are not merely enablers or facilitators. The claim to neutrality can reinforce and legitimise existing power relations. Practitioners need to be clear about what they stand for – and against.

---

2. Acting in solidarity: practitioners should proactively seek opportunities to engage in a critical and committed way with communities and social movements for progressive social change.

3. Taking risks: critical and creative learning is necessarily unpredictable and open-ended. Exploring official problem definitions and challenging taken-for-granted ways of thinking can be a liberating process.

4. Developing political literacy: politics needs to be made more educational and education made more political. Learning to analyse, argue, cooperate and take action on issues that matter requires a systematic educational process.

5. Working at the grassroots: democracy lives through ordinary people's actions; it does not depend on state sanction. Practitioners should be in everyday contact with people on their own ground and on their own terms.

6. Listening to dissenting voices: activating democracy is a process of creating spaces in which different interests are expressed and voices heard. Dissent should be valued rather than suppressed.

7. Cultivating awkwardness: democracy is not necessarily best served by the conformist citizen. This means that the educational task is to create situations in which people can confront their circumstances, reflect critically on their experience, and take action.

8. Educating for social change: collective action can bring about progressive change. Learning for democracy can contribute to this process by linking personal experience with wider political explanations and processes.

9. Exploring alternatives: learning for democracy can provide people with the opportunity to see that the status quo is not inevitable, that 'another world is possible'.

10. Exposing the power of language: the words used to describe the world influence how people think and act. Learning for democracy involves exploring how language frames attitudes, beliefs and values.

Source: Learning for Democracy Group (2008)

Health, happiness and wellbeing

> The biosphere or ball of life (bio means life) includes the air, the water, the minerals, the trees, the rivers and the oceans, let alone the fish, the birds and the animals. It is easy to see that everything is in motion within and without. All are involved in a great dance, and we too are part of that dance. We do not simply live on the Earth. We are part of the Earth, and just as each part of a body is dependent for health on all the others, so our own health and well-being is linked up with the health and well-being of the Earth. (Hope and Timmel, 1999, p 13)

This quote, from *Training for transformation*, takes us to the health and wellbeing of people and the planet, framing our action within an interconnected ecosystem in which everyone and everything is interdependent. It places our current crises of social justice and environmental sustainability in a self-destructing paradigm of alienation, one that is fragmented and disconnected from the whole. This is why we need to be able to think in terms of interconnected systems.

We are starting to think in more connected ways these days, and we are beginning to realise that success, rather than being measured in terms of profit, can be measured in terms of wellbeing. This can be seen as a measure of human flourishing: happy people and a happy planet are the ultimate measures of human success, embracing social, economic, health and environmental inequalities. When things are unequal they are out of balance, and this leads to instability and uncertainty.

The New Economics Foundation (in Coote, 2015) proposes a new social settlement that builds on Beveridge's vision but which tackles our current crises of widening social inequalities, escalating threats to the natural environment and the concentration of power in the hands of 'wealthy elites'. Here is a fundamental denunciation of neoliberal ideology of great significance for community development, arguing that the economy should be serving the people and the planet rather than ruling people and planet. It is a proposal based on inclusion and collaboration, encouraging wider dialogue on the kind of society we want to create and action to change the course of history. To this end, they outline three interconnected goals: social justice, environmental sustainability and a more equal distribution of power.

Three goals for a new social settlement

Goal 1: Social justice

We have defined this as: *An equal chance for everyone to enjoy the essentials of a good life, to fulfil their potential and to participate in society.* Wellbeing, equality, and satisfaction of needs are central to our understanding of social justice.

Goal 2: Environmental sustainability

We have defined this as: *living within environmental limits and respecting panetary boundaries, ensuring that natural resources that are needed for life to flourish are unimpaired for present and future generations.*

Goal 3: A more equal distribution of power

We have defined this as: *distributing power more equally, through the formal and informal means by which people participate in and influence decisions and actions at local and national levels, and between groups where economic, social and cultural factors combine to create inequalities.*

Source: Coote (2015)

Movements for change are in evidence. For instance, when I was at the Hay Book Festival in 2010, I went to a talk by Richard Layard, the economist and also the co-founder of Action for Happiness, which was launched as a mass movement for social change in 2011. How refreshing to hear an economist in particular saying that society cannot flourish without a shared purpose, a common good that connects the self to the whole, not only giving us back the responsibility for others that has been eroded in the rise of individualism, but also responsibility for the sustainability of the planet. Action for Happiness calls for us to aspire to another worldview that favours cooperation and rejects competition, a world in which all people can flourish without excessive inequalities, a world in which children all have a right to be loved, valued and included in families, communities and societies the world over. This is the ultimate in empathy and compassion, and is what is needed to counter the alienation created by profit. Instead of prioritising profit, elevating status and consumption, being obsessed with our appearance, possessions and income, we could invest in the wellbeing of others, in families, communities, the workplace, societies and the world (Williamson, 2011).

Global agreement of the need for new ways of measuring progress has to reflect holistic values and replace the inadequate measures that are currently used. We are slowly realising that the current system is corrupt – built on competition, it inevitably favours the powerful and disadvantages the vulnerable. The Happy Planet Index is a way of measuring progress differently, based on the wellbeing of people and the planet (www.happyplanet.org). The progress nations are making in promoting good lives for their people in an endeavour to create sustainable planetary wellbeing for all and for future generations is the basis for success. The third global report (Murphy, 2012) still indicates that we are living on an unhappy planet, and that high and sustainable wellbeing is within the grasp of only nine countries, that eight of those are in Latin America and the Caribbean, that in Western Europe, Norway is highest, at 29th, and that the US is 105th out 151 countries. The overall message is that good lives do not have to cost the earth, that wellbeing is often the highest in countries that are not having the greatest environmental impact (Abdallah et al, 2012). The insistence in times of recession that the imperative is to restore the market economy with its profit imperative as the only way of recovery has to be seen as paradoxical and undesirable. It is a message projected into public consciousness in newspaper and TV headlines that needs to be changed to 'another world is possible' (Fisher and Ponniah, 2003).

In this chapter, we have taken a look at the purpose, principles and practice of community development as a radical, political activity committed to social justice and environmental sustainability. I have traced the history of community development's emergence as a distinct practice with a social justice imperative underpinned by transformative, non-negotiable values that locate practice not only at a grassroots level, but also at a structural level, where discrimination is woven into the fabric of society. For these reasons, we cannot put our practice into action without contextualising it in its political times. I introduced the notion of placatory practice as that form of practice that sits on the surface, making life just a little bit better around the edges, but radical, transformative practice as the practice of social justice, identifying the root sources of discrimination that lead to massive inequalities in society. To make a difference, we need to work towards an integration of theory and practice, *praxis*. To this end, I introduced Paulo Freire's *critical pedagogy* as the basis of an authentic praxis for community development, bridging the problematic divide between theory and practice that often leaves us operating from a point of 'thoughtless action' (Johnston, in Shaw, 2004, p 26), and therefore wide open to being hijacked as agents of the state, delivering top-down policies that are often doing more to widen inequalities than to practise social justice. To practise empowerment we need theories that help us to understand the way that power works in society, and once this is understood, people act together to bring about change for the better. This led us to have a look at social, economic and environmental justice in order to understand the injustices our current world order is creating. Then we had a look at health, happiness and wellbeing as measures of success. These are themes I will develop in subsequent chapters.

The cost for pursuing economic development as progress has led to unsustainable lives for people and the planet. Wilkinson and Pickett (2010, p 254), in their ground-breaking work, *The spirit level*, identify the contradiction: 'further improvements in the quality of life no longer depend on further economic growth, the issue is now community and how we relate to each other.' More than that, there is evidence that the narrowing of income inequalities in rich countries makes them more responsive to the needs of poorer countries, suggesting, indeed, that equality is better for everyone (Wilkinson and Pickett, 2010).

Let's finish here by reminding ourselves that, 'The secret is compassion towards oneself and others, and the principle of the Greatest Happiness is essentially the expression of that ideal. Perhaps these two ideas could be the cornerstones of our future culture' (Layard, 2005, p 235).

Theory in action 1

Community development as the practice of social justice

Issue

A socially just society is based on equality and mutual responsibility, one that values human rights and recognises the right to the dignity of everyone. In this sense, poverty becomes a human rights issue that can only be achieved from a social justice perspective, and social justice cannot be understood without paying attention to economic justice and ecological sustainability.

Evidence

As an example, read this evidence from The Royal Society:

The 21st century is a critical period for people and the planet. The global population reached 7 billion during 2011 and the United Nations projections indicate that it will reach between 8 and 11 billion by 2050. Human impact on the Earth raises serious concerns, and in the richest parts of the world per capita material consumption is far above the level that can be sustained for everyone in a population of 7 billion or more. This is in stark contrast to the world's 1.3 billion poorest people, who need to consume more in order to be raised out of extreme poverty.... The Earth's capacity to meet human needs is finite, but how the limits are approached depends on lifestyle choices and associated consumption; these depend on what is used, and how, and what is regarded as essential for human wellbeing. (The Royal Society, 2012, p 4)

Analysis

Wellbeing covers our lives as a whole, reflecting how satisfied we feel about being alive on every dimension. Of course it is affected by our genetic make-up, our innate disposition, our sense of purpose and our resilience, and this affects the choices we make; but it is profoundly influenced by the culture and times we are born into, which affects our health, our safety, our work, our opportunities, our status and the realisation of our potential. If we believe that to aspire to human flourishing means that as many people as possible should experience wellbeing, then it seems to make sense that the best society is going to be one that creates the greatest potential for all. This carries with it a responsibility for everyone to have the opportunity for a good life, and a responsibility to hand over a world that is capable of offering the greatest wellbeing to future generations. Yet, in Britain and the US, despite massive economic growth, people are no happier than they were in the 1950s. Now, if we set this within the reality that while economic stability affects happiness, long-term economic growth has little bearing on it: unemployment reduces happiness in equal proportion to bereavement (NEF, 2004), and trust is a major determinant of happiness (only 30 per cent of people in the UK feel that most people can be trusted, but in Scandinavia it is over 60 per cent). This suggests that the impact of poverty and the quality of human relationships are core to quality of life.

Action

The New Economics Foundation (NEF) is a leading UK organisation committed to social, economic and environmental justice, ideas and action.

We aim to improve quality of life by promoting innovative solutions that challenge mainstream thinking on economic, environmental and social issues. We work in partnership and put people and the planet first.... Austerity policies have put communities and organisations across the UK under intense pressure. While the negative social consequences are well documented, less attention has been paid to the range of creative responses to austerity measures from local authorities, housing associations, grant-makers and funders, charitable and voluntary sector, campaigners and activists. (NEF, 2015)

In its report, *Responses to austerity*, NEF (2015) builds on its previous research into the social impact of austerity policies on vulnerable communities. This report concentrates on the action that communities are using to struggle for social justice despite the damaging policies that have decimated public sector funding. NEF's aim is to build a strong knowledge base to inspire communities to act for change by drawing on examples that communities have been putting into practice already. These come into three categories:

- **Adapting:** making austerity more liveable or workable.
- **Challenging:** speaking or acting against austerity.
- **Imagining:** becoming advocates of alternatives and wider structural change.

The report provides a vital source of information and action for community development. Visit NEF's website at www.neweconomics.org/publications/entry/responses-to-austerity and read *Responses to austerity* (2015).

In summary, NEF says:

> A growing body of evidence demonstrates that austerity policies in the form of cuts to welfare and services aggravate social inequalities, fail to reduce government debt and are unnecessary. Individuals and organisations have been deeply affected by public spending cuts and have reached the limits of survival strategies. In a difficult context, various groups are seeking new and creative ways to respond. Driven by the aims of promoting wellbeing and tackling inequality, they are taking action to mitigate the effects of austerity, to challenge it, and to imagine alternatives.

NEF's argument concentrates on levels of action:

1   Groups are mobilising to adapt, challenge and imagine alternative responses to austerity policies.
2   Organisations are finding ways to maintain and even expand their operations.
3   A UK-wide movement is needed to support sustainable change.

To join them in 'fighting for social justice in times of austerity', get together with your team of activists and practitioners to plan how you could join in this movement for change. Use their examples to trigger creative ideas, and plan how you could develop or locate a project that could add to the strength of those 'fighting for justice in times of austerity'.

In the next chapter, I introduce the life and ideas of Paulo Freire as the basis of a Freirean approach to community development practice. This offers practitioners a coherent structure for developing theory and action for change.

TWO

Paulo Freire's critical pedagogy

In practice, one of the biggest challenges to igniting the community development process is to find a way through the hopelessness that oppression usually brings. Subordination robs people of self-belief. The challenge of community development is to create the conditions for people to become confident and autonomous, able to act together to bring about change. So what can Paulo Freire, the Brazilian adult educator, offer this process?

Paulo Freire, as Peter Mayo says, 'achieved iconic status among educators and a whole range of cultural workers striving for greater social justice … who imagine a world not as it is now but as it should and can be' (Mayo, 2013, p 9). The reason for Freire's popularity around the world is that he not only helps us to theorise oppression, but he also helps us to develop liberating practice that brings about change. This is the essence of liberating praxis. And the beginning of that process is, as Nita Freire says, discovering hidden knowledge (Freire, N., 2014), hidden in the taken-for-granted contradictions of everyday life, so familiar that we do not even notice. In this chapter I explore the relevance of Paulo Freire's critical pedagogy as a practical tool for weaving theory and practice together into an integrated social justice approach to community development.

Easy introduction to the relevance of critical pedagogy

By critical pedagogy, Freire means empowering education, education that questions everyday life, identifies contradictions, makes critical connections with the structures of society that discriminate and acts to change things for the better. In fact, it is a perfect fit with community development! It is a term that is often used interchangeably with popular education, 'popular' meaning related to poor and marginalised groups of people, a form of informal education that has social justice at its heart. In this sense, it is education that sides with oppressed people, with the intention of creating a more fair and equal society. It is based on the idea that education that does not focus on the disadvantaged is inevitably going to privilege the privileged, therefore maintaining the unjust structures of society that discriminate against the least powerful. Freire's influential book, *Pedagogy of the oppressed* (1972), understood in this way, simply means popular education. Its roots lie in the lives and struggles of everyday folk, which is why it focuses on stories that come from experience.

Its overriding purpose is not to make life a little more tolerable for those who are oppressed, but to create a society that is more just, equal and fair through progressive social and political change. This cannot be done without an analysis of power and how it serves the interests of the privileged by exploiting the disadvantaged. Its process is critical pedagogy, a collective rather than individual learning based on critical consciousness, involving questioning and exposing the links between knowledge and power, leading to a new knowledge that informs action for change. At the heart of the process is an understanding that education is not neutral: it is either strengthening the status quo by deepening the structures of discrimination that create social inequality, or it is questioning, exposing and changing these structures to create a new future based on fairness, justice and sustainability. In summary, critical pedagogy focuses on the *politics and power* of everyday life through a process of *education and learning* that emerges in *critical consciousness*, the foundation of *collective action* for change.

Freire offers not only a theory, but also the tools to apply the theory in practice. This is the strength of his legacy. Rather than a person of abstract ideas, he lived his life as an unfolding praxis in itself, a way of *being*, not just a way of *working*. Dedicated to social justice, his approach to education was not top-down, but a process of learning in mutual, reciprocal, equal relationships. His pedagogy was developed from his own learning with oppressed people from a wide range of cultural backgrounds, not as an authority figure, but as a co-learner, true to the values of the critical pedagogy that became his lifework. There are many thinkers who influence our minds, but few who also speak to us on an emotional level to engage both thinking *and* feelings as knowledge. Freire is one of those rare people who excite the intellect with the passion to act.

Central to Freire's critical pedagogy is a process of **conscientisation** (or *conscientização* in Portuguese). This involves setting the context for people to question their reality by interrupting the taken-for-granted acceptance of everyday life. Looking at life situations from a distance gives rise to a more questioning perspective on why situations are as they are. The act of questioning begins to identify the contradictions we live by but have not noticed because they are so familiar. This is done in dialogue groups (**culture circles**, in Freire's terminology), where a relevant issue for the community is captured in, say, a photograph, and taken out of context, helping the group to see it from a different perspective in order to question why it should be so. Dialogue deepens, and connections begin to be made between disempowerment and structural discrimination. This new way of seeing the world, an awareness of the way that power advantages some people and disadvantages others, leads to collective decisions on what to do about it. Critical pedagogy really is as simple as that!

This chapter will take you deeper into understanding how to use critical pedagogy in your own practice. First, I want to share some thoughts about how to prepare for this approach by understanding the thinking behind it.

Dehumanisation

Freire used the term **dehumanisation** to emphasise the ways in which oppression robs people of their right to be fully human in the world. For individuals to be healthy and for society to function well, we have to create a system that offers people the chance to develop their potential as a contribution to the whole. Self-determination and personal autonomy lead to a collective autonomy, a more fully functioning and engaged society. In this way, difference/diversity replaces domination/subordination as a way of life that dismantles excess privilege for the few with a common good for all.

Poverty is a dehumanising experience that creates a sense of powerlessness, destroys confidence and self-belief, limits opportunities, and robs people of their hopes and aspirations. Community development's commitment to social justice involves believing in people to such an extent that they believe in themselves! This is the foundation of empowerment and the beginning of social change. I suppose we could see it as a transformative step to restoring the fundamental right to be fully human and engaged in the world. As a practitioner, the first step in the process of change, therefore, is to fully believe in people's capacity to be thinking and conscious, capable of acting together to change their lives and to change the world. Without this belief, it is impossible to work with the concept of *empowerment*. Everything about your verbal and non-verbal behaviour will reflect doubt and uncertainty, and this will reinforce *disempowerment*. This suggests that the first step on the path is one of *self-reflection*.

Pause for thought...

Self-reflection is an important part of developing a critical approach to practice. We need to be open to exploring our own inner attitudes, lurking deep inside, if we are to have a critical engagement with the world. Without this, our non-verbal language projects our prejudices and expectations, and sometimes this can be the opposite of what we say! Do you believe deep down inside that people are fully capable, but that life circumstances have robbed them of the right to think and to act consciously? Take time to examine the thoughts that come into your mind. What assumptions and value judgements do you make about people? Think of the times when almost unconscious judgemental thoughts have become conscious to you. What are the challenges to believing that people are capable of being thinking, active participants in the process of change?

We are all products of these times in which swathes of poor people have been labelled 'welfare scroungers', intent on ripping off 'benefit Britain', so it is not easy to be aware whether these ideas are influencing our practice. This places us as participants in the process of becoming critical as much as anyone else. Perhaps we can never be sure that we have purged ourselves of the negative stereotyping of people around us, but we can make sure that we become more conscious of judgemental thoughts.

The next step is to listen from the heart to the stories that people tell, taking them seriously, and caring. This simple act of everyday compassion is powerful. Many people have never been listened to or taken seriously. So, giving the space for voices to be heard is the first act of empowerment, and it equalises power relations between people as mutual, reciprocal acts of human caring. We could call this an act of re-humanisation, restoring the right to become fully human. In itself it is an empowering encounter.

Think about the times when you have not been taken seriously, ridiculed or humiliated, and remember the impact it had on your self-esteem. Imagine how it feels to be labelled by society, never to be listened to or taken seriously from childhood, and you begin to get an idea of how that experience consistently erodes confidence, denies opportunities and reduces life chances. It is important to understand that the most powerful way to control people is to colonise minds with stories of *superiority/inferiority*. If everything about your life reflects that you are capable and respected, you will flourish. If you are told stories that demean and diminish your identity, your gender, your culture, your faith, your age, your social background and everything about your life reflects this, then it will diminish your confidence, destroying hopes and aspirations to be the person you could be. Understanding the way that power works systematically to silence people is at the core of Freire's thinking. And once we begin to question these power relations of superiority and inferiority, the blinkers lift, and we see power in action in everyday life, all around us.

Structural discrimination

The next stage is to begin to question dehumanising experiences that people have in their everyday lives as not random and personal, but systematically structured into society in relations of *domination* and *subordination*. Paulo Freire saw this process as *critical pedagogy*, a term that simply means teaching people to question their everyday reality to become more critically conscious. Once we start to see the world differently, we act differently, and the key to unlocking the energy of self-belief lies in exposing the contradictions we live by as myths that are told by a dominant ideology that seeks to maintain the status quo. The most powerful of these under **neoliberalism** has been the story of the 'welfare scrounger', which has been so persuasive in convincing the general public that all people on benefits are work-shy and irresponsible, it has created widespread support for policies that target the most vulnerable in support of global corporate interests.

Freire's approach involves identifying and questioning the contradictions we live by in order to identify the root causes of social injustice. For instance, becoming aware that 80 per cent of the repayment of the economic crash, caused by the greed of the wealthy, is being paid for by the poorest in UK society is an unacceptable paradox that is being lived out in reality, and not systematically challenged. At the same time, there is massive resistance to increasing taxation levels paid by the swelling numbers of excessively rich to redistribute wealth to an acceptable level in order to reduce social divisions. This is justified by a parallel process of labelling poor people as feckless and undeserving to justify the dismantling of the public sector. The result is that the UK is the most divided country in Europe. **Pathologising** poor people as responsible for creating their own oppression is a myth that deflects attention from the discriminatory structures of society that are widening social divisions to a point of unsustainability. The process of change begins in the community, and Paulo Freire offers us both the ideas and the practical tools to develop a critical approach to practice that tackles the issues from the grassroots with a global reach.

Paulo Freire and the power of ideas to transform practice

Paulo Freire's ideas transformed my understanding of power at the same time as giving me the tools to transform my practice. In turn, I have worked with thousands of practitioners and students who get excited by these ideas, and see their increasing relevance in today's political context. In 1997, I met Paulo Freire in Omaha, Nebraska, not realising that his death was imminent. His humility, together with his uncompromising commitment to *liberating education* as the right to become fully human in unjust societies, was palpable. His emphasis on praxis, bridging the gap between thinking and doing, came with his challenge that we cannot expect this to be a passive process. He talked of the way he continued to work at understanding ideas, and suggested that we should all expect to read, exploring the relevance of ideas to the way we see the world, discussing them with others, and integrating them into practice. When we do this, we build the bridge that links theory and practice.

Freire's belief was that education is a fundamental right for everyone, from the cradle to the grave, and that a holistic approach to knowledge (knowing that comes from feelings and experience as well as the intellect) leads to a greater wisdom for a fair and healthy democracy. A paradox that sits well here is the understanding that a divided society is an unhappy, unsustainable society that diminishes the wellbeing of everyone, rich and poor alike. Yet we have created a worldview that elevates profit above human wellbeing, justifying why some people should be excessively rich at the same time as others are unacceptably poor. A holistic approach to making sense of life incorporating feelings, experience and intellect exposes these contradictions we live by and raises questions. By the same token, a fragmented approach to making sense of life based on pragmatic facts conceals

Figure 2.1: Paulo Freire, 1921–97

prejudice and discrimination, obscuring the root sources of oppression. Critical praxis takes a holistic approach to knowing the world, using stories of everyday life as the key to social change. It is founded on freedom of thought and freedom of being as the essence of empowerment, and locates a profound love for people and the world as essential components of a critical approach, not only to work, but to life!

So, based on what I have said about experience and feelings being vital to community development's theory and practice, let's explore some aspects of Freire's life story that influenced his ideas.

Paulo, the boy: early experiences that influenced his ideas

Paulo Freire was born on 19 September 1921, in Recife, North East Brazil. His father was an army sergeant and his mother a seamstress, fluent in French (as well as her first language, Portuguese), and the mother of four children. Paulo was the youngest of the four, but two older children died before he knew them. It was a happy childhood, with an affectionate father and a quiet and tender mother. He learned to read with his parents under the shade of the mango tree in their garden, with the ground as his blackboard and a twig as the chalk, described by his good friend Gadotti as 'a living, free, unpretentious preschool' (1994, p 2).

This happy childhood was changed forever at the age of eight, with the impact of the world economic Depression. He was 'woken up from his dream when his family lost everything with the 1929 world crisis of capitalism' (Freire, N., 2014). Along with most North East Brazilians, his family was plunged into a struggle for survival, and the family moved the 12 miles from Recife to Jaboatão in 1931, where life seemed easier. The harsh experience of poverty caused him to reflect, not only on his own personal pain, but also on the injustices faced by the majority of the Brazilian population. As an 11-year-old child, he was puzzled by the way people were silenced rather than angered by their suffering, and made his mind up to change things so that children did not experience the misery of poverty and hunger. This personal experience at such a young age taught him the profound impact of poverty on life chances. He talked about trying to read and learn, but, 'I didn't understand anything because of my hunger…. It wasn't lack of interest. My social condition didn't allow me to have an education. Experience showed me once again the relationship between social class and knowledge' (quoted in Gadotti, 1994, p 5).

Pause for thought …

Freire talks about how his education was limited by hunger. Think about the impact of poverty in your own community. Set this within the facts: the UK, the most divided country in Europe, has levels of inequality that compare with Nigeria. One in three children is growing up in poverty, and this figure is rising, one in seven children goes to school without breakfast and one in eight does not get a cooked meal. Why does a rich country, such as the UK, choose not to feed its poorest children?

Freire's father was only 52 when he died, and Freire was only 13. The short time they shared together had such an impact on the young Paulo that it stayed with him all his life, and in a dialogue group with Walter de Oliveira in 1996, the year before Freire died, he talked about both the right and the responsibility we have to work at becoming who we are, despite external forces that could prevent this happening. Freire told the following story about the lessons he learned from the life he shared with his father:

> It is very strange today that I am seventy-five years old and older than my father at his death. He died in 1934 and I feel his presence almost as if he were here now. Such was his influence and presence in my childhood. In our short experience my father gave me a lot. He gave me a serious testimony of respect for others…. With him I learned tolerance. For example, he was a Spiritualist, a follower of Allan Kardec, the French philosopher…. My mother was Catholic. Of course, he was not a churchgoer…. He did not accept the ways of believing God offered by the Catholic Church. This was in the first part of the century, constituting a fantastic example of his openness and his courage. I remember when I was seven years old there was a one-week mission in the parish we lived in, which I participated in and I was trained for my first communion in the church…. And he said to me "I will go with you". You cannot realize how that speech marked me until now. That was a deep understanding of tolerance, of respect for the different…. He could say, "No it is a lie, I cannot leave you free to commit a life, to participate in such a life". On the

contrary, he went to the church and gave me a fantastic example of the absolute and fundamental importance of solidarity, of how respect for the other is absolutely indispensable, how to discuss changes and how to discuss transformation with respect. (Freire and de Oliveira, 2014, pp 48–9)

Reflecting on his life with his father, Freire learned the meaning of freedom, respect and solidarity.

His father's death brought his schooling to an abrupt halt until his older brother went to work and brought money home for food. Once the Freire family began to eat more, Paulo began to learn again. But it was the education of the streets that gave him a different way of making sense of the world, a deep understanding of the way that poverty works to silence and dehumanise people. The life he shared with young people from poor families around him educated him into a different way of seeing the world. He later came to understand that it contained the truth of their lives. This experience built on the culture of freedom and respect for difference that he laid as a foundation for his life.

He did not go to high school until he was 16. What humiliation he felt being taught with younger children of 11 and 12! And by the time he got to Recife University to study law, he was over 20. He qualified and worked as a lawyer, then as a high school Portuguese language teacher, and finally, as an adult educator once he came to realise that *liberating education* was his passion.

Freire: his adult life and work

It was when he was working as a high school teacher that Freire met Elza, a primary school teacher: 'My meeting her was one of the most creative meetings in my life' (quoted in Gadotti, 1994, p 4). It was Elza who encouraged him to study, to develop the work that made his mark in the world, and who visited him in prison in 1964 with food, not only for him, but for his cellmates too. She continued to be a huge influence on his life and work, from the time they married when he was 23, until her death 40 years later. With Elza, he became involved in the radical Catholic Action Movement, but quickly came to see the contradictions between the church's teachings and the privileged lifestyles of its congregation.

As an activist, he discovered the reluctance of the powerful to give up their privilege, that consciousness among the privileged does not inevitably result in action for change. Reflecting on his own action, he captured the need for critical reflection: 'I said many beautiful things, but made no impact. This was because I used my frame of reference, not theirs' (Freire, quoted in Mackie, 1980, pp 3–4). He was compassionate and committed, but that was not enough: he needed to suspend his own way of seeing the world and be open to hear and empathise with the many truths shaped by diverse experiences. 'I was taught by them that the right way to think was concrete, real, everyday life with all its connotations, nuances and contradictions ... they are teaching me to *think right*' (Freire, N., 2014).

Benevolence is not transformative, and power is seductive: real change comes from tolerance, respect for others, a commitment to freedom and the right to think and the right to be. This was a deepening in practice of the 'absolute and fundamental importance of solidarity' that he learned from his life with his father.

Sharing the lives of people in poverty led him to name the *culture of silence* that he had recognised as a child in Jaboatão: the way that oppression creates passive acceptance of unjust conditions because people blame themselves for their suffering. This formed the foundation of his critical pedagogy. He realised that literacy is embedded with ideas about the pecking order in society, the status quo, and that teaching people to read and write from a critical perspective can sow the seeds of questioning the taken-for-grantedness of the injustices deep-rooted in everyday life. Once people begin to see that their circumstances are not due to their own inadequacy, it restores the dignity to act for a more fair and just world.

The profound insight of his thought began to emerge when he was appointed Director of Education at SESI, an employers' organisation for workers and their families. It was here that he saw the contradictions between formal education and the reality of the lives of the working class more clearly. He began to realise that liberation would not be handed over from top down, but had to be demanded as a right from grassroots activism. This insight led Freire to understand the democratic principle involved here: in freeing themselves, oppressed people also free their oppressors.

His activism at this time, the Movement for Popular Culture and the active practice of democracy, became the focus of his doctorate from Recife University in 1959. This led to a chair in History and Philosophy of Education at the Recife University until 1964, when he was imprisoned. In 1962, he became director of the government's regional adult literacy programme in North East State Brazil, a popular education movement designed to cope with massive illiteracy in Brazil. His radical teaching was based on the belief that everyone is capable of engaging in **critical dialogue** once they see its relevance to their lives. Here we see the connection between thought and action emerging as praxis. After this regional appointment, Freire became director of the national literacy programme (Taylor, 1993).

During this period, there were widespread experiments with his approach to mass literacy. By 1963–64, there were courses for coordinators in all Brazilian states, and the plan was to establish 2,000 culture circles, community groups that would reach out to involve two million people in critical dialogue (Holst, 2006). Literacy is a liberating praxis in Freire's eyes; people learn to question at the same time as learning to read. Rather than assimilate the images often found in reading books that reflect the dominant ideology, for example, a White, heterosexual family, with a stay-at-home mother and a father who goes out to work, he used line drawings to capture images relevant to poor people's everyday experiences to start the process of questioning life's contradictions. For example, this might start off with a drawing of a coffee bean, but critical dialogue would take questioning deeper into why they are grown and who benefits from the profits of their production. When I was in Nicaragua in 1985, I saw these materials in use, very simply reproduced on poor-quality paper, but enormously effective in encouraging people to question their reality in order to see unequal power relations in action. I talk more about how to use this approach in the next chapter.

Freire's profound insight into literacy as a vehicle for critical consciousness, based on exposing the links between education and power, led him to be seen as an enemy of the state when the multinational-backed military coup took place in Brazil in 1964. Freire was arrested, stripped of his professorship and imprisoned. His trial lasted for 75 days, and he was accused by one of the judges as being a 'traitor to Christ and the Brazilian people' (Gadotti, 1994, p 35). His attempts to implement a national literacy programme that encouraged poor people to read, write and think had him labelled a subversive, a threat to the status quo (Mayo, 2004).

In prison, it became clearer to Freire that *education is politics*, and he was convinced that social change must come from grassroots action. Although the charges were dropped, when he was offered political asylum in Bolivia, he accepted, fearful for his life if he stayed in Brazil. Fifteen days later there was a coup in Bolivia, and he was, in turn, exiled to Chile, where he continued his work at the Institute for Research and Training in Agrarian Reform. Chile gave him the opportunity to re-evaluate his pedagogy in theory and practice from this different cultural and political perspective, to question Brazil from across the border.

Freire was in Chile from 1964 to 1969. His approach to critical pedagogy was used in the United Nations (UN) School of Political Sciences, where seminars were held on his work. He wrote *Education: The practice of freedom* in 1965 based on notes he brought with him from Brazil, written from more of a reformist rather than radical ideology. During his time in Chile, he was stimulated by Marxist thought, and became involved in powerful working-class organisations (Torres, 1993). The influence of this thought and action was reflected in *Pedagogy of the oppressed*, first published in Portuguese in 1968. According to Holst, Freire's work in this Chilean political context influenced his theoretical development and, in turn, influenced his ideas on action to make *Pedagogy of the oppressed* one of the most significant books on popular education to this day (Holst, 2006).

One of the most important dimensions of Freirean pedagogy is that it can only be transformative if it is situated in its social, political and economic context, and when it becomes a collective approach to social change. His compassion with the pain of those experiencing poverty filled him with the passion to understand oppression and to come up with a strategy for change. 'To find explanations, he studied Marx, but the historical materialist dialectic didn't give him all the tools to understand what was going on in the most intimate of those beings whose education had been denied ...' (Freire, N., 2014). He turned to a wide range of theorists to help his thinking, including Sartre, Marcuse, Che Guevara, Fidel Castro, Merleau-Ponty, the critical theory of the Frankfurt School, and African thinkers Amilcar Cabral, Frantz Fanon and Julius Nyerere. This eclectic approach to ideas, together with the lived experiences of working with people in the community, deepened his conceptual thought and practice.

In 1969–70, he spent time at Harvard as Visiting Professor at the Centre for the Study of Development and Social Change. Then, in 1970, he moved to Geneva as principal consultant to the Department of Education of the World Council of Churches. He stayed in this post until 1980, as an adviser on educational reform. During his time there he developed popular education approaches with diverse groups of people.

Throughout this period, Freire's influence spread, and his critical pedagogy became increasingly seen as a practical tool for popular educators engaged in political/cultural projects around the world. The concept of *conscientização* (conscientisation) gave fresh insight into the political nature of popular education as a process of liberation. Freire's recognition escalated, speaking at conferences, acting as a consultant to projects throughout the developing and industrialised nations, and advising governments. It was during the first six years of this long period of exile that his most celebrated work, *Pedagogy of the oppressed*, was written and brought him recognition as a seminal thinker of his time (Mayo, 2004).

After the amnesty of 1979, he went back to Brazil the following year and began 'relearning Brazil' by reading Gramsci and also 'listening to the popular Gramsci in the favelas' (Torres, 1993, p 135). By 'popular Gramsci', he means not that the people in the 'favelas', the shanty towns, had read Gramsci, but that Freire, after reading Gramsci, could hear in these stories of everyday life the ways that top-down power subordinated them. This happened to me after reading Freire: I could hear and see Freire in action everywhere around me. These are the ways in which ideas change the way we make sense of the world: we begin to see in new ways. Freire spent at least two afternoons a week with people in their communities, listening to their experience of life and the way that they made sense of it. This is what he means by creating *critical praxis* out of lived experience – we apply theory in action, and out of that action we, in turn, deepen our theory. Gramsci saw this as a *unity of praxis*: theory and practice become an inseparable part of each other in cycles of action and reflection.

Although his original interest was in the relevance of people's education in developing countries, particularly through literacy, health, agricultural reform and liberation theology, he also worked closely with radical educators in North America and Europe, arguing that issues of exploitation and discrimination exist everywhere. The influence of Freirean pedagogy has spread far and wide as a major influence for those committed to a more fair and just world. The inescapable paradox is, as Torres puts it so well, that political pedagogy 'in industrialized societies is nurtured by notions of education and social change developed in the Third World' (Torres, 1993, p 137).

Freire joined the Workers' Party in São Paulo, and for six years led its adult literacy project. When the Party was elected in 1988, he was appointed São Paulo's Secretary of Education.

Figure 2.2: Freire 'listening to the popular Gramsci in the favelas', 1980

On his 62nd birthday in 1983, Paulo Freire received a letter from 24 children from Gustavo Teixeira School in São Pedro, São Paulo State, asking him to 'continue loving children for ever'. His reply was to address them as 'Dear Friends from the First Grade', and that he was 'very happy to see you had such a lot of confidence in me when you asked me to continue loving children' and 'I promise I will never stop loving children. I love life too much. With love from Paulo Freire' (quoted in Gadotti, 1994, p xx). This reminds me of Gandhi's words to the angry mill workers of North Lancashire when he came to apologise for his embargo on English-woven cotton. He explained that millions in his country were starving and needed to spin and weave for themselves. At one point, he added, 'Please tell them that I love all children of the world as my own' to the man with the microphone, who, in turn, said 'Mr Gandhi says to tell you that he loves all children of the world'. The microphone picked up Gandhi's softly spoken voice: 'That's not what I said! Of the world, I love all children of the world *as my own.*' I puzzled over this before working out why those three extra words made so much difference. Then it dawned on me that loving all children of the world as much as our own is a political position that counters self-interest and individualism. If we love all children of the world, we will not support policies that starve the children of poor families. This insight into praxis, not only integrating theory and action but also emotions and intellect, was central to the important feminist project on knowledge, difference and power of Belenky's work on women's ways of knowing as connected knowing. It emphasises experience and feelings as legitimate knowledge that underpins action for change (Belenky et al, 1986,

1997). This awareness links Freirean pedagogy with feminist pedagogy, combining theory, politics, experience and feelings to provide us with the possibility of becoming effective agents of change for social justice.

When Elza died in 1986, Freire lost his long-time companion and colleague. He then married Ana Maria Araujo (Nita) in 1988, a friend of the family and a former student, who shared his life and his work until his sudden death in 1997 (Mayo, 2004). Freire remained active to the end. In the last 10 years of his life he was Secretary of Education in São Paulo (1989–91), and taught at the Pontifical Catholic University in São Paulo. He also wrote prolifically, and gave inspiring talks around the world. I was lucky enough to hear one of his last talks at the Pedagogy of the Oppressed conference, initiated by Doug Paterson at the University of Omaha at Nebraska in March 1996. Both Freire and Augusto Boal, his Brazilian colleague, author of *Theatre of the oppressed*, were conferred with honorary doctorates by the university during the conference. This organisation, now Pedagogy and Theatre of the Oppressed, holds an annual conference in different venues in the US, and the many Freire Institutes worldwide offer resources to continue the development of his work. Nita Freire was at the Freire Institute's conference at the University of Central Lancashire, Preston, UK, in 2014, giving a keynote speech to promote the ongoing development of Freire's work. A professor in her own right, she is a significant figure in the Freire Institute movement.

Ideas do not develop in a vacuum; they develop in relation to life experience. Understanding Freire's life story offers an insight into the way that his ideas were formed from life experience based on his identity, his cultural background and his political times. I will now set the scene for Freire's key concepts, the practical application of his work that is the focus of the next chapter.

Becoming critical: new possibilities for knowing and being

The way we see the world affects how we act in the world. This is fundamental to understanding Freire's approach. The stories we are told from the time we are born about our place in society, by, for example, family, community, teachers, and the media, have such a strong influence on how we make sense of the world around us that they are internalised as *common sense*. These assumptions are *taken-for-granted* as unquestioned truths, and are hard to break through without an interruption in our thinking. This idea of an interruption in our taken-for-grantedness is the kick-start to critical consciousness.

When asked, 'What can we do in order to follow you?', Freire, in his own inimitable way said, 'If you follow me, you destroy me. The best way for you to understand me is to reinvent me and not to try to become adapted to me' (Giroux, quoted in Freire, N. and de Oliveira, 2014, p 7)! To understand his thinking, it is important to reflect on how he speaks about his father's impression on his understanding of freedom: freedom to think and freedom to be.

Education for Freire is not abstract, prescriptive or a training ground: it is the foundation of individual autonomy and social agency, learning from the past through the contradictions of the present, fired by a collective sense of social responsibility for a common good. In the pursuit of these ends, he was more concerned with asking better questions than telling people the answers (Giroux, quoted in Freire, N. and de Oliveira, 2014, p 8). For Freire, education is the practice of freeing minds through a culture of questioning which opens the mind to intellectual curiosity because of its relevance to everyday life experience. This is education for social justice with a responsibility to others and the world. It begins by respecting people's experience, voices and beliefs as the first step to self-belief and empowerment on a journey of solidarity for a common good.

Freire was preoccupied with identifying social contradictions that expose grand narratives of domination as serving the interests of power and privilege. He was clear that what he offered was not an abstract theory or a fixed formula, but a continuing, evolving, universal approach that needs to be adapted to its particular political times and its specific cultural/social context within an ethics of 'pragmatism, love and solidarity' (McLaren and Giroux, quoted in Gadotti, 1994, p xiv).

This approach, so often defined as one of love, humility, hope and faith by Freire, gives rise to the values of reciprocity, mutuality, respect and trust that define everything about a Freirean approach to community development. Based on an ideology of equality, it frames the skills that define our practice. As McLaren and Giroux poetically express, it is 'a pedagogy of laughter, of questioning, of curiosity, of seeing the future through the present, a pedagogy that believes in the possibility of the transformation of the world, that believes in history as a possibility' (Mclaren and Giroux, quoted in Gadotti, 1994, p xvii). But underlying this is the important connection between knowledge and power; understanding that dominant knowledge serves economic social and political interests, and that critical pedagogy provides us with the conceptual tools needed to question inequalities and injustices. This paves the way towards a 'collective vision of what it might be like to live in the best of all societies and how such a vision might be made practical' (Shor, quoted in Macrine, 2009, p 120).

Pause for thought...

This is an idea that Freire developed conceptually: we take for granted our everyday circumstances, and internalise the contradictions we live by unquestioningly as common sense. It is only when we look at these contradictions in a different light that we see that they make no sense at all, and that is when we begin to question. For instance, think about the contradiction of a nation choosing to reduce a third of its children to growing up in poverty, not only limiting the life chances of its next generations, but limiting the potential for all society. Think of scenes from everyday life in your community, and reflect on the life chances of children born into poverty against those born into privilege. Yet, mostly these everyday paradoxes are unquestioned, accepted as natural and normal, and therefore acceptable.

Creating learning contexts enables people to come together and critique what is happening in their lives in order to see the way that power is part of everyday existence. This is the route to critical consciousness, a way of seeing inequalities woven through all aspects of life, from the personal to the structures of society. These critical spaces are the context for questioning the world around us, exposing its contradictions in order to act collectively to change things for the better. At this point, let's explore how to take this idea into practice as theory in action.

Community development as critical pedagogy

Freire places great emphasis on praxis, a unity of action and reflection, so that practice (or doing) and our thinking about what we do (theory) are bound together in one process, applying theory in action, and developing theory from that action. This becomes transformative praxis when it situates people in their political context, identifying and questioning the unjust contradictions of everyday life. Freire's critical pedagogy is a process of critical consciousness leading to action for change, in which personal problems are questioned in relation to political times that embed structural injustices within the very fabric of society. The process is one of empowerment combined with the knowledge to analyse and collectively act together for change. The overall aim is to deepen democracy by transforming unjust power relations by understanding the historical conditions that have created the present injustices in order to change the future.

Freire's critical pedagogy is not only based on analyses of power, helping us to understand how power relations are part of everyday life, but he offers a conceptual toolkit for us to use in practice to understand the connections between knowledge and power. This is the foundation for what Freire calls *liberating education*. Dominant ideology is based on the social construction of knowledge that is sold to society as common sense, a way of accepting the dominant order of things according to values that often serve the interests of the most powerful rather than the least powerful. Becoming critical involves exposing the assumptions that create this reality. Paulo Freire's contribution is to demonstrate the importance of praxis, so that theory in action is our intention as we go about our everyday practice. It is the only way we can make sense of the political context of people's lives and the impact it has on their reality. This is why Freire insists that theory is embedded in people's stories of everyday life, and why this is the foundation of our practice.

By questioning what is happening around us, we tease out the beginning of a new way of seeing the world. This forms the basis of acting together collectively to bring about change from a critical, more analytic perspective. It is as easy as that, but when practised on a large scale, it can change the world, simply by creating the context for people to see the world differently. This insight into the political nature of education underpins critical pedagogy. The starting point for Freire is to see that education can never be neutral: its political function is always to liberate or to domesticate. If we fail to understand this, we overlook the ways in which power and domination are woven through the very fabric of society, persuading people to accept their lot. We also miss the point that our role as critical educators is to develop the context for liberating education in order to expose the sources of discrimination that create structural inequality. This new way of seeing the world leads to action for change, opening up possibilities for a world built on social justice values. It is a *pedagogy of hope* that carves its way through hopelessness and restores human dignity; it is a *pedagogy of love* inspired by compassion for people and the planet.

From this perspective, a practitioner is a popular educator, a critical pedagogue who, driven by a sense of agency and informed by an ideology of equality, forms mutual, reciprocal relationships with people, approaching education as a process that calls for us to learn as much as we teach. Together, we learn to see the political in personal lives as a process of mutual discovery. We never tell people what to think. Telling people what to think merely replaces one form of oppression with another: this approach is all about freeing people's minds to think and act for themselves. This, in itself, shifts the balance of power to locate everyone on the same side, in mutual commitment to dismantle what is unfair and unjust, and to create a world of possibility in which everyone and everything has a chance to flourish.

Freire's personality reflected this love of life: his sense of presence, his attention to people, and the seriousness with which he engaged in every encounter. This understanding helped me in my own practice to see empowerment in every encounter I had with people. When this slipped, I was reminded.

A story: Mindfulness in everyday encounters...

One day, Brenda came up to me, angrily demanding to know what she'd done to offend me. Taken aback, I asked her what she meant. "I was coming out of the Co-op last Thursday, and you walked straight past me with your nose in the air and a frown on your face. What have I done to upset you?" Last Thursday? Puzzled ... then I gradually remembered the stress of trying to balance the community centre accounts in time for the auditor's visit. I must have been so preoccupied, I didn't even notice Brenda coming out of the Co-op. I looked at the distress on her face, and realised how careless it was of me not to notice her, how easily my body language could be taken as a personal insult, even more especially in this community which was so used to being treated harshly. Thank goodness she felt able to challenge me. It was a lesson to pay attention in the moment to the quality of every encounter, and if I didn't learn it, there could be many others who walked away rather than challenged me. No encounter with me should ever damage or diminish anyone, if I am practising what I preach!

Freirean conceptual tools offer practical approaches to critique society's inequalities and injustices, at the same time as developing a vision of a practical utopia based on the belief that collective action can bring about social change. Within the process itself, Freire offers value-based skills that equip us to be both self-critical, reflecting on our inner attitudes and qualities, and to have a critical engagement in the world, to see everyday contradictions that reveal power in action.

Theory in action 2

Becoming critical

Issue

There is a discrepancy between what community development says it is about in theory, and the reality of what is happening in practice. To legitimately claim a social justice principle, social justice has to be the goal for every stage of practice, from personal encounters to collective action. To do this, we have to work at becoming critical.

Evidence

There is little evidence to suggest that community development is making a significant contribution to social justice outcomes for a more fair, just and sustainable society. Dilution and underfunding threaten the transformative dimensions of practice, but it is more important than ever to keep that critical edge in place in political times in which social divisions are widening alarmingly. Becoming critical involves understanding how power discriminates and acting together to change the source of that power. That means we have to think and act at all levels, local to global.

Analysis

An analysis of power in today's political context is called for. Noam Chomsky, one of the most influential critical thinkers of our times, talks very simply about the nature of power in current political times, and the need to unravel free trade agreements, such as the Transatlantic Trade Investment Partnership (TTIP), in order to understand how corporate interests use anti-democratic principles that threaten public services. Driven by big businesses in the US and the European Union (EU), it is intended to remove barriers to free trade and investment, but it leaves the public interest vulnerable: policies that support a common good by promoting social equality, protecting the environment or supporting public health can be challenged by foreign investors as acting against the interests of free trade (Chomsky, 2015).

Chomsky believes that countries with more freedom control people through the media rather than by force. He asks whether any social system has a legitimate right to impose controls that limit the potential of people. Social obedience maintains control, subordinating large numbers of people, but why do people obey when power collapses in the face of dissent? Nothing will ever change if people take-for-granted the roles they have been given.

What we are seeing is beyond capitalism. It is a new system that is supported by the nation state, which uses taxpayers and public sector cuts as a safety net for corporate interests when unacceptable risks crash, for example, the 2007 banking crisis, in which the UK diverted resources from its poorest people to pay 80 per cent of the deficit. In this sense, the state is serving global corporate interests by bailing out unacceptable risks using ordinary people as a safety net. If we are going to be able to challenge this highly developed global system, we need to dismantle the structures of power, not by devolution, but through social movements (Chomsky, 2015). This is where community development comes in!

Figure 2.3: Theory in action: action in theory

Action

In relation to the need for dissenting voices to speak to power, consider: 'An Act of Dissent is a simple way of saying, "No, I do not accept this and, [...] my silence may be construed as acquiescence"' (Thomas, 2015, p 8). Read some of the 100 Acts of minor dissent tested by Mark Thomas and discuss the use of peaceful disruption tactics to 'interrupt' the collective flow of acquiescence. Similarly, read Saul Alinsky, well-respected Chicago activist, and explore the ways he used disruption tactics to dismantle the course of power (see Alinsky, 1972, 1976).

Go to the Noam Chomsky website (www.chomsky.info) and select 'Pedagogy of the oppressed' from the audio and visual list. Listen to Noam Chomsky talking about Paulo Freire in his political times and his continuing relevance in today's political context. Then think how short-term objectives can be set within the longer-term goal of social change. How can a participatory democratic shift to keep control of local resources and the talents of local people become part of a movement for a common good for all? How can you link your local community development to collective action for change through social movements? Paulo Freire's critical pedagogy offers community development an approach to practice that is capable of situating local practice within this complex bigger picture in cycles of action and reflection, a critical living praxis.

Freire inspires the optimism that a new world is not only possible, but it could be built on cooperative values that place human flourishing and planetary flourishing at its heart. This dismantles the competitive worldview of profit wrung from the exploitation of people and the planet as a measure of success, replacing it with a worldview built on cooperation with human and environmental wellbeing as its measure, not just bridging the theory–practice divide, but fully integrating a way of knowing the world with emotions and experience, as knowledge equips us with the tools to identify the contradictions that come from fragmented knowing. The next chapter takes a more in-depth look at Freire's key concepts to help you to develop this approach in your own practice.

THREE

Kick-starting Freire in everyday practice

WASHING ONE'S HANDS OF THE CONFLICT BETWEEN THE POWERFUL AND THE POWERLESS MEANS TO SIDE WITH THE POWERFUL, NOT TO BE NEUTRAL.

This chapter introduces Paulo Freire's specific concepts in a simple and direct way so that you can begin to build them into a Freirean approach to practice. There are examples along the way that offer suggestions how to apply these ideas in everyday action. In the previous chapter we looked at Paulo Freire, the man and his thoughts, in his historical, cultural and political times. Now let's take a look at how these key principles can be applied in current practice.

One of the challenges for community workers is to overcome the apathy, hopelessness and dehumanisation created by living in poverty, captured in Freire's concept of a *culture of silence*. This is a direct result of the *pathologising of poverty* that is so much part of the 'welfare scrounger' image, persuading people to accept their poverty as a consequence of their own inadequacies rather than a consequence of power relations and structural discrimination. We are looking for practical ways to break through the *dehumanising* impact of this dominant message, that somehow poverty is a result of personal irresponsibility, to kick-start the energy for change.

Critical consciousness, collective action and social transformation

As a jumping off point, let's contextualise Freire's key concepts within the rich imagination of his thinking. This avoids any sense of them being an eclectic, random group of ideas, but rather an integrated range of concepts that together provide an approach to community development practice which raises its transformative potential. This point is important. If the concepts are used in an *ad hoc* piecemeal way, they will be tokenistic rather than transformative. By this I mean that they might make life appear a bit better on the surface, but will not go down deep enough to challenge and change the structures of society that embed discrimination in everyday life.

At the heart of Freire's critical pedagogy is the development of critical consciousness, *conscientisation*, a way of seeing the world with all its contradictions, a process that starts by simply creating the context for people to question their everyday experience. The purpose of this is to look beyond what we unquestioningly accept and take for granted in everyday life. Seeing situations with fresh eyes lifts the blinkers: we see the contradictions of life that are unjust and that lead to social inequalities. This locates the community worker as an educator in a process of *education for liberation*.

Of course, this in itself is not enough to be transformative without collective action for change. This is precisely why the concept of *empowerment* is always a collective and not an individual process: personal empowerment is only truly empowering when it leads to collective action for transformative change. The process begins in *dialogue* in a community group; from there it moves into local action, but it never stops at the boundary of community. Transformative change reaches outside the community, linking local groups to movements for change that have the collective power to transform structural inequalities on a much bigger scale. For these reasons, community workers committed to social justice need to be aware of the process as a whole, and locate local projects within this more extensive process. If we stay at the level of the local community project, we are failing to situate personal lives within the political, social and economic context of their times, and so fail to identify the discriminatory forces that are prescribing life chances according to forces of domination and subordination. In these ways, community development is about deepening democracy, acting together to create a society in which everyone is valued, heard and respected, one that we might see as participatory democracy.

Freire's profound insight into the nature of oppression politicised community work in the early 1970s. Still, all these years on, he offers the conceptual tools for us to develop our ideas appropriately for these current, rapidly changing times of crises for both social justice and environmental sustainability, the twin pillars of community development. Here I will introduce you to Freirean key concepts in order to fill your toolkit with the basics for this approach. In subsequent chapters, I will unfold a critical re-reading of his work from our many new insights into the complexity of oppression in all its overlappings and intertwinings, including the ways in which social justice links to environmental sustainability issues.

Pause to search...

... the internet for the growing number of Freire institutes across the world, from Ireland to India, which reflect the current interest in and commitment to a burgeoning movement for social change based on critical consciousness. They also provide courses and resources to support community development practice.

Figure 3.1: Freire Institute movement

education · empowerment · transformation

Source: Reproduced with permission of the Paulo Freire Institute

Paulo Freire's key concepts

This section introduces some important key concepts that are the foundation of a Freirean approach to any practice that has a social justice intention. The fundamental belief underpinning Freire's critical pedagogy is that human beings are subjects, able to think and act for themselves, and from this point of view, everyone is capable of seeing the world critically in order to change it for the better. When I use the word 'critical' in this way, I mean questioning everything to get beyond the taken-for-grantedness that we all live by. In order to change these entrenched attitudes, the challenge is to discover how to break through the powerful dominant narratives that write the mass of people off as Objects (see p 50) incapable of taking responsibility for themselves, let alone for society.

The stories that we are told carry powerful messages that become internalised and controlling. If you think about it, internalised ideas are far more powerful than external controls: they do not have to be policed from outside, the message just has to be persuasive, maintained, and then it does its own controlling from inside our minds. Freire's life purpose was to identify a process of critical discovery through which oppressed people could free their minds and become aware that *they* hold the key to transformative social change. The simple act of discovering some control over life's circumstances is empowering, energising and brings with it a sense of self-belief. It restores dignity. It also comes with a sense of identity, affirming who we are.

So we are looking at this as a liberating practice that is about freeing minds, seeing the world through a different lens of infinite possibilities, and acting together to turn possibilities into reality.

Action/reflection

The gaping chasm between theory and practice is an ongoing weakness for community development. It reduces the potential of practice to achieve a social justice outcome. Paulo Freire emphasised the importance of a unity of theory and practice that weaves thought and action together in *praxis*. This process builds theory in action and action as theory in a cycle that is rooted in everyday experience, quite different from theory that is abstract, fragmented and decontextualised from people's lives. This is precisely why Freire insisted that his ideas had emerged from his own identity, his culture, his experience and his political times, and why he told us that this approach could not be superimposed on any context. We have to work at using the concepts as tools that help us to make sense of what is happening in the here and now, specific to our current political times but located in a past–present–future perspective.

It reminds me of the social activist bell hooks who, at a time when Freire was being criticised for seeing life from only a class-based perspective, and failing to address 'race' and gender, took a paradoxical stand: she acknowledged that Freire had given her the tools to define her own experience of racism as a Black American woman, a subject in resistance, at a time when early White feminists

Figure 3.2 Action and reflection: a dialectical contradiction!

were not engaging with Black women's struggle. It was a reminder that we need to acknowledge our intellectual debts and build on an evolving body of knowledge. A synthesis of action and reflection offers us a way of building theory in action in order to get to grips with the constantly changing context of our practice. If we fail to do this, we resort to 'thoughtless action' (Johnston, quoted in Shaw, 2004, p 26), and this leaves us wide open to either *placatory practice* (a surface-level reaction to the symptoms of oppression) or *pure activism* (uninformed action), neither of which is useful. Critical reflection leads to informed action, and this is the only way to bring about sustainable change.

Later in this book, I introduce emancipatory action research (EAR) as an approach to praxis, a way of integrating experience, education and action, the investigation of social reality with critical consciousness, in cycles of action and reflection that are central 'prerequisites for participation' (Tandon, 2008, p 288).

Dehumanisation

Freire's use of dehumanisation is important in understanding the nature of power relations. Oppression is the unjust abuse of power by privileged social groups over subordinated groups in order to exploit them and to deprive them of privileges in society. Dominant groups benefit from this systematic exploitation of subordinated groups, whether they have individual oppressive attitudes or not, because dominant attitudes become assimilated into public consciousness as an ideology, a truth that is not questioned and therefore becomes embedded in the structures of society as common sense.

Pause for thought...

Think of the power relations between Black and White people in, for instance, South Africa, or in the richer countries of the West, such as the US or the UK, and reflect on ways in which personal prejudice becomes embedded into the fabric of society as structural discrimination. Think of the dominant narratives that encourage attitudes of domination and subordination based on racism. Consider the ways in which gender relations between men and women privilege men and subordinate women. Then think about the ways that people experience multiple discrimination based on overlapping oppressions, for instance, poor, elderly, Black women. People experience personal prejudice that is acted out in everyday life. But think about the ways that even those who are privileged but not consciously prejudiced automatically benefit from discrimination when attitudes of superiority and inferiority become embedded in the structures of society. Freire captures the way that oppression dehumanises both oppressors and oppressed. So, if oppression dehumanises both, how do you see this in relation to the violence of the English riots of 2011 (see pp 79–81)? How does this sit in relation to Freire's concept of a culture of silence?

When discrimination becomes so deeply embedded in the assumptions of the institutions that govern society, supported by cultural stereotyping in the media, it is unquestioned and becomes systematically reproduced to a point that anyone with privilege has an interest in maintaining the status quo, even those who would not readily identify themselves as prejudiced. In these ways, oppression refers to relations of domination/subordination between social groups and between societies. Social injustice refers to the discriminatory, dehumanising practices that result in the destruction of life chances through poverty, unemployment, poor education, homelessness, poor health and premature death which interact to exploit oppressed groups to the advantage of the dominant by denying fair distribution of resources. Social justice practice aims to tackle disadvantage, not only at a personal or community level, but also at a structural level in order to dismantle the self-perpetuating processes of subordination. *Dehumanisation* is the term that captures the way that subordinated groups are robbed of their humanity. But Freire also considers that the very act of dehumanising robs the powerful of their humanity too, which is why he talks about the oppressed not only regaining their own humanity, but restoring the humanity of the oppressors (Freire, 1972).

Conscientisation

Conscientisation is a process of awareness that begins as people start to question their everyday reality and make connections between their personal lives and the political structures of society that creates this reality. This critical insight alters a sense of personal failure, connects to the shared circumstances of others, and creates the conditions for collective action for social change. Freire refers to conscientisation as 'the deepening of the coming of consciousness' (Freire, 1993, p 109), so whereas 'there can be no conscientization without coming first to consciousness … not all coming to consciousness extends necessarily into conscientization' (1993, p 109). By this, Freire means that false consciousness permeates our being in such convincing ways that everyday truths are obscured and distorted by dominant ideologies. To get to the heart of these truths we need curiosity, critical reflection and rigour to take us a step further than critical consciousness in order to locate our practice in a position where it can make a difference to social injustice.

Magical consciousness

The process of becoming critically aware is seen by Freire to have three levels that are reflected in the language of people: magical, naïve and critical consciousness. **Magical consciousness** is the level at which people are reduced to a passive and unquestioning state about the injustices in their lives. The harshness of life tends to be accepted as fate, and explanations are often shrugged off as inevitable and unchangeable. How often have you heard people say that they must have done something bad or been wicked in a past life to explain away the injustices of their suffering in the present? In an interview with Christine Morris in 1996, Freire described his quest for understanding the power of this silencing:

> It was hard for me to understand how these people dealt with reality. They used to explain pain, discrimination because of destiny or god's punishment. For me, this ideology paralyzed the people and maintained stratification. We had to learn the power of the counter attack because to stay in fatalism helps the dominant. (Morris, 2008, p 57)

Naïve consciousness

Naïve consciousness involves some insight into the nature of individual disadvantages, but does not connect these with structural discrimination. At this level of consciousness, people tend to blame themselves, saying that their life circumstances are due to their own inadequacies. Think of how many times you have heard people say that they are not clever, should have worked harder, or studied more at school. This individualisation of failure leads us to see the *student as failing education*, rather than *education failing its students*. It links to thoughts about Freire's insistence on critical pedagogy needing to listen to the language of the people and be relevant to their culture. Education that is relevant to dominant social groups reinforces disadvantage in subordinated social groups. In these ways, the traditional education system often plays a hegemonic role in maintaining the interests of the privileged in society.

Critical consciousness

Critical consciousness is a way of seeing the world that connects personal lives with their political context. This exposes the contradictions we live by, making connections with the way that discrimination is woven into the structures of society, reaching into people's being, shaping lives in ways that privilege some and disadvantage others.

False generosity

False generosity is a term originally coined by Engels that influenced Freire's thinking about the way that empty gestures give the appearance of equality without changing the underlying structural conditions that are causing inequalities. An example of this might be seen in the way that welfare benefits can be improved to subsistence level to help people to survive, but without asking why unemployment is a feature of society, why there are no sustainable employment opportunities for large numbers of people. This links to Marxism's *false consciousness*, the way that subordinate groups are persuaded to accept inequalities by pathologising their situation rather than politicising it.

Education is never neutral

Education is a political process: it can never be neutral. The political nature of education means that it is either **domesticating**, in other words, teaching people to accept their lot without questioning, or liberating, teaching people to question everything. To take a neutral stand is to ignore the profoundly political nature of education, and ignoring it, we let it do its damage. Freire was insistent that social justice educators have a responsibility not to attempt to be neutral.

Banking education

Freire refers to the **banking** approach to education as the system that upholds the teacher as powerful and all-knowing, pouring information into the unquestioning minds of learners, who are seen as controllable Objects. The educator is active, the Subject, and the learners passive, or Objects. This is referred to as the banking method because it makes deposits in the minds of learners, filling them with facts that are detached from reality, convincingly and unquestioningly, as a real truth. This is the traditional method used in a hierarchical model of education. It is a process that transmits knowledge based on dominant interests in society, and therefore reinforces the existing order of things, the status quo.

Cultural invasion

Freire's concept of **cultural invasion** refers to the colonisation of one social group by another. The process results in the 'invaded' losing their own culture because the dominant culture of the invaders imposes the values that come to be internalised as superior and desirable. In this way, the invaded assimilate the values of the dominant culture and become alienated from their own culture, subordinated and powerless in relations of oppressor/oppressed. The oppressors own the thinking and are active Subjects; the oppressed absorb these alienating ideas and become passive Objects.

This raises questions about any form of education based on seeing learners as Objects decontextualised from their world, rather than Subjects active in their world.

Oppression – overwhelming control – is necrophilic; it is nourished by love of death, not life. The banking concept of education, which serves the interests of oppression, is also necrophilic. Based on a mechanistic, static, naturalistic, spatialized view of consciousness, it transforms students into receiving objects. It attempts to control thinking and action, leads women and men to adjust to the world [of oppression], and inhibits their creative power. (Freire, 1972, p 72)

Figure 3.3: Banking knowledge as unquestioned truth

Practice of education for critical consciousness

Community development workers are committed to social justice, and this involves liberating people from oppressive relations by interrupting the taken-for-grantedness of everyday life and becoming critical. Freire offers practical ideas for creating the learning context for people to question the contradictions they live by which act in the interests of maintaining power and privilege, in order to value their own experience, history and culture in creative ways that restore confidence and self-belief. This is the basis for working with identity: first, individual autonomy and then, the collective autonomy that leads to collective action.

Freire's belief in working with marginalised groups was based on his experience of the resistance of privileged groups to hand over power. He understood that for change to be sustainable, it is the 'oppressed' who free themselves *and* the 'oppressors', because in a divided world, there are no winners.

Critical pedagogy is a form of liberating education that is rooted in the culture and experience of everyday lives. Critical educators accept people as capable thinking beings who, through a process of critical consciousness, begin to see the everyday contradictions as structural injustices that divide society. It is this awareness that inspires them to get involved in the process of change. This can never be a transfer of knowledge from educator to learner, but is the beginning of a *mutual* discovery – new ways of knowing lead to the co-creation of new knowledge.

Listening from the heart

In order to understand the stories of the people and the relevant issues of everyday life in the community, it is important to be out and about getting to know people, **listening from the heart**. This is only possible if it comes from a deep trust that people are capable of intellectual thought and capable of acting on that knowledge to bring about change. Without this, everything about our actions will betray a lack of trust, and that, in turn, will undermine the process of self-belief.

At every stage of the process, belief in people's infinite potential forms the foundation of our practice. If we want to understand what people are sad, happy, worried, angry or fearful about, we need to be skilled at the art of relaxed, informal conversations that build empathy and trust in order to hear what concerns them. This is how to begin to understand the way that bigger picture issues are reaching into the heart of communities and affecting local lives.

Figure 3.4: Listening from the heart

People have a right to know why you are interested in them, and this is an opportunity to build openly trusting relationships as the basis of ongoing mutual partnerships in the process of change. Freire believed that it is necessary to listen to people and really hear the way they talk about their everyday lives, expressing their stories in their own language and culture. The spontaneous conversations of the community are everywhere – in the market, the shops, on buses and trains, in homes, in the laundrette, in the hairdressers, cafés, supermarkets, in pubs, schools, community centres. Talk to people. Begin to recognise common themes that generate energy or passion or curiosity in people: these are the themes that begin a Freirean approach to practice.

Generative themes

Generative themes are the relevant issues and concerns that emerge from the stories of people's everyday lives. They are called 'generative' as they generate passion because they are relevant to people's experiences, and that releases energy from the apathy of hopelessness that comes from having no control over life's circumstances. You will know they are generative themes because they will repeatedly come up in the stories that you hear. Your team of local activists and community workers will be familiar with these themes after spending time in listening spaces.

> People will act on the issues on which they have strong feelings. There
> is a close link between emotion and the motivation to act. All education
> and development projects should start by identifying the issues which
> the local people speak about with excitement, hope, fear, anxiety or
> anger. (Hope and Timmel, 1984, p 8)

Problematising

A **problematising** approach is based on the generative themes that emerge from listening to the community. Talk together about the stories that people are speaking about with feeling. Which are the most common themes? They might be poverty, unemployment, lack of play facilities, inadequate public transport, parenting … a crisis in the community, or something you would have never anticipated! Your team now needs to prepare material that will stimulate dialogue in groups. To do this, we develop **codifications** of the theme.

Codifications

Capture some aspect of the theme you have identified as a scene from everyday life. Freire originally used line drawings, but equally photographs, drama, video, story, poetry and music are effective forms of codification, depending on their relevance to the community group (or culture circle, in Freire's terms). 'Codification' simply means the medium that is used to capture the essence of everyday issues to present it to the group. Taking an experience out of its context enables people to see it with fresh eyes, rather than from the taken-for-grantedness of everyday experience. The more relevant the theme, the more likely it is to generate interest, emotion and action. To be effective, it must be set in the familiar, everyday lives of people, *coded* in their language and culture, drawing on their experience and encouraging them to question.

In order to prepare codes:

- Choose a theme that is relevant and generates strong feelings.
- Capture a familiar scene from everyday life that relates to the theme.
- Make it simple, unambiguous and obvious.
- Select the best form of capturing this, perhaps a photograph, or a cartoon, mime, play, poetry, song.

Culture circles

We might call what Freire termed 'culture circles' community groups. This is where the learning context is created. It is important that the values of community development form the basis of this experience – mutual respect, reciprocity, dignity, equality and trust. Each person must feel that they are active participants, that they have a voice, are heard in their own words, and are taken seriously. Remember

Figure 3.5: Culture circles

that *listening from the heart* reflects high regard, building mutual respect and self-esteem. The aim is to develop critical consciousness, to go deeper into an issue of relevant community concern in a trusting context.

Role of the animateur

Animateurs are critical educators who stimulate learning and change with community groups. The term in English, 'animator', is often linked to animation in film, which is why I have chosen to use the French term *animateur* – it captures the way that Freire saw this role as that of a critical educator committed to working in a mutual way with participants to stimulate critical dialogue. There are three key components to this approach: passion, critical consciousness and action.

This also links to the work of Augusto Boal (2008), who used performance to capture expressive scenes from everyday experience in order to explore political questions. Boal was a Brazilian activist and later a politician, a contemporary of Freire's. To explore examples of using drama as a method of consciousness, see the inspiring work of The Lawnmowers Independent Theatre Company in Gateshead, North East England, a 'theatre for change' company run by and for people with learning difficulties (see www.thelawnmowers.co.uk).

A critical educator uses a horizontal, not hierarchical, model – that of co-learner and co-teacher. It is a mutual relationship in which the educator is as open to learn as to teach, and the participants are as open to teach as to learn. People make critical connections when they link cultural, political, social and economic issues with their everyday life experience. This counters the apathy and disaffection symptomatic of a *culture of silence*. Critical pedagogy is a form of learning based on questioning answers rather than answering questions, in a process of 'extraordinarily re-experiencing the ordinary' (Shor, 1992, p 122). The cornerstone of Freire's theory is that every human being is capable of critically engaging in their world once they begin to question the contradictions that shape their lives.

In relation to codifications, a critical educator, without using any power or influence, simply sets the context for questioning:

• What can you see?
• What's going on?
• Do you recognise where it is?
• Who's there?
• What's happening?
• How do you think they are feeling?

Figure 3.6: Teaching to question

The questions are designed to probe deeper into the issue, and in doing so, critical connections are made with the structural roots of personal/local issues. The questioning will gradually turn away from the codification, and focus more on critical dialogue within the group itself.

Dialogue

Dialogue is at the heart of the process of critical consciousness. It involves mutual, respectful communication between people, engaging the heart and mind, the intellect and emotions. It involves a relinquishing of the traditional power of the educator, and this in itself is an enormous challenge. We have many assumptions about the power of the teacher. The animateur has a relationship with the participants on a mutual basis as educator-learner with learner-educators. In other words, instead of the educator as the controller of knowledge, this repositions the educator as open to learn as much as to teach. In this way, the roles of educator and learner become mutual and interchangeable: everyone becomes a co-learner/co-teacher.

Dialogue embodies the values of community development, encouraging people to relate to each other in ways that are mutual, reciprocal, trusting and cooperative. It involves horizontal communication between equals who are mutually engaged in a process of critical inquiry. By listening to the stories people tell about their lives and engaging in critical dialogue, the community worker is able to establish strong relationships based on an understanding of local culture; in turn, everyone involved develops a sense of confidence and trust. To be more fully open to others in listening to and telling our stories, we need to be humble, letting go of our view of the world to develop a form of 'connected knowing' (Belenky et al, 1986) in which we suspend our own truth in order to more fully hear the truths of others. As we learn to practise our values in action in these ways, dialogue becomes a key tool for consciousness, between Subjects, rather than Subject and Objects: 'It is a humanizing speech, one that challenges and resists domination' (hooks, 1989, p 1312).

Dialogue seeks out further information on the case in point, which eventually leads to action for community projects related to the issue. In the first instance, this may be credit unions, LETS (local exchange trading systems), housing projects, a residents' association, cooperatives, action for safe road crossings or play areas, a community café, a literacy group, a reminiscence group or a women's writing group – the possibilities are endless. These local projects are the beginning of a process of increasing critical consciousness and collective action that leads to greater potential for change by moving out from the person, the group, the community, in increasingly collective organisation – networks, alliances, campaigns and movements for change.

Praxis

Praxis is the unity of theory and practice that comes together in action and reflection. In other words, it is a form of education that is rooted in everyday life, involving, as Freire said, reading the word and reading the world. In this way, instead of theory becoming detached from action, it is woven together and deepened in action as we work together to co-create knowledge that comes from experience, rather than unquestioningly accepting knowledge that is detached from life. In a process of action and reflection, theory in action and action as theory, a unity of praxis is built.

Critical self-reflection is an essential part of the process of praxis. **Reflexivity** calls on us to go into the nooks and crannies of our inner being, where the unconscious attitudes and assumptions that we have internalised lurk. Identifying them brings them into our consciousness where we can challenge and change them. Freire urges us to question our ideological beliefs, to identify where prejudice has crept into our being and influences our action. It is by changing our innermost attitudes that we alter the way we make sense of the world (epistemology), and this, in turn, changes the way we act in the world (**ontology**). Reading the world in these ways locates knowledge as power related to the world, to our histories, to the present, and to change for the future. In praxis, we are constantly deepening a more critical understanding of ourselves in relation to the world, in order to act collectively to change it.

Freire argued that critical consciousness and action for change are a living praxis, a unity, and that it is impossible to separate the two. These **dialectical** opposites, theory and action, come together as a unity of praxis once we understand the relevance of each to the other. It is only as a unity of praxis that our thinking becomes critical and our action becomes relevant. Rather than an intertwining of 'thinking' and 'doing', a unity of praxis suggests a critical way of 'being', a 'critical living praxis'. Community development needs to 'aspire to become an association of truly serious and coherent people, those who work to shorten more and more the distance between what they say and what they do' (Freire, 1997, p 83).

> At all stages of their liberation, the oppressed must see themselves as people engaged in the vocation of becoming more fully human. Reflection and action become essential. True reflection leads to action but that action will only be a genuine praxis if there is critical reflection on its consequences. To achieve this praxis it is necessary to trust in the oppressed and their ability to reason. Whoever lacks this trust will fail to bring about, or will abandon, dialogue, reflection and communication…. (Freire, 1972, p 41)

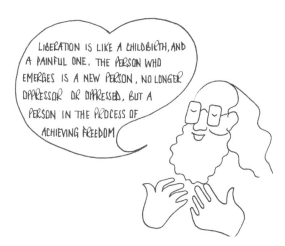

Collective action

Freire insisted that empowerment is a collective experience, that true freedom is to work to transform all society (Freire, in Shor and Freire, 1987). Our practice can never afford to see empowerment as personal freedom; it is only when it becomes part of a collective movement that it is part of a process of liberation. Critical pedagogy is a process that begins in personal empowerment and extends to critical, collective action, from local projects to movements for change through projects, campaigns, alliances and networks.

On a more collective level, Freire urged critical educators to build communities of solidarity, a form of networking to provide the context for problematising the increasing globalised inequalities created by neoliberal globalisation (Darder, 2009, p 574).

Horizontal violence

The concept of **horizontal violence** helps us to understand this in practice. Horizontal violence refers to dehumanising acts against people who are acting together in solidarity, a form of divide-and-rule that is a symptom of the power relations of the top-down system.

This is an illusion of democratic power, because although it is located in the community, it is not representative of the community, and it is destructive rather than liberating. The swing towards counter-oppression gradually stabilises as relationships based upon mutual respect, dignity and equality are established.

Narratives of the people

For Freire, theory and practice is found in the **narratives of the people**. By listening to the everyday stories that local people tell about their lives, community workers become familiar with the common, shared experiences that make up community life. These are the generative themes that are relevant to local people, and therefore offer a key to the codifications that will hold people's interest and generate dialogue. They ignite the passion for change, the energy to act.

In these ways, listening is the basis of empowerment. It is a fundamental skill that calls for humility and acceptance, a form of listening that hears from our hearts, not our ears. Freire believed in the capacity of love to transform, not a superficial love, but an innate joy of life and compassion for people. He challenged us to educate our fears and to transform fear into courage, a courage born of love and moral responsibility.

A culture of tolerance and trust

Distinct values frame Freirean critical pedagogy and are non-negotiable. These values have both influenced community development and are embedded in our statements of practice: mutual respect, dignity, equality, trust, reciprocity and humility. Tolerance is another of these values; without it there can be no authentic democratic dialogue, according to Freire. It is really important to understand that this does not mean that we put up with unacceptable behaviour that falls outside the boundaries of our values, just as we do not meet one violent act with another, but stand firm with dignity against anything that is dehumanising.

Without trust in the infinite capacity of people to co-create knowledge from their own reality in the process of becoming critical, and trust that they can act together to transform the world, change will not happen.

Theory in action 3

Getting to grips with Freirean concepts

Issue

Cultural invasion, the imposition of the values and beliefs of a dominant culture in ways that marginalise people in order to dominate them, results in dehumanisation. This is often related to a culture of silence, generating apathy, hopelessness, loss of self-belief and resignation to the way things are. Becoming critical is as essential for the community worker as the catalyst for empowerment and action as it is for participants in a mutual process of conscientisation. The challenge for community development workers is to establish relationships based on mutuality, reciprocity and trust in order to break through the culture of silence that Freire identified as a child when he experienced the contrast of being plunged into extreme poverty from a life of relative comfort. This can only be achieved as part of a critical living praxis, one in which theory is embedded in everyday practice. I say this because Freire does not work as a partial approach. As Paula Allman says, 'we cannot take hints from Freire or use bits of Freire; we must embrace the philosophy as an integral whole and attempt to apply it accordingly' (Allman and Wallis, 1997, p 113). Without this, it cannot reach its full potential for contributing to social change. Without the process of conscientisation and collective action, individual acts of kindness remain tokenistic rather than transformative.

Evidence

> Our advanced technological society is rapidly making objects of us and subtly programming us into conformity to the logic of its system to the degree that this happens, we are also becoming submerged in a new 'Culture of Silence'. (Freire, 1972, p 15)

Freire refers to poverty as a 'crime against humanity' (Freire and Macedo, 1995). Figure 3.7 shows a photograph of a street in Easington, a former mining town in County Durham in 2013. To seek evidence for the claim that poverty is a crime against humanity, in the light of such concepts as cultural invasion, a culture of silence, dehumanisation, etc, let's consider statistics on life expectancy related to poverty and privilege (taken from www.theguardian.com/society/2015/apr/30/life-expectancy-increases-gap-widens-rich-poor-imperial-research and summarised below).

The life expectancy gap between rich and poor continues to widen. Latest available statistics (from 2012) comparing the North–South England divide show that men in Blackpool can expect to live to 75.2 years, the lowest life expectancy in the country. But men in the City of London, where life expectancy is highest, live an average of 83.4 years. Evidence shows that the eight-year gap in men's lifespan between rich and poor districts reflects the size of the gap between England and Wales as a whole – and Sri Lanka or Vietnam! The seven-year gap for women is as large as that between the UK and Malaysia or Nicaragua. These facts come from a research study published in the medical journal *The Lancet*, in which poverty and austerity policies are blamed for rising social inequalities and reduced life expectancy

Figure 3.7: 'Northerners die earlier than Southerners, new research shows "shocking" North–South divide'

Source: *The Huffington Post UK*, 11 June 2013 © Getty

in poor areas. It predicts that these inequalities will worsen as the impact of poverty targets children in more disadvantaged social groups and communities. On top of this reductions to National Health Service budgets and privatisation of services will reduce the quality of health care and worsen inequalities further. Similar trends in within-country health inequalities can be seen in the US. Research shows that as social conditions worsen, particularly for children and younger people, health inequalities rise.

Analysis

A theoretical analysis is essential if community development is to maintain its claim to be a practice committed to social justice. Here is a set of concepts related to a Freirean approach to practice. Read through them and see if you can start to understand their relevance to the 'integral whole' that Paula Allman talks about in relation to Freirean pedagogy:

- Conscientisation
- Magical consciousness
- Naïve consciousness
- Critical consciousness
- False consciousness
- Domesticating/liberating education
- Banking education
- Cultural invasion
- Generative themes
- Problematising
- Dialogue

- Dehumanisation
- Collective action
- Horizontal violence
- Praxis
- Culture circles
- Narratives of the people
- Animateur

Action

Based on your understanding of the last two chapters, reflect on these key concepts, and jot your understanding down. Think of examples from everyday life.

In your dialogue group, share your understandings and your examples.

Play the Freire game! Write each of the concepts listed above on a card. Each player selects a card and introduces it to the group in a mutual, non-competitive way. The group listens, and then adds to or questions the initial interpretation, giving examples of Freirean concepts in practice where possible, until the group as a whole are satisfied with the analyses.

Freire thought that whether we are teachers, trainers, social workers or community workers, when we are working in the community with people, whether we are conscious of it or not, we are engaged in a political act. If we fill their heads with facts, telling them what to do or how to think, we reinforce the system of power and domination that is creating social inequalities. Distracting people from making critical connections with the social, cultural and economic systems that keep so many oppressed, prevents them from questioning the reality of their lives and claiming their right to become more fully human.

> Critical reflection on practice is a requirement of the relationship between theory and practice. Otherwise theory becomes simply 'blah, blah, blah', and practice, pure activism. (Freire, 2001, p 30)

These key Freirean concepts contribute to a practical theoretical toolkit that builds theory in action, bridging the disconnection between theory and practice for social justice. Freire insisted on the importance of praxis in the process of transformative action for change. When theory and practice become so intertwined that they cannot be detached from each other, practice becomes a process of generating theory in action and generating action from that theory. It moves us nearer to a unity of praxis, ie praxis as a way of being.

Freire talks about critical reflection on lived reality as being the key to transformative action. This is what he calls *authentic praxis*. Without this, transformative change for social justice is not possible, and action becomes pure activism while theory becomes armchair revolution (Freire, 1972, 2001). The important concept of praxis will be a recurring theme throughout the book, and these Freirean concepts will form the foundation of a critical living praxis that will be built on in easy stages as we move forward.

You are now equipped with a conceptual toolkit for kick-starting Freire in your everyday practice. The basis for this process is to create interruptions in the taken-for-granted acceptance of daily life that silences people into submission. The process of empowerment calls for analyses of disempowerment. Understanding the ways in which power works to silence people helps us to expose and dismantle its impact. This is what I will move on to in the next chapter.

FOUR

Power: disempowerment and empowerment

In the last chapter I talked about Freire's concept of conscientisation as a process of becoming critical, questioning everyday life and its contradictions. This is the basis of unfolding an understanding of power and how it weaves its way into our lives, permeating the surface of our skins to become so taken-for-granted it is accepted unquestioningly as *common sense*. The process of empowerment has to interrupt the taken-for-granted assumptions that lead us to accept the unacceptable as 'normal'. For Paulo Freire, *conscientisation* is a process that begins by *problematising* ordinary scenes from everyday life by decontextualising them to present them in another form, *codifying* familiar situations so that they are seen in a different way, a way that raises questions. These codifications (photographs, stories, drama, etc) present interruptions in the everyday taken-for-grantedness of our lives.

Putting his critical pedagogy into action, Freire got *animateurs* to spend time in marginalised communities, living among people, listening to their daily life situations to identify their common concerns or *generative themes*. These were then codified, represented as drawings to get dialogue going in *culture circles*. This might have been a picture of the *favela*. The animateur would start by asking participants why favelas exist, why local people stay, who benefits.... Only after dialogue would people learn words connected to the dialogue and begin the literacy process. This is what Freire meant by 'reading the world before reading the word', that teachers have a responsibility to do more than hand over information – they must ask the questions relevant to people's lives in order to allow them to become *more fully human*.

> How can I teach peasants in Brazil without helping them understand the reasons why thirty-three million of them are dying of hunger.... I think teaching peasants how to read the word hunger and to look it up in the dictionary is not sufficient. They also need to know the reasons behind their experience of hunger.... What I would have to tell these thirty-three million peasants is that to die from hunger is not a predetermined destiny. I would have to share with them that to die from hunger is a social anomaly. It is not a biological issue. It is a crime that is practiced by the capitalist economy of Brazil against thirty-three million peasants. I need to also share with them that the Brazilian economy is not an autonomous entity. It is a social production, a social production that is amoral and diabolical and should be considered a crime against humanity. (Freire and Macedo, 1995, p 379)

Freire believed that power structures the world over are much the same, creating not only poverty, hunger, illness, violence, underachievement in school, unemployment, loss of self-belief and hopelessness, but also premature death. Freire calls this a crime against humanity.

Ontology, or a theory of being, refers to the way we see ourselves in relation to the world around us, helping to make sense of why we live life as we do. Once we start to question why situations are accepted as normal, we realise that we are often making sense of nonsense, making acceptable the unacceptable face of dehumanisation. *Epistemology*, influenced by ontology, is a theory of knowing or how we make sense of the world, and this is influenced by particular values. So if dominant **hegemony**, the stories told by the powerful, persuade us to see the world in terms of a natural order of superiority/inferiority, we see ourselves in relation to this idea and accept our place. However, if we question the world around us and begin to explore values of equality and diversity, this will lead to different ways of knowing, and, in turn, to different ways of being.

This simple idea, that if we see the world differently we will act differently in the world, is at the very heart of critical pedagogy. Seeing critically leads us to act critically. Empowerment, as a collective process of becoming critical, opens up the possibility of change through collective action. Epistemologies and ontologies are part of a living theory, or practical theory that evolves from everyday life in order to transform the way things are for the better. Theory and practice become synthesised into praxis as we create theory as part of life itself, a critical living praxis. To begin the process of change we need to have theories that help us to understand the rules we live by, how they are agreed by society as a whole, and how they become embedded in everyday life; for this we turn to critical theorists.

> Critical theorists begin with the premise that *men and women are essentially unfree and inhabit a world rife with contradictions and asymmetries of power and privilege.* (McLaren, 2009, p 61; emphasis in original)

As critical educators we seek theories that are dialectical, that locate the individual as one who both creates and is created by society, to the extent that it is impossible to understand one without the other. In this way, 'critical theory helps us focus *simultaneously on both sides of a social contradiction*' (McLaren, 2009, p 61; emphasis in original). By focusing on this idea, you can see that any site of domination is also a site of liberation, but it is only by understanding the nature of power that we are able to transform it into empowerment.

Ideas do not emerge in a vacuum; they emerge in a time and place, and build on ideas and experience that have gone before in order to make sense of the present. In this sense, theories are never right or wrong; they contribute to a collective understanding that builds on a past–present–future continuum. Hence our emphasis on becoming critical as an inner process of deep reflexivity and an outer process of making critical connections in what Judi Marshall terms 'inner and outer arcs of attention' (Marshall, 2001, p 44).

Empowerment needs an analysis of power to be transformative. Otherwise, it remains a personal, individual act of self-belief rather than a political, liberating movement for change. Empowerment is therefore the ability to make critical connections in relation to power and control in society in order to expose the contradictions that lead to privilege on the one hand, and poverty on the other. It is vital that we have these tools of analysis in our conceptual toolkit in order to develop practice that has a social justice potential.

I like the terms *actionless thought* and *thoughtless action* (Johnston, quoted in Shaw, 2004, p 26). For me, they capture the urgency to bridge the persistent gap between theory and practice that reduces the potential of community development. Actionless thought, thinking without doing, is simply *armchair revolution*: thoughtless action, conversely, is *pure activism*, intuitive and unexplainable. Critical reflection and dialogue weave thought and action together in praxis, as a unity that involves theory-in-action and action-as-theory, each building on the other from lived experience to form what Freire called an *authentic praxis* (Freire, 1972, p 41).

Figure 4.1: Bridging the gap between theory and practice

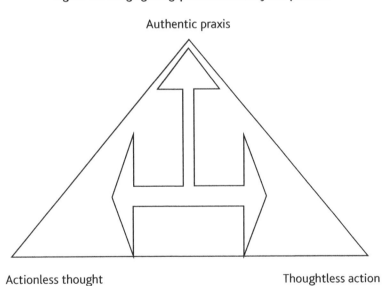

Authentic praxis

Actionless thought   Thoughtless action

This diagram, as you can see, connects the flow between *thoughtless action* and *actionless thought* to achieve a synthesis in *authentic praxis*. This simply means that ideas are not capable of transformation without action: action is not capable of transformation without ideas. Together they offer community development practice the potential for transformative change through authentic praxis. Critical pedagogy involves seeing the world through a critical lens to identify the contradictions we live by, and this is why Freire insisted that our theory and practice is to be found in the simple stories of everyday life.

In the process of dismantling false consciousness to expose relations of domination and subordination, we need to explore theories of power. Unfortunately, there is no single theory of community development that includes every idea that we need to put into action. We rely on an eclectic mix of theories that, together, offer ideas that make practice more critical. Freire was profoundly influenced by the ideas of Antonio Gramsci, so let's take a look at what Gramsci has to say about power. To start with, it is important to understand the political context that formed him and shaped his ideas, much as we need to explore the relevance of his ideas in current times.

Figure 4.2: Antonio Gramsci: 1891–1937

Antonio Gramsci

Mussolini imprisioned Antonio Gramsci for 10 years, until Gramsci's death in 1937, for nothing more than taking a dissenting position on fascism by encouraging people to think more critically. Prior to this, he had been a political journalist and activist, and his deep concern about power in Western societies was based on this praxis (for a more detailed discussion of Gramsci's life and ideas, see Ledwith, 2011). Gramsci's understanding of the way that power permeates society, persuading us to think and act in ways that support dominant interests, has had a profound impact on community development theory since his *Prison notebooks* were published in English in 1971. This coincided with the publication of Freire's *Pedagogy of the oppressed*, highly influenced by Gramsci's ideas, and together, the wide availability of these two books transformed the social justice potential of community development practice by helping us to understand the ways in which power works to dominate/subordinate, as well as offering ideas for practice interventions.

Hegemony

Gramsci was preoccupied with the changes he witnessed in Italy during the rise of fascism. Social control, he noticed, was more subtle than force alone. He extended the traditional Marxist concept of *hegemony* (the ways in which a dominant group asserts control over other social groups) to include not only **coercion** (state control through the law, the police and the armed forces), but a parallel process of **ideological persuasion** as well. Persuading people to **consent** to the dominant social order by embedding dominant attitudes and values in cultural institutions, such as schools, the family, mass media, religious organisations, and so on, involves a more subtle form of power that reaches inside our minds, convincing us to consent to life as it is, and unquestioningly slot into our prescribed place in the order of things. Dominant attitudes are sold to us as common sense, and we internalise these attitudes, even though they may not act in our interests. He saw this process working through moral leadership, with teachers and others in positions of influence in our personal lives reinforcing dominant ideas sold as truth, as common sense. Hegemony, in these ways, asserts control over knowledge and culture, affirming the ideas of the dominant culture and marginalising and silencing others.

Pause for thought...

Wink (2010, p 42), for instance, tells a story about a high school in an African-American community where the principal stormed into a classroom and threw a pupil out, saying that rap music and break dancing were against the rules: "We set the rules, and when we do, we mean business!" In this example, the rules and the physical policing by the principal are *coercion* in action; the dominant White culture, threaded through the curriculum to the exclusion of Black cultures, resulted in the dominant ideology being seen as normal and acceptable. Ideological persuasion, on the other hand, is embedded in the culture of an institution. In schools, this may be transmitted in a staffroom which nurtures conversations that judge the worth of pupils. This is certainly what I experienced in the staffroom. These attitudes become absorbed into the minds of teachers, who then play a role in transmitting their expectations on to the children in their care. The messages are so powerful children are persuaded to see their own potential through the eyes of the teacher. Without an analysis of power, teachers are unaware of the role they play through their own power and status, and schooling inevitably remains hegemonic: a site where the dominant control ideas that maintain their dominance, and the subordinated accept these ideas and maintain their subordination (Mayo, 2004). In these ways, the system becomes self-perpetuating, reinforcing the status quo with a flexible balance of coercion and consent.

Gramsci's insight into the nature of ideological persuasion deepens understanding of power relations by demonstrating the interplay of these contradictory forces, *coercion* and *consent*, in a dialectical top-down and bottom-up relationship. The development of a counter-hegemonic process that interrupts the moral leadership of the powerful is central to Gramsci's thinking. A different way of making sense of the world plays an essential part in the process of change by creating hope that change is possible. Gramsci saw the importance of critical education in opening people's minds to the possibility of change, releasing the intellectual potential inside each of us to question, think and act in alliances for change between diverse social groups.

Intellectuals

> All men [and women] are intellectuals: but not all men [and women] have in society the function of intellectuals. (Gramsci, 1971, p 9)

By this, Gramsci means that even though we do not all have the status of intellectuals, we all have the potential for intellectual thought.

Gramsci did not think that the process of becoming critical would erupt spontaneously. He saw **traditional intellectuals** playing a particular role in triggering the process of change.

Traditional intellectuals

Traditional intellectuals are those who, despite their privilege, have a social conscience that is bigger than their loyalty to their own class. They are the catalyst in the process of change by creating the context for questioning lived reality. Although Gramsci saw this role as vital in setting the wheels of change in motion, he was not convinced that their commitment would be sustained; if push came to shove and the going got tough, he believed they would defect in the face of persecution. Nevertheless, having cut the ties to their own class, traditional intellectuals have a useful role to perform in unlocking the process of critical consciousness and action for change. Looking deeper to see those who have chosen to live and/or work in marginalised communities, I would count Jonathan Dale as a traditional intellectual. He gave up academic status at St Andrews University to live and work as a community worker in Salford. Now retired, he is still a Quaker activist. Here he gives some insight into his ideology at a talk he gave at a Quaker conference on economic justice and the sustainable global society at Friends House, London, on 24 September 2011:

> One of the challenges, of course, is what right do we have to our privileged share of the earth's resources? The earth's resources, the world's resources, the split between ourselves and people who are much poorer than ourselves, the split between ourselves and those of

future generations who may not have what we have because we have used so much of the collective entitlement up.

Karl Marx wrote in *Capital*: 'From the standpoint of a higher economic form of society, private ownership of the globe by single individuals will appear quite as absurd as private ownership of one man by another. Even all simultaneously existing societies taken together are not the owners of the globe. They are only, in translation, its temporary beneficiaries and like good heads of households they must hand it down to succeeding generations in an improved condition.' (Dale, 2011)

Bob Holman was a Professor of Social Policy at the University of Bath who gave it up from a Christian faith perspective to live and work in Easterhouse, Glasgow, as a social worker/youth worker. He is now retired but active in the Social Work Action Network (SWAN). In 2012 he refused his MBE to resist a tokenistic status in his fight for a just society. In his own words:

My proposed MBE was 'for services to the community in Easterhouse, Glasgow'. Last week, I was at a community project called Family Action in Rogerfield & Easterhouse (Fare), which I helped to start 22 years ago. Serving at the cafe was a man who has been a volunteer since the start. He cannot manage paid employment but his loyalty is such that he has been elected to Fare's board of directors. Another long-term helper works six days a week as a security guard on minimum wage. He takes one holiday a year and joins the under-canvas camp where he toils as a cook. Fare's grants have been cut – so much for the 'big society' – and three staff were to be made redundant. The rest of the workers, nearly all local residents, agreed to a 7% cut in their own modest incomes so that the three could be kept on. And many more. Why should I get a royal reward for services to Easterhouse and not them?

I am an egalitarian. I believe that a socially and materially equal society is more united, content and just. The royal honours system is designed to promote differences of status. It is made clear that those who are made knights or dames are socially superior to those given CBEs, OBEs or MBEs. But all are socially above those without honours. These imposed differences hinder the co-operation, interaction and fellowship, which are the characteristics of equality. Refusing a royal honour is a small step but one in the right direction. (Holman, 2012)

Traditional intellectuals play a vital initial role by acting as catalysts in the process of transformative change by questioning everyday experience as you see from the testimonies of Jonathan Dale and Bob Holman. They bridge the divide between theory and practice.

Organic intellectuals

In line with his belief in the intellectual potential of everyone, Gramsci used the term **organic intellectuals** to refer to those who emerge from their own culture to take a key role in the process of change. Every social group produces individuals who possess 'the capacity to be an organiser of society in general, including all its complex organism of services, right up to the state organism, because of the need to create the conditions most favourable to the expansion of their own class ...' (Forgacs, 1988, p 301). The difference with organic intellectuals in Gramsci's eyes is that they are much more likely to stay true to their class of origin. This reminds me of Cathy McCormack, an inspirational community activist from Easterhouse, Glasgow, who is an organic intellectual in every sense of the concept. She learned about popular education in Nicaragua after becoming politicised in a housing campaign in Easterhouse in the 1980s:

> It was only through my experience in Nicaragua that I started to understand the truth. Now I was getting to the roots of my own poverty. That's when I really became involved in the international struggle for justice.... I wanted the people in both communities to learn and benefit from each other's experience. So I established the Greater Easterhouse Nicaragua Solidarity Link Group.... (McCormack, 2009, p 116)

> Whether you live in a village in Central America or in a Glasgow scheme, the people's experience is still the same and they want their voices heard. When I started on this journey, I was politically ignorant but I was able to make sense of things and start making connections. I was experiencing an education no university could have given me, but it was a shattering education because I was realising how badly human beings could treat each other.... (McCormack, 2009, p 104)

Cathy brought popular education to Easterhouse from her encounter with Freirean pedagogy in action in Nicaragua. At this time, after an intensive Training for Transformation programme in Ireland, she set up with others the Popular Democracy Education Resource Centre (PODER) in Easterhouse, which led to her involvement in the Scottish Popular Education Forum, aiming to bring popular educators together from all over Scotland in movement for social change.

I had the great pleasure of meeting Cathy in Edinburgh in 1999, when she came to talk about her experience at the International Association for Community Development (IACD) conference in Edinburgh. Her book, *The wee yellow butterfly* (McCormack, 2009), is a vital resource for community development workers who want to understand the work of organic intellectuals.

Praxis

Gramsci emphasised praxis in the process of change. The term he frequently used in his prison notebooks, 'philosophy of praxis', is the concept of a unity of theory and practice. 'For Gramsci the philosophy of praxis is both the theory of the contradictions in society and at the same time people's practical awareness of those contradictions' (Forgacs, 1988, p 429). This concept of critical praxis is of great relevance to our current context in which community development theory and practice have been falsely separated, leaving practice open to misinterpretation:

> The history of education shows that every class which has sought to take power has prepared itself for power by an autonomous education. The first step in emancipating oneself from political and social slavery is that of freeing the mind. I put forward this new idea: popular schooling should be placed under the control of the great workers' unions. The problem of education is the most important class problem. (Gramsci, quoted in Davidson, 1977, p 77)

This 'problem of education' is precisely why community development is first and foremost about learning to question.

Stuart Hall and Antonio Gramsci

Stuart Hall is seen as the UK's leading cultural theorist, and probably the most influential Gramscian thinker of our times. Hailed as the 'godfather of multiculturalism', he arrived in Britain from Jamaica in 1951 to go to the University of Oxford on a scholarship. 'Three months at Oxford persuaded me that it was not my home. I'm not English and I never will be. The life I have lived is one of partial displacement. I came to England as a means of escape, and it was a failure' (Stuart Hall, quoted in Williams, 2012). This tongue-in-cheek comment made in an interview only a year before his death denies the pivotal location that this 'partial displacement' offered him as a Black intellectual in the truly Gramscian sense of the concept.

In 1964, Richard Hoggart founded the Centre for Contemporary Cultural Studies at the University of Birmingham, and invited Hall to join him as its first research fellow. In 1968, Hall became acting director, and in 1972, director of the Centre, laying the foundations of cultural studies by taking popular, low-status social groups seriously, tracing interweaving threads of culture, power and politics to analyse youth sub-cultures, popular media and gendered and ethnic identities. In 1979, he became Professor of Sociology at The Open University, and coined the term 'Thatcherism' in a visionary article, convinced that it marked a profound cleavage in British political history.

Stuart Hall is a traditional intellectual who has demonstrated the relevance of Gramsci's analysis of power in current times, most particularly when he spoke out about Thatcherism when there were few, if any, other prominent voices offering an understanding of what was happening to British politics. Shrewdly, he named Thatcherism as a new hegemonic project, emerging out of the postwar consensus on the welfare state to sell new ideas as common sense, ideas that justified a major shift to the right of politics. His analysis was that this was a new **historic bloc**; in Gramsci's terms, a new balance of political, social and economic forces operating in favour of maintaining the status quo constructed in response to crisis.

Hall identified that Thatcher had succeeded in selling free market neoliberalism as a common-sense alternative to the welfare state, an ideology built on profit rather than welfare. Important to note is that his analysis was only possible with the help of Gramscian concepts that named and shamed hegemony in action, selling a common sense so powerful that the British political system has shifted to a right-of-centre position which fails to challenge its logic and its consequences. As a result, social inequalities are increasing, public sector institutions of the old welfare state are being dismantled, and three decades of neoliberalism have permeated public consciousness to such an extent that no other system can be imagined. And by failing to imagine that any other system is possible, even at a historical conjuncture created by the collapse of neoliberalism, the drive is to create more of the same:

> The crisis consists precisely in the fact that the old is dying and the new cannot be born. (Gramsci, 1971, p 276)

Sally Davison interviewed Stuart Hall in 2011 to explore how he saw Gramsci's contribution. The common-sense ideas that cement a hegemonic alliance of dominant interests can be disrupted by a crisis, such as the current financial crisis, to present the possibility of change. Hall argues that neither Blairism nor Cameronism represented conjunctures 'capable of change' but were part of a continuing neoliberal project that replaced capitalism with market forces. Hall's gift to us is to emphasise the relevance of Gramsci, whose notion of hegemony gives those who work for social justice an incisive understanding of power and the way to challenge and change its hold in popular consciousness (Davison, 2011).

Since the early 1970s, when Gramsci and Freire made a major contribution to community work theory, the world has changed dramatically. Building on the strong foundation of Gramsci and Freire, new ideas will be introduced as this book unfolds, adding to our understanding of community development practice. At this point, from Gramsci's position in providing an essential insight into the power of ideas to colonise our minds, persuading us to accept the dominant order of things as common sense, I want to add Foucault to the mix. His ideas extend Gramsci's by taking the concept of power as a top-down combination of coercion and consent reaching from above to control how we think and behave, to add power as a web-like structure woven between and within us all.

Foucault

> For Foucault, power comes from everywhere, from above and from below; it is 'always already there' and is inextricably implicated in micro-relations of domination and resistance. (McLaren, 2009, p 72)

Foucault saw power everywhere, not only on a mega level of state and the local level of civil society, but permeating the micro-relationships of everyday life. As with Gramsci, he saw knowledge and power as inseparable, but rather than Gramsci's top-down analysis of power, Foucault also saw networks of power permeating the surface of life. This adds to community development's emphasis on critical consciousness as a liberating process, placing critical education at the heart of transformative change. He, like Gramsci, was preoccupied with how people become the conscious subjects of history through intellectual freedom.

By this, I mean that in questioning our lived experience, we expose the contradictions we live by, and in seeing the world through a different lens, we claim our power as Subjects in the world. Once again, it reminds us that the key to unlocking grassroots action for change lies in freeing the mind from the chains of false consciousness that persuade us to be passive Objects, to become 'self-determining agents that resist and challenge power structures' (Danaher et al, 2000, p 150).

Foucault has been embraced into the evolving body of literature searching for an analysis of power for critical praxis to help us to understand the ways in which a social hierarchy is constructed through power/knowledge relations and reinforced in everyday encounters. Some have the privilege to assert a truth as a statement of power; others accept its truth and transmit it in a cumulative process, reinforcing power structures at street level (Giroux, 2009). This calls on us to identify the ways power embedded in classed, racialised and gendered relations becomes reinforced in the practices and discourses of everyday life:

> Power must be analyzed as something which circulates, or rather as something which only functions in the form of a chain. It is never localized here or there.... Power is employed and exercised through a net-like organization. (Foucault, 1980, p 98)

In these ways, power is 'an active process constantly at work on our bodies, our relationships, our sexuality, as well as on the ways we construct knowledge and meaning in the world' (Darder et al, 2009, p 7). Power is embodied in our selves as well as embedded in society, not only out there in structures of domination, but also in sites of resistance interacting within the relationships of those who claim to be on the same side.

> Critical educators argue that *praxis* (informed actions) must be guided by *phronesis* (the disposition to act truly and rightly). This means,

in critical terms, that actions and knowledge must be directed at eliminating pain, oppression, and inequality, and at promoting justice and freedom. (McLaren, 2009, p 74)

As McLaren points out, *empowerment* means not only setting the context for participants to understand the world around them, but also to find the courage to name what is wrong. This is what Freire meant by **denunciation**. We need to be able to understand power in order to denounce it, and by denouncing it, we create an interruption, in which to build counternarratives of human flourishing, **annunciation**. In these ways, much as Gramsci redefined *hegemony* to include power as ideological persuasion interacting with coercion, so Foucault argues that we must direct our attention from a concentration on the role of the state and the institutions of civil society to include the micro levels of social interaction:

> Hegemonic or global forms of power rely in the first instance on those 'infinitesimal' practices, composed of their own particular techniques and tactics, which exist in those institutions on the fringes or at the micro-level of society. (Foucault, 1980, p 99)

Pause for thought...

When stories go unchallenged, they silently seep into the public mind (McNiff, 2012). Giroux, referring to Foucault, warns that a society that 'neither questions itself nor can imagine any alternative to itself ... [feeds] ... the growing ineptitude, if not irrelevance, of (in)organic and traditional intellectuals, whose cynicism often translates into complicity with the forms of power they condemn' (Giroux, 2009, p 177).

Thinking of power in this way, rather than only a polarity between the state and civil society, we are more able to see how dominant ideology reaches into the processes of life permeating people's relationships in every interaction, influencing attitudes, identities and perceptions (Foucault, 1980). For instance, when Owen, my younger son's Black British friend, came to stay with us after our move from culturally diverse Manchester to predominantly White Lancaster, he told me, "The gaze lingers for just a little bit too long as I walk up the street." It lingers, of course, just long enough to make a disempowering statement that Owen is Other. Power relations, according to Foucault, are acted out in everyday encounters to embed dominant attitudes in the fabric of life.

Theory in action 4

Hegemony in action

Issue

Gramsci's greatest legacy is his analysis of hegemony as the interplay between *coercion* and *consent*. Hegemony is always struggling to maintain its power, and to do that it relies on the collective support of the people. This is why the dominant narrative is so crucial in convincing the public in general that 'more of the same' is called for, that 'there is no alternative', by instilling fear of uncertainty, instability or insurrection.

Evidence

Mark Duggan, a 29-year-old Black man, was shot dead by the police in London in 2011. This sparked riots that spread through the major cities of England. Parliament was recalled for a debate on public disorder. David Cameron, Prime Minister, appealed to the public: "It is criminality, pure and simple – and there is absolutely no excuse for it." In further television appearances he asserted that these were criminals with gang affiliations. The story was told so powerfully that it provoked fear in people. This supported coercive tactics: the imprisonment of those involved, and the eviction of their families from public housing.

Cameron recalled Parliament for a debate on public disorder on 11 August 2011:

> What we have seen on the streets of London and in other cities across our country is completely unacceptable, and I am sure that the whole House will join me in condemning it. Keeping people safe is the first duty of Government. The whole country has been shocked by the most appalling scenes of people looting, violence, vandalising and thieving. *It is criminality, pure and simple – and there is absolutely no excuse for it.* We have seen houses, offices and shops raided and torched, police officers assaulted and fire crews attacked as they try to put out fires. We have seen people robbing others while they lie injured and bleeding in the street, and even three innocent people deliberately run over and killed in Birmingham. We will not put up with this in our country. We will not allow a culture of fear to exist on our streets, and we will do whatever it takes to restore law and order and to rebuild our communities.

> First, we must be clear about the sequence of events. A week ago today, a 29-year-old man named Mark Duggan was shot dead by the police in Tottenham. Clearly, there are questions that must be answered, and I can assure the House that this is being investigated thoroughly and independently by the Independent Police Complaints Commission. We must get to the bottom of exactly what happened, and we will.

> Initially, there were some peaceful demonstrations following Mark Duggan's death and understandably and quite appropriately the police were cautious about how

they dealt with them. However, this was then used as an excuse by opportunist thugs in gangs, first in Tottenham itself, then across London and in other cities. It is completely wrong to say there is any justifiable causal link. It is simply preposterous for anyone to suggest that people looting in Tottenham at the weekend, still less three days later in Salford, were in any way doing so because of the death of Mark Duggan. Young people stealing flat-screen televisions and burning shops – that was not about politics or protest, it was about theft. (Cameron, 2011, emphasis added)

Analysis

'It is criminality pure and simple' was absorbed into the public consciousness as common sense, supported by media coverage. Most people failed to ask why this would happen, what had contributed to a breakdown in law and order. We could see hegemony in action as both coercion and persuasion in action.

There was a UNICEF backlash that suggested a likely breach of international law on children's rights as expressed in the UN Convention on the Rights of the Child (1989). Locking up children under Article 37 of the Convention, is only to be used as a last resort to stop a child reoffending, yet 45% of all under-18s arrested in the riots had no previous criminal history. There were also a few political commentators, such as the Archbishop of Canterbury at the time, Rowan Williams, who stood up in public to say that unless we do something to create decent lives for our young people, we will see more riots to come. We heard little about the research into 'What prompted civil unrest?' undertaken by *The Guardian* in partnership with the London School of Economics (LSE) (Lewis et al, 2011), in which 270 participants in the riots were interviewed from key areas – London, Birmingham, Liverpool, Nottingham, Manchester and Salford. The findings indicated that the main contributing factors were poverty, policing, government policies, unemployment and a response to Mark Duggan being shot by the police. Only 32 per cent mentioned any association with gangs.

In the midst of all this, youth unemployment hit a million, and the Director of the Child Poverty Action Group (CPAG) challenged the government for breaking its own laws by failing to meet the conditions enshrined in the Child Poverty Act 2010, that is, ending child poverty in the UK by 2020. Since then, the goal posts have been shifted: in July 2015, the Conservative government announced its intention to redefine poverty to include family breakdown, debt and addiction. Poverty then becomes not just a lack of money but a moral judgement. This coincides with moves to repeal the Child Poverty Act 2010 amid further cuts to the welfare budget (Wintour, 2015).

Action

Investigate coverage of the English riots of 2011 in the media. Discuss your findings in relation to Gramsci's concepts of hegemony.

In your dialogue group, look at the cartoon on the following page, and then read the extract under 'Evidence' above from Cameron's speech in the parliamentary debate.

Figure 4.3: Prime Minister David Cameron's response to the English riots in 2011

PUBLIC SECTOR CUTS OR ENGLISH RIOTS?

What do you think the cartoonist is trying to present in terms of contradictions over the notion of criminality? Who is the victim and who is the criminal?

How do you compare the different interpretations put on the English riots by Rowan Williams, UNICEF and CPAG in the 'Analysis' section above? Relate any of the ideas that emerge to situations in your own community that create hopelessness or discontent.

Stuart Hall on the 2011 English riots

Read Stuart Hall's comments on the English riots below. What does he add to your debate?

> The riots bothered me a great deal, on two counts. First, nothing really has changed. Some kids at the bottom of the ladder are deeply alienated, they've taken the message of Thatcherism and Blairism and the coalition: what you have to do is hustle. Because nobody's going to help you. And they've got no organised political voice, no organised black voice and no sympathetic voice on the left. That kind of anger, coupled with no political expression, leads to riots. It always has. The second point is: where does this find expression in going into a store and stealing trainers? This is the point at which consumerism, which is the cutting edge of neoliberalism, has got to them too. Consumerism puts everyone into a single channel. You're not doing well, but you're still free to consume. We're all equal in the eyes of the market. (*The Guardian*, 11 February 2012)

Speaking truth to power

> To tell the truth, to arrive together at the truth, is a ... revolutionary act. (Gramsci and Togliatti, 1919)

Gramsci's comment links to the Quaker concept of 'speaking truth to power', and to Stephen Kemmis's notion of 'telling unwelcome truths'. Seeing truth as a revolutionary act, Gramsci means that the courage to name the uncomfortable reality of inequalities as unacceptable injustices plants seeds of dissent. Interrupting the collective silence in this way, by exposing it as *nonsense* rather than *common sense*, a dissenting voice rings through the unquestioning apathy to open a crack where the light of change can shine in on an unjust system.

Failing to question inequalities justifies continued targeting of the poor and marginalised. For instance, in 2008, when Killeen accused successive UK governments of a violation of human rights for failing to change the unjust images of the 'welfare scrounger' embedded in public consciousness since Thatcherism, he was suggesting that we now have 'povertyism' sitting alongside racism and sexism as a new structural inequality based on poor people being worthless. This links to the Freire quote on 'a crime against humanity' at the start of this chapter.

Also explore how the following evidence might be hidden deeper by racism, patriarchy or homophobia:

- In 1993 Stephen Lawrence, aged 18, was killed within 10 seconds in an unprovoked racist attack.
- Every minute the police in the UK receive a domestic assistance call, yet only 35 per cent of domestic violence incidents are reported to the police, and one woman is killed every three days (Women's Aid; www.womensaid.org.uk).
- In 2010 Dominic Crouch, aged 15, committed suicide by jumping off the roof of a six-storey block of flats after homophobic bullying at school.

As the old system crumbles, a crisis erupts:

> In this interregnum a great variety of morbid symptoms appear. (Gramsci, 1971, p 276)

In conclusion

In Gramscian terms, dominant hegemony internalised as common sense gains public consent. In current times this gives way to neoliberal policies continuing to govern for the market against the people! Gramsci saw critical education as the way to dislocate common sense in a process of identifying and challenging power in preparation for revolutionary change at a point of conjuncture, a crisis of the current system. Stuart Hall identifies the current conjuncture as an opportunity for change. But if we fail to see local practice in its wider political context, our practice is decontextualised, in danger of pathologising victims of injustice. At best, decontextualised practice can only be placatory, making life a little bit better on the surface, but failing to change a system into which relations of domination and subordination are embedded. Effective interventions need to see forces of power critically.

Gramsci's significant contribution was to add to the traditional Marxist analysis of hegemony the notion of ideological persuasion. This has been powerfully acted out since the rise of Thatcherism in the UK through a dominant narrative of the 'welfare scrounger', replacing an ideology of welfare with an ideology of the market. Elevating profit over people, it gives rise to escalating wealth in the pockets of the privileged as the poor become progressively poorer. This is enhanced by a systematic dismantling of public sector provision that protects the most vulnerable in society. Three decades of this dominant narrative, without counternarratives that change the story to one of more compassionate alternatives, leave it so firmly in public consciousness as an unchallenged truth that gross inhumanities become accepted as normalities. If we see more critically, we act more critically. Gramsci located praxis at the heart of social change. But the act of breaking through the taken-for-grantedness that results from dominant 'truths' sold as common sense will not happen without an intervention, Gramsci felt. He saw a key role as that of the traditional intellectual, a privileged person who becomes committed to the cause of social justice, as a catalyst in the process of change, unlocking the critical consciousness of subordinated people, and releasing the energy to act collectively in alliances for change. The concept of critical education and collective action through critical alliances are central to Gramsci's thought. But this cannot happen if the time is not right, and this is where the concept of conjuncture is vital. Before his recent death, Stuart Hall talked about our current historical conjuncture – a point at which social, political, economic and ideological contradictions have become condensed in the crisis caused by market fundamentalism being sold as global common sense. His point is that Gramsci's analysis is a means of understanding the complexity of power relations in today's political context, and that crisis is an opportunity for change. He felt that we have three choices:

- more of the same
- a transformed version of the same
- or relations that are radically transformed based on social justice.

Crisis is an opportunity, a crack where the light shines in. But becoming critical is an essential part of action for change:

> Look, Gramsci, the Italian Marxist, believed in pessimism of the intellect, optimism of the spirit. You must look at what's happening now. If it's unpropitious, say it's unpropitious. Don't fool yourself. Analyse the conjuncture that you're in. Then you can be an optimist of the will, and say I believe that things can be different. But don't go to optimism of the will first. Because that's just utopianism. (Stuart Hall, quoted in Williams, 2012)

Stuart Hall is emphasising that action will not result in transformative change unless the analysis on which that action is based is critical. In order to change power it is necessary to understand power. For that reason, in the next chapter I will explore 'race' and gender analyses, and the ways in which power acts as an interlinked, overlapping, intertwined complexity.

FIVE

Paulo Freire and anti-racist feminism

After the English version of Freire's *Pedagogy of the oppressed* became widely available in the early 1970s, there was an immediate feminist backlash. In the first place, this was because of his assumed use of dominant male language (for example, 'men', 'he', 'his'), and then for his simplistic oppressor/oppressed analysis that hides more complex 'race' and gender differences. Since then, the feminist critique has developed a wider analytic perspective, suggesting that the sound basis of Freire is worthy of a feminist re-visioning of his work. In this chapter, I begin by outlining the development of feminism before exploring the 'close and troubled relationship' between Freire and feminism (Shor, 2000, pp 2-3). This forms the basis for exploring Patricia Hill Collins' thinking on the complexity of intersectionality as an analysis for re-visioning Freire.

Women in movement

Mary Wollstonecraft's *Vindication of the rights of women* (1792) was the first great feminist book. Her ideas were based on the relationship between intellect and power, that women are deliberately kept ignorant and persuaded to 'feel' rather than 'reason'. Although she did not name sexism, she identified power in relation to male domination and the control of women: women had no place in society, only in relation to men. Her argument was that society benefited from educating women as well as men. Mary was a radical: she ran a school, helped her sister

Figure 5.1: Suffragette

escape from an abusive husband, helped an American lover smuggle stolen goods from French aristocrats to finance the French Revolution, travelled alone with her child, and published her adventures ... a woman before her time! She was accepted as an intellectual and radical in London circles, and saw education as the key to achieving gender equality. Her ideas continued to influence women until, more than a century later, the suffragette movement erupted.

Three distinct periods of modern feminist activism are widely acknowledged, even though there is no full agreement on how to

85

characterise them. Generally speaking, they can be summarised as first wave, second wave and third wave feminism.

First wave feminism is seen as the suffrage movement of the late 19th and early 20th centuries, with British suffragettes, led by Emmeline Pankhurst, prominent in the struggle for equal voting rights and property rights. Their tactics were confrontational: chaining themselves to railings to provoke police reaction, pouring harsh chemicals into mailboxes, breaking windows and setting fire to unoccupied buildings to draw attention to the struggle. Many were locked up in Holloway Prison, London. Their strategy was to go on hunger strike to highlight the cause, but they were savagely force-fed and often injured. Women in Britain over the age of 30 who met certain property qualifications were finally given the right to vote in 1918, and in 1928 voting rights were given to all women over the age of 21.

The Second World War changed women's aspirations. Governments conscripted men to fight, so needed women in the workplace taking on male-dominated trades. Once war was over, the story changed, and women were persuaded back into the home. But the iconic image of Rosie the Riveter, used by the US Government to recruit female workers during World War II, became a widespread symbol of women's empowerment far beyond that of a war propaganda tool, raising issues of workplace rights.

The women's liberation movement gained momentum in the late 1960s and early 1970s, broadening the debate to a wide range of issues: equal rights around sexuality, the family, the workplace, reproductive rights, political representation and human rights issues such as domestic violence and marital rape. Simone de Beauvoir, the French philosopher, had highlighted the treatment of women throughout history in *The second sex* (1949), making a major impact on feminism. But it was the publication of the American feminist and activist, Betty Friedan's

Figure 5.2: Rosie the Riveter

Source: Adapted from WWII poster by J Howells Miller c1942

The feminine mystique (1963) that is credited with igniting the Women's Liberation Movement (WLM), or *second wave feminism*, from the late 1960s, and this is the movement that has had the greatest impact on women's lives. It began in the US, but quickly spread to the UK, Europe, and eventually into a worldwide movement for change.

British feminist theorist and writer Sheila Rowbotham produced a pioneering book, *Hidden from history* (1973), a pivotal study of history in Britain through women's eyes from the mid-17th century to the 1930s, showing how class and gender, work and the family, personal life and social pressures have shaped and hindered women's struggles for equality, questioning not only the present day, but the very way that history is recorded in favour of men. 'The personal is political' became the rally cry of second wave feminism, connecting personal experience with larger social and political systems. This emphasis on power and insight into structural discrimination made second wave feminism of the 1960s and 1970s distinctive from first wave feminism of the 1920s, which was concerned primarily with achieving the right to vote.

In *third wave feminism*, during the 1970s and 1980s, feminists became divided over the issue of pornography. Andrea Dworkin, the American radical feminist and writer, was prominent in the anti-pornography divide with second wave feminists. She linked pornography to rape, child abuse and other forms of violence against women. *Pornography: Men possessing women* (1981) and *Intercourse* (1987) are her best-known books. She identified ways in which right-wing women undermine all women, but it was her claim that all heterosexual intercourse degrades women that divided feminists. From the early 1990s to the present, some feminists identify with the third wave as a backlash against the second wave's lack of concentration on multiple identities, sexual freedom, diversity, Black women and cultural differences, as well as the key issues around equality

Figure 5.3: 'The personal is political'

Going deeper into second wave feminism

Throughout the 1960s and into the 1980s, second wave feminism grew from grassroots activism, women coming together in leaderless community groups to discuss common lived experiences, and analysing these as different from men's everyday reality. This was theory in action at grassroots level, co-creating new knowledge long before it was hijacked and incorporated into academic settings. This was a period when the impact of critical thinkers like Freire and Gramsci freed people's minds to question their life experience. The new social movements of the time, not only feminism, but others such as the anti-racist/civil rights, gay and lesbian and green movements rose from grassroots settings, based on a new awareness that questioned the status quo, and acted together for social change.

Second wave feminism was radical and based on equal rights. Driven by a critique of inequality, women rose to demand change. It did not take long to realise that as well as being 'hidden from history', the reality of women's lives is obscured by class analyses of power offered by male theorists to such a degree that they hide more truths than they reveal. During these two decades, despite antagonism and resistance from men, meeting in women-only groups was a regular feature of everyday life, at the centre and on the margins, as were alliances between groups in struggle. It was a time when street protests were commonly visible, and marches would include women standing up in numbers against injustice: 'Free Nelson Mandela', anti-Thatcherist chants of 'Maggie, Maggie, Maggie, Out! Out! Out!', solidarity with Nicaragua, Greenham Women's support groups, Women Against Pit Closures, and many more were in abundance. It was a time of action and change, and this should not be overlooked. Critical consciousness and collective action led to liberating policy and legal reforms, even though we still have a long way to go.

Pause for thought...

Watch the film *The Imitation Game* (2014) which tells the life of Alan Turing, the talented mathematician and computer pioneer who deciphered the Nazi Enigma code during the Second World War to end the war two years earlier, saving countless lives. He was a gay man at a time that same-sex sexual activity was criminalised as unnatural and immoral. In 1952, Turing reported a burglary at his home that attracted attention from the police. He was subsequently prosecuted for homosexual acts in 1952, but accepted oestrogen treatment (chemical castration) as an alternative to prison. Two years later, at the age of 41, he was found dead, officially recorded as suicide.

The Sexual Offences Act 1967 decriminalised homosexual acts in private between two men over the age of 21 in England and Wales. The Criminal Justice (Scotland) Act 1980 and the Homosexual Offences (Northern Ireland) Order 1982 followed. Lesbian, gay, bisexual and transgender (LGBT) rights came to prominence as a new social movement after these Acts were brought into force, but it was not until the Equality Act 2010 that LGBT rights were honoured. In 2009, the British Prime Minister, Gordon Brown, made an official public apology

---

on behalf of the British government for 'the appalling way [Alan Turing] was treated', and the Queen granted Turing a posthumous pardon in 2013. Roy Jenkins, Home Secretary at the enactment of the Sexual Offences Act 1967, commented: 'those who suffer from this disability [homosexuality] carry a great weight of shame all their lives' (quoted during parliamentary debate on 4 July 1967 by *The Times*).

Find out about the activism that led to these changes in legislation to protect gay men and lesbian women. What can you discover about alliances that not only strengthened women's roles in society, but also made it a better place for all?

During the years of street activism, there were also theoretical struggles. It was easy to see that the traditional Marxist class analysis subsumed women's oppression into the working-class struggle. It was less easy to understand how the same dichotomous thought, in turn, trapped White women's thinking inside a male/female analysis, overlooking the interlinking nature of multiple oppressions and the need for a politics of difference. In other words, White women saw the category 'Woman' as an all-consuming category, and failed to understand the experience of being a woman was also defined by 'race', sexual preference, age, culture and 'dis'ability in all sorts of combinations. Today, we are much more aware of the complex nature of a matrix of oppressions linked to social justice, and the ways in which these engage with environmental justice.

Pause for thought...

Take, for instance, domestic violence and the refusal of the police to intervene in 'domestics' that led to women being denied the protection that was their human right. The women's refuge movement, pioneered by Erin Pizzey in the 1970s, strode boldly into public consciousness from 'behind closed doors'. Mother of four children, her own experience of violence at the hands of her husband, a wealthy, successful Somerset doctor, led to her opening Chiswick Women's Aid in 1971, the first refuge for women, which marked the start of the Women's Aid movement.

Domestic violence is an example of the type of experience that feminists challenge as hidden from view by a class analysis. In 1979, Pizzey's book *Scream quietly or the neighbours will hear* (Pizzey, 1979) made an indelible mark on the political dimensions of women's personal experiences. In a Freirean feminist way, she used the raw honesty of the stories of the abused women who sought shelter with her to theorise ways in which women's experience differs from a class analysis.

So the context of second wave feminism was one of action and analysis. Not only were women united in groups, but also collective action, campaigns and alliances were the order of the day, and everywhere women asserted their moral authority to do what was right. This became the basis of a way of claiming intellectual freedom to see and act in ways that created a world free from suffering and domination for all. The power of patriarchy was recognised as prominent in the creation of everyday reality.

Feminism has had a powerful influence on community development. The ways in which women at grassroots level have demonstrated that *the personal is political* have been transformative, for both theory and practice. In community development at this time, women's groups sprang up everywhere. In my own practice, Hattersley Women for Change, despite male opposition, opened the Women's Room in the community centre as a space where women could come together to talk about their lives, make sense of their experiences, and act to change the way things were. A weekly programme of events took shape, from women writing together to bricklaying for women, linking into campaigns and action on poverty as well as acts of solidarity through International Women's Day.

Prior to second wave feminism, women's experience, in the home and community, was seen as 'soft' and apolitical. These altered perspectives led to an analysis of the way in which the public/private divide has oppressed women for generations by creating the myth that politics stops at the boundary of our community, and certainly at the thresholds of our homes.

Feminist critiques of Freire

It did not pass unnoticed that the key players in the critical pedagogy movement were male! Patti Lather is one of the leading feminist theorists to critique critical pedagogy, with its emphasis on experience-based knowledge failing to address women's experience. Her work focuses on women as intellectuals, and on building a knowledge base from personal narratives in a rethinking of authority and power in order to question patriarchy (Darder et al, 2009). This is exactly what Chiswick Women's Aid, Abasindi Black Women's Cooperative Moss Side, Hattersley Women for Change and the thousands of other grassroots projects did at the time to create a rich theorising of life from experience, challenging a purely class analysis as hiding more truths than it reveals.

Kathleen Weiler acknowledges the liberation pedagogy of Paulo Freire and the profound importance of his work (Weiler, 1994). In turn, she questions Freire's assumption of a blanket term like 'oppression' as a catch-all for every experience as well as his non-specific goals for liberation. A feminist pedagogy, she claims, offers a more complex vision of a pedagogy of liberation. She identifies three ways that a feminist pedagogy could build on and enrich Freirean pedagogy: by questioning the role and authority of the teacher; recognising the importance of personal experience as a source of knowledge; and exploring the experience of people of different races, classes and cultures.

Patricia Hill Collins says that, 'every idea has an owner and that the owner's identity matters' (Hill Collins, 1990, p 218). By this, she recognises that our identity is formed out of who we are, in all our complexity. For instance, the backlash of feminism against Freire's emphasis on the male was followed by the Black feminist backlash against second wave feminism's assumptions that White women's experience is the same as Black women's. Freire subsumed women into his male assumptions about oppression from a class perspective, much as White feminists subsumed Black women into a White interpretation of gender oppression.

In response to the feminist backlash against Freire's thinking in *Pedagogy of the oppressed*, bell hooks talks about making a commitment to work from a 'lived understanding' of people's lives rather than accepting as authentic the distortion of a 'bourgeois lens', citing Freire:

> … authentic help means that all who are involved help each other mutually, growing together in the common effort to understand the reality which they seek to transform. Only through such praxis – in which those who help and those who are being helped help each other simultaneously – can the act of helping become free from the distortion in which the helper dominates the helped. (Freire, from *Pedagogy in process*, cited in hooks, 1993, p 151)

This idea challenges the benevolence implicit in Band Aid or other acts of charitable giving because they do not change the power relations that create social injustice. Within this understanding of the importance of alliance between all those committed to social justice, hooks was able to see the key role that Freire played in her own consciousness, providing a conceptual structure that gave her critical insight into her own experience of racism, when 'the radical struggle of Black women to theorise our subjectivity', to understand ourselves as subjects in resistance, was not welcomed by early White feminists (hooks, 1993, p 151).

Freire always said that the struggle belongs to us all, that we all have both a right and a duty to transform society into a better place, and that his contribution is not a blueprint but a strategy based on his own experience for us to adapt to our current cultural and political contexts.

Strengths of Freirean and feminist pedagogy

Freirean and feminist pedagogy are both founded on popular education for critical consciousness as a tool for understanding the nature of structural discrimination. Seeing the world critically opens up the possibility for collective action for a just and sustainable world. Freirean and feminist pedagogies agree that dominant attitudes need challenging, and that all people have a basic human right to be respected participants in their world. Freire, offering the conceptual tools for understanding the nature of oppression, a process of conscientisation, and the importance of culture and history in the struggle for change, complements feminism. Feminist pedagogy diverges from Freire, however, in its challenge to patriarchy as a fundamental oppressive structure that echoes through women's lives, complexified by the idea of multiple oppressions that intersect.

In these ways, we begin to understand why, despite Freire's compatibility with second wave feminism's emphasis on the personal as political, he received harsh criticism from feminists. His response was that *Pedagogy of the oppressed* needs to be set in its historical and cultural context. It cannot be read as if it were written yesterday and retrospectively criticised, with the benefit of hindsight, using conceptual tools that were not available at the time it was written (Freire and Macedo, 1995). The influences of postmodernism and an increased understanding of *difference* have challenged the assumptions of metanarratives that are based on a universal, collective experience as reducing lived experience to a simplistic unity.

A theory of liberation that glosses over divisions in society, attempting to universalise experience shaped by gender, 'race', ethnicity, age, sexuality, 'dis'ability and so on, entrenches those divisions still further. hooks challenges feminist thinkers who separate feminist pedagogy from Freirean pedagogy: 'For me these two experiences converge.... I have taken threads of Paulo's work and woven it into that version of feminist pedagogy I believe my work as a writer and teacher embodies' (hooks, 1993, p 150).

> Words seem not [to] be good enough to evoke all that I have learned from Paulo. Our meeting had that quality of sweetness that lingers, that lasts for a lifetime, even if you never speak to the person again, see their face, you can always return in your heart to that moment when you were together and be renewed – that is a profound solidarity. (hooks, 1993, p 154)

Feminist pedagogy, like Freirean pedagogy, places everyday stories at the heart of the process of critical consciousness. The 'personal is political' leads to a critical understanding of the nature of structural oppression, and the way that we are shaped in all our differences by structures of power that permeate our lives. By exploring the political nature of everyday encounters, we move towards the critical consciousness necessary to change oppressive structures.

It seems strange now, but in the second wave feminism years, we were remarkably clumsy in our understanding of the complexity of oppressions, and I remember large gatherings of women where our thinking was exposed as simplistic, top-down, ranked-order, status-related wearing of the badges of oppression. Our thinking was not equipped for complexity. So, while Freire is criticised for not dealing with the specific nature of the subordination of women within a class analysis, as second wave feminists, we made many mistakes in not recognising racism. The assumption of a universal sisterhood rendered Black women invisible. This ethnocentric approach overlooked cultural and historic relations, and in its preoccupation with the male/female dichotomy became oblivious of the hegemonic White, female, often middle-class focus (Anthias and Yuval-Davis, 1992). We moved from one form of fragmented consciousness to another.

Defining 'woman' in relation to 'man' misses the way in which 'race', class and gender intersect with each other. These images are 'key in maintaining interlocking systems of race, class and gender oppression' (Hill Collins, 1990, p 68). So, in building this eclectic approach to theorising practice for social justice, our next port of call is a deeper look at Patricia Hill Collins, whose contribution to the complexity of power and subordination took thinking into the nature of intersecting, overlapping and interlocking oppressions.

Patricia Hill Collins

I want to build the work of Patricia Hill Collins into our conceptual toolkit of community development theory at this point, and to concentrate on her immense contribution in challenging and transforming our thinking about the complexity of intersecting oppressions. She is distinctive because her emphasis on identity politics located at the intersections of overlapping oppressions offers us knowledge that has the potential to change the world. This knowledge came from her own lived experience as a Black American woman, but while committed to this, she retained a focus on the importance of the bigger issues of all human dignity in a socially just world. Her thinking was that if we limit our action to our individual causes, we will never achieve world change, so she placed 'US Black women's experiences in the center of analysis without privileging those experiences' as more important than other oppressions (Hill Collins, 2000, p 228). She saw African American women at the crossing point between two of the most powerful systems of oppression, 'race' and gender, and identified how this understanding should alert us to scrutinising the intersections where other inequalities come together in interlocking systems of oppression.

Hill Collins offers a Black feminist epistemology, a way of knowing that is different from the dominant way of seeing the world:

• Alternative epistemologies are developed from narratives of lived experience.
• New knowledge emerges from dialogue in mutual co-creation.
• All knowledge is value-laden, and should be tested by empathy and compassion. A more holistic knowledge will heal the intellect–emotion divide so much part of Eurocentric, positivist knowledge, and will embrace the researcher as present and part of the process of alternative knowledge creation.
• Personal accountability is vital in the process of building knowledge from lived experience because it embraces the character, beliefs, values and ethics of the knowers, and as such is a 'truth'.

Knowledge only exists in relation to the context in which it is defined. How we see truth depends on how we see ourselves, how we live our lives and how we relate to others; it therefore carries a moral responsibility. It is never neutral or sterile, and all of us live at intersections of cross-cutting interests defined by social identities of class, 'race', gender, sexual identity, culture, religion and nationality. Hill Collins talked about '*safe spaces* where Black women speak freely', and these are the spaces I refer to as critical spaces, where participants can be free to speak without recrimination. For Collins, there are three primary safe spaces for African American women: their relationships with one another; the Black women's blues tradition that captures the suffering of slavery within the hope of a transcendent collective consciousness; and through the voices of Black women authors.

These three safe spaces provide opportunities for self-definition that she saw as the first step to empowerment. In other words, if we fail to define ourselves, we will be objectified as 'Other'. But, 'by definition, such spaces become less "safe" if shared with those who [are] not Black and female', despite their intention to create 'a more inclusionary, just society' (Hill Collins, 2000, p 110). Changes in thinking alter behaviour, and in these ways, 'the struggle for a self-defined Black feminism occurs through an ongoing dialogue where action and thought inform each other' (Hill Collins, 2000, p 30). Just as White feminist thought has emerged from White community development, Black community development has been the context for Black feminist thought. In these ways, Black feminism identifies themes of oppression – racism, misogyny, poverty, and so on – and rearticulates them within the narratives of everyday life for Black women.

Patricia Hill Collins sees this as different from critical consciousness inasmuch as new insights into experience are re-inserted into an ongoing constant dialogue: 'Rather than viewing consciousness as a fixed identity, a more useful approach sees it as continually evolving and negotiated. A dynamic consciousness is vital to both individual and group agency' (Hill Collins, 2000, p 285). She saw Black intellectuals as specific to the process as praxis researchers, set on digging deeper into the nature of oppression and bringing about social change as a consequence. Just as with Gramsci's definition of the *organic intellectual*, she sees the lived experience of *Black feminist intellectuals* as defining themselves while co-creating knowledge, therefore anchored to their commitment to the cause 'when the obstacles seem overwhelming or when the rewards for staying diminish' (Hill Collins, 2000, p 35).

Hill Collins' *matrix of domination* identifies four interrelated systems of power in society: structural (law, polity, religion and economy); disciplinary (organisations that manage oppression – consider racism and sexism in education, employment, etc); hegemonic (ideology and consciousness through language, images and narratives); and interpersonal (everyday life). It is the interpersonal that Hill Collins saw as our first port of call in becoming aware of the way in which our 'thoughts and action uphold someone else's subordination' (Hill Collins, 2000, p 287).

Critical race theory

Critical race theory (CRT) is complementary to Freire: both involve 'seeing' oppression in action from lived reality. Exposing the invisibility of racism and the power of Whiteness, personal stories from experience are used to theorise action, and counternarratives of change are used to create new possibilities for social justice. CRT is based on power being embedded in the structures of White hegemonic societies systematically discriminating against people from a 'race' and ethnicity perspective. Systems of law, education, health, criminal justice and so on institutionalise racism.

CRT also recognises intersectionality, the way that sexism and classism interweave with racism and other oppressions to compound disadvantage. In this sense, CRT as a paradigm (a framework of ideas) sits well with Freirean thought and complements Patricia Hill Collins. It also complements the work of people like Peggy McIntosh in engaging with Whiteness as an unconscious silence with an absence of racial identity, but an assumed, unrecognised status and power. CRT uses stories to capture the lived experiences that silence and disempower (Ladson-Billings and Tate, 2006), or, as Diane Warner, a Black colleague of mine, uses it, 'screaming silences' (Serrant Green, 2004) that capture the juxtaposition of Black/White relationships in scream/silence dynamic in the 'micro-aggressions' of daily life (Dixson et al, 2005). The challenge in using story as an exposé of power and discrimination is to focus on the power of the storyteller in the process. If the White storyteller has the confidence, commitment, status and experience to expose the violence inflicted on Others' lives, how can she ensure that she is seeing critically? Whiteness studies focus on White experience to expose that assumed, invisible, unconscious power.

> Imagine a world where a group of people is continually placed at the bottom of the social pile; in schools, in the labour market, in housing. Imagine that this group is blamed for its own misfortune: its members are seen as lazy, their families 'dysfunctional'; they're just not smart enough. But what would happen if groups started to pass more tests more frequently that the dominant group? (Gillborn, 2008, p 90)

Gillborn's problematising, from a dialectical perspective, gets us to imagine a dominant ideology based on fear in stark relief. If White power permeates everyday life, shaping the world to the advantage of White people, then it is not in the interest of being White for power to equalise (Gillborn, 2008). This is why action for change can be acts of 'false generosity', as Gramsci would say, acts of *tokenism* that give the illusion of a move towards fairness, justice and equality. But, if Whiteness is the avoidance of facing up to the privilege of being White, and acknowledging the way it is embedded in both the thoughts and structures of society, as seen in Whiteness studies like that of Peggy McIntosh, then the rejection of one's own complicity in White privilege meets CRT in alliance for thought and action for social justice.

Pause for thought...

Imagine a Black woman and a White woman, both British, colleagues and close friends, visiting Chicago together. Excited by Hull House, the settlement established by Jane Addams in 1889 modelled on Toynbee Hall in the East End of London as a centre for social reform, they paid a visit. Hull House was a community of university women whose aim was to provide social and educational opportunities for working-class people from the surrounding area, many of them European immigrants. This was of interest to the two women, both committed and involved in action for Black and White women working together for social justice. As they stood side by side talking to the two White women from Hull House who were welcoming and eager to explain their work, the White woman failed to notice that the attention was on her, that she was the one being spoken to and speaking back, that the conversation eliminated the Black woman. How did it feel to be ignored, not respected, seen as less important in this cross-cultural but White conversation? The White woman eventually looked over to her friend, being aware of her silence too late. She was no longer beside her, there was no sign of her: she had not announced her departure, and neither had she been noticed leaving. Alarmed, the three White women searched everywhere, not able to think of what would cause her to disappear. Distressed, her White friend in desperation searched outside the building and spotted her standing at a bus stop across a wide road, alone. Their eyes met with anger from one side and relief from the other.

This is a story of my travels with Paula, engaging me in the *micro-aggressions* of daily life, taking me outside the comfort and privilege of my Whiteness to be faced with her screams and my silences. These 'screaming silences' became part of my painful education into the nature of racism as a screaming daily experience, and my unconscious silence around White power. Think about your own experiences in relation to 'screaming silences'. (Paula's story is developed in **Theory in Action 5** on p 99.)

CRT's radical assertion that it is not in the interest of dominant White society for power to equalise is criticised for simplifying the intentions of White people. Nevertheless, it helps to focus critical attention on 'race', leading us deeper into the profound inequalities of ethnic groups, despite Britain's increasing ethnic diversity (Lawrence, 2012). In turn, many Black women have rejected feminism as White, particularly as Black feminism is often seen by Black men as collusion with a White racist oppressor. This pressure for Black women to prioritise Black unity can make it harder to address the intersections of racism and sexism (Pratt-Clarke, 2010).

Environmental justice and sustainability

Freire and the Freirean movement have been accused of overlooking the environmental crisis (Bowers and Apffel-Marglin, 2004). Freire's emphasis on critical consciousness in relation to class is seen to be based on Western concepts of humanity, freedom and empowerment. This subordinates indigenous belief systems founded on biodiversity, suggesting that critical pedagogy 'fractures knowledge and supports the further alienation of human beings from nature' (Darder et al, 2009, p 17). Critiques like this sharpen our thinking around the relationship between social justice and environmental justice. Community development has integrated social justice and environmental justice into its purpose, so let's take a look at their interconnection.

The eco-pedagogy movement developed from critical pedagogy, influenced by Freire to prioritise culturally relevant knowledge related to environmental justice. This grew out of discussions at the Earth Summit in Rio de Janeiro in 1992, designed to prioritise an ecological ethic for humanity: 'the construction of a planetary citizenship, so that all, with no exception or exclusion, may have healthy conditions, in a planet able to offer life because its own life is being preserved' (Darder et al, 2009, p 18). It extends Freire's 'love for all life' from diversity to biodiversity. Paulo Freire was working on ecopedagogy when he died, and some of these ideas are included in his posthumous *Pedagogy of indignation* (2005a).

Other examples of Freire's ongoing influence on action for social and environmental justice and the connectedness between community, empowerment and sustainability include Blewitt's (2008) work under the banner of 'The Converging World', a charity that links people to address issues related to education, poverty and environment developed by local, community-led sustainability groups. The Coffeehouse Challenges started this off, based on the coffee shops of 18th-century London which were the context for dialogue and action on big issues of the times. A series of meetings in Starbucks in Bristol led to residents of Chew Magna, a nearby village, looking at how they wanted their community to develop. Just one person who was a common denominator in both processes gathered support and organised a series of coffeehouse conversations in the village on moving towards a zero-waste society, and each time numbers grew:

> The first response was surprising – something had tapped deeply into the consciousness of the local population and had released energy. Not only were people concerned, even anxious, but it was apparent that they were keen to make something happen. When, one evening, more than forty people turned up, it was too late to stop the momentum and soon four groups formed to take action. (Roderick with Jones, 2008, pp 18-19)

Indigenous cultures evolved successfully in respectful harmony with their natural environments. Seen in this way, cultural diversity becomes essential for biodiversity. Local economic projects with values for a future based on both social justice and environmental justice respect this balance.

Pause to search...

The New Economics Foundation (NEF) promotes social, economic and environmental justice. Its intention is to transform the economy so that it works in the interests of people and the planet. Go to www.neweconomics.org and discover some ideas for local projects that sow the seeds for a balance of social justice and environmental justice. Take the ideas back to your community and share them.

Ecofeminism

Ecofeminism's commitment to the environment comes from making a critical connection between the destruction of the environment and the oppression of women. Without this analysis, some essential connections can be missed. For instance, Riordan (2008) claims that:

- women in poverty are most at risk from dangers associated with climate change;
- women are largely ignored in climate research, policy and development;
- women are key actors in developing local coping strategies for climate change;
- women are critical agents of change in communities;
- women's skills and leadership are crucial for the survival and recovery of all;
- women's empowerment is needed for the sound management of environmental resources;
- women possess initiative, creativity and capacity to find grassroots solutions for climate change.

Without a gender analysis there is an unrecognised burden on the world's poorest women as well as limits on the effectiveness of action for environmental change (Riordan, 2008, p 49).

Feminist principles of 'harmony, co-operation and interconnection challenge male principles of competition, "discrimination", extremism and conflict' (Young, 1990, p 33). Women continue to be active in organising and theorising an alternative worldview based on harmony and cooperation, non-violence and dignity, a view that embraces both public and private, local and global, humanity and the natural world in equal measure. It reflects women's concerns for preserving life on earth over time and space.

We need new ways of knowing, new stories about connection, and responsibility for people and place.

Loci of oppressions matrix

Radical community development, and by this I mean a critical approach to practice that locates it at the heart of a movement for social and environmental justice, calls for a pedagogy of diversity for our times. I see a Freirean, anti-racist feminist pedagogy as a step towards this. Informed by analyses of class, patriarchy and racism as overarching structures of oppression that intertwine with each other, this model takes intersectionality through different contexts at different levels in a complex system of connections for domination and subordination. A Freirean-feminist-anti-racist pedagogy is also profoundly concerned with other aspects of difference and diversity, seeking a worldview that is equal, harmonious and respectful of all life on earth. This worldview is not possible within an ideology of neoliberalism based on profit over people and the planet. In other words, neoliberalism is an ideology incapable of reform because its success depends on exploitation and profit, with no accountability for human or environmental wellbeing.

The loci of oppessions matrix is a tool for a Freirean-feminist-anti-racist pedagogy for radical community development practice. It holds the potential for identifying overlapping, intersecting analyses of power that take thinking and action from a local to a wider collective potential for change.

Theory in action 5

Freirean anti-racist feminism using the loci of oppressions matrix

Issue

The search for a *critical living praxis* would benefit from a re-visioning of Freire through a feminist and anti-racist lens. Seeing the potential of his ideas from a position of *difference and diversity* offers a critical repositioning which takes stock of many different ways of knowing the world in order to challenge power in all its complexity.

Evidence

Not only are social inequalities increasing the world over, but they are increasing rapidly in rich countries. For example, child poverty in the UK affects one in three, and is increasing, and world child poverty affects one in two, making children the social group at greatest risk of poverty. We know that children's poverty is linked to family poverty based on 'race', class, gender, 'dis'ability and cultural dimensions (see Chapter Six). Clearly, in times of rapid change, we need analyses that give insight into the complex nature of *discrimination* if practice is to be effective in contributing to social justice.

Patricia Hill Collins identifies why a class analysis or a gender analysis is insufficient to understand the complexity of power, because alone they overlook the way that 'race', class and gender oppressions are intersecting, interlocking systems.

This seems helpful in our quest to explore the way these interconnected systems work. Her ideas complement those of Freire and Gramsci. Re-read the section on Patricia Hill Collins on p 93, and consider her use of the concepts of intellectuals, consciousness and alliance.

Analysis

The three-dimensional model in Figure 5.3 might help to capture the complexity of intersectional thinking in a simpler form. (i) *Difference* ('race', class, gender and so on) on one axis; (ii) *context* (family, workplace, streets, schools and so on) on another; and (iii) *levels* (local, national, global and so on) on a third form a complex set of interrelationships that interweave between axes, but also intertwine on any one axis. The elements are not fixed; they are interchangeable on each face. Imagine this as a Rubik's cube, each section capable of changing and being re-examined in relation to the whole. In locating these complex

Figure 5.4: Loci of oppressions matrix

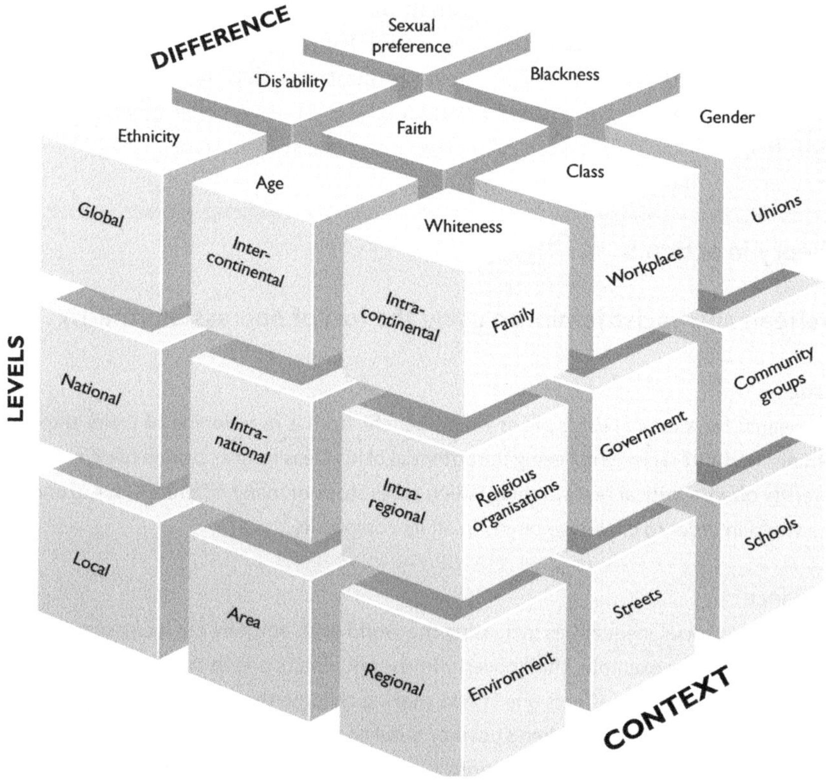

intersections, we begin to understand the root causes of oppression, and in doing so, identify potential sites of change.

So, for example, the model not only helps us to explore the interrelatedness of 'race', class and gender on one face, but to locate this within an environmental context, and on a local level. Then, if the level is shifted from local to, say, global, different but related issues emerge. The model gives no answers. Its purpose is to stretch our thinking in multidimensional ways, and in doing so, to pose questions that deepen our analysis and make our practice more critical.

Action

Paula: A continuing story of the 'micro-aggressions of daily life'

Using the loci of oppressions matrix, identify from the narrative below where the intersections of power are acted out in Paula's everyday life.

> In Lancaster, a predominantly White community, whenever I saw Paula from a distance, I noticed her proud and dignified stature slumped, and her eyes cast down to the pavement. One day at work, she greeted me with a big smile, and told me the story of Duncan, my 17-year-old younger son:

"I was walking up from town, deep in my own thoughts, feeling that I don't belong here as I did in Manchester. 'Yo Paula!', echoed across the street. I looked up, and there was Duncan driving his pizza delivery van, waving out of the window with a big grin on his face, so pleased to see me. It made me feel part of the place."

I laughed when I heard this, knowing that Duncan would indeed be so happy to see Paula out and about. We moved to Lancaster from Manchester at the same time as Paula, and Duncan had grown up in a multicultural community, with many close Black friends in his life.

In the years that we were both friends and colleagues, Paula and I used to travel to the US on work trips. I walked through passport control and customs, confidently assuming that I would not be searched. Gradually, I realised that every time Paula was the one chosen from the line of White visitors to the country to have her bag checked. These were not random acts. I used to walk over and demand to know whether there was a problem, but was always told it was 'routine'. Paula had learned to accept it as part of her life. Despite our mutual research into the problematic relations of alliances between Black and White women, we only partially addressed the very painful ways in which this got acted out in our friendship – and there were many! Paula was often furious that I had more privileges and was less challenged. But when she took me into one of the most volatile Black areas of Chicago, she was at home, she belonged, and I received the gaze as outsider, dislocated from my assumed comfort, and acutely aware of the danger of being different, of being a White women in a Black community. Over the years until she died, my deep friendship with Paula bounced through these challenging and painful experiences, educating me into racism as a lived experience.

Figure 5.5: Paula: my sister in resistance

> When Paula was taken ill and rushed to hospital, I followed the ambulance nose-to-tail in my little VW Polo, anxious not to lose her in the power and bureaucracy of the hospital. By the time I parked and got to the ward, she was already in bed, her beautiful features framed by the starched white linen pillowcase. The doctor interviewing her looked up at me, "And who are you?" To my amusement, in her illness, she raised her head from the pillow, looked him directly in the eye, daring him to challenge her, "She is my *sister!*" He looked at her Blackness then at my Whiteness, but backed off. In that moment, I realised that she was acknowledging my authenticity as a sister in resistance.

When you become familiar with the loci of oppressions matrix, use it as a training tool, introduce it to colleagues, local activists, managers and policy-makers to demonstrate intersectional thinking. Develop storytelling skills: encourage people to share personal narratives that capture the contradictions of everyday life, and use these as the focus of analysis, with the help of the loci of oppressions matrix, to demonstrate that the *personal is political*.

In conclusion

> The point of getting people to think critically is to enable them to create true democracy – what Fromm, Marcuse, West, and others regard as the cornerstone of socialism – both at the micro and macro level. If adults think critically they will be demanding worker cooperatives, the abolition of private education, the imposition of income caps, universal access to health care based on need not wealth, and public ownership of corporations and utilities. Critical thinking framed by critical theory is not just a cognitive process. It is a developmental project, inevitably bound up with helping people realize common interests, reject the privatized, competitive ethic of capitalism, and prevent the emergence of inherited privilege. (Brookfield and Holst, 2011, pp 58-9)

Brookfield and Holst, in naming critical pedagogy's purpose of creating true democracy, focus attention on the need for understanding the complexity of intersecting, overlapping oppressions. The loci of oppressions matrix helps us to get to grips with the systems of power that create an unequal world. But at the same time we need to incorporate new technologies into community development action. At this point I will take these ideas on intersecting oppressions into an analysis of poverty.

We are in new feminist times in which there is evidence of new grassroots feminist activism, with people mobilising online as the internet opens up dialogue between women in different countries, women who may be isolated in their communities, in order to understand each other's lives and to act together to tackle inequality and injustice, to make the world a better place. Take Freire's concept of dialogue in the role of conscientisation, and apply it to the idea of safe spaces for creating **critical dissent dialogue**. Hill Collins talks about 'safe spaces where Black women speak freely' without recrimination. How can this be related to online activism? How can you use online connections in your own work?

Bloggers and young activists are finding each other under the Twitter hashtag TYFA (Twitter Youth Feminist Army), for example. Lili Evans set up a blog with a friend (jellyandlilipop.wordpress.com) to connect young feminists using social media as a tool, and has started a face-to-face feminist group at her school:

> I guess I became a feminist when I actually looked at the world and saw how unfair it was. Women. People of colour. LGBT people, who have much harder lives for no good reason. I set up the Twitter Young Feminist Army with two other girls who are sadly no longer on Twitter because of the misogynist abuse directed at them. But mostly there's a great community online. Quite a lot of young girls are isolated, maybe their friends aren't interested in feminism and they are a bit scared of joining groups of older women, so we help them connect. At our age you get told not to wear short skirts to school and then you get shouted at by men in cars on the way home anyway, and realising that it's wrong and that there are other people out there who share your views is great. The thing I'd really like to see happen is equal pay, and access to better sex education and contraception advice for younger people. (Lili Evans, 15, quoted in Tracy McVeigh, *The Observer*, Saturday, 1 June 2013)

Having looked at intersectionality and the complex nature of overlapping, interlocking oppressions, it becomes much clearer as to why one generic category 'oppressed' is insufficient to make sense of the way that discrimination works. In the next chapter, we explore the way that poverty reinforces discrimination.

SIX

Poverty: 'a crime against humanity'

Privilege is maintained through power relations in ways we have explored in the last few chapters. Some social groups are advantaged and others disadvantaged in a process of domination/subordination. In the last chapter, the work of Patricia Hill Collins demonstrated the complex nature of oppressions that add to Freire's oppressor/oppressed analysis; multiple, intersecting forms of discrimination that get stitched into the fabric of society at mutually reinforcing levels, from personal prejudice to structural discrimination.

Gramsci's development of the traditional Marxist concept of hegemony, explored in Chapter Four, gives insight into the way that we are persuaded to see some social groups as more worthy than others, and in accepting this story we consent to discrimination as common sense, allowing it to be sewn into policy and practice. Policies, in turn, reinforce divisions of poverty and prosperity that are not questioned, and we accept the unacceptable as normal. Dominant stories are so convincing that they seep beneath the surface of our skins to such a point that we tolerate the way things are without considering alternatives.

The Second World War influenced popular thinking about faring well in society, and the British welfare state marked a watershed in social justice thinking in the postwar years, becoming 'a beacon of social care in the world. Any society that treats its people with respect is a healthy society. This makes sense, not only in terms of human rights, but also economically. Poverty comes at an enormous cost to everyone, destroying potential, and creating social problems, so collectively it is a wise decision to support people rather than to punish them.

In this chapter, I take a look at poverty, explore its links with discrimination, and offer some ideas for practice.

Peter Townsend

Peter Townsend and Brian Abel-Smith published *The poor and the poorest* in 1965, making a massive impact on people's understanding of *relative* poverty. This is known as the 'rediscovery of child poverty'. Townsend, a tireless campaigner and researcher into child poverty, was a co-founder of Child Poverty Action Group (CPAG) in 1965, its chair for 20 years and life president from 1989. He died in 2009, but his work leaves an important legacy for all those involved in the struggle against social injustice.

In 1979, Townsend defined poverty as follows:

> Individuals, families and groups in the population can be said to be in poverty when they lack resources to obtain the type of diet, participate

in the activities and have the living conditions and amenities which are
customary, or at least widely encouraged and approved, in the societies
in which they belong. (Townsend, 1979, p 31)

His definition makes it clear that in rich societies like the UK, poverty must be
understood in relation to general living standards. Yardsticks for *absolute* poverty set
measures for people's survival: yardsticks for *relative* poverty measure *social inclusion*
rather then *social exclusion*. Poverty deprives people of the resources to flourish.
This refers not only to income, but to the complex, interlinked disadvantages
that reduce life chances offered by education and health, *or* the wellbeing offered
by an attractive environment and a trusting community. It is money that largely
determines the amount of control people have over their life circumstances.

Townsend was the single most important person to develop understanding
of the way that poverty is structured into people's lives not as an *absolute* state
of being, but as a *relative* injustice. His driving belief was that poverty analyses
need to be translated into action, and that popular education is at the heart of
the process of action for change. This did not stop at national level – he saw the
interconnected issues of world poverty and its 'race' and gender dimensions as
part of the same problem:

> No longer can the trend in the poor countries be separated from that
> in rich countries. The problems ... are increasingly the product of
> economic and political powers exercised by the international agencies
> and the MNCs [multinational corporations]....There needs to be 'real
> world' coalitions ... as a basis for principled international redistribution.
> (Townsend, 1995, pp 10-12)

His belief was that poverty is a global issue influenced by trade, aid and
development policies that do not act to benefit poorer countries, an understanding
that poverty connects the richest in rich countries to the poorest in poor countries,
was before its time. The privileged in rich industrialised countries play a role in
creating social inequalities on a world scale. As a critical commentator on world
poverty, Townsend urged a radical overhaul of global institutions and a human
rights approach to child poverty to establish an 'international welfare state' that
embraced fairer systems of resource distribution and redistribution (Yeates and
Deacon, 2011, p 257).

Townsend was heartened by UNICEF's attention to child poverty, and talked
about the UK escalation in child poverty as a 'neglect-filled Anglo-American
model which unless there is massive investment in children we will head for
economic catastrophe' (Townsend, 1995, pp 10-12). As early as 1986, he was
vocal about privilege as a poverty problem:

> More attention must be given to the exposure of excessive and
> unnecessary privilege, as much as excessive and unnecessary power.

It is impossible to raise the poor without simultaneously diminishing the rich. (Townsend, 1986)

This concept of lowering the ceiling of privilege in order to lift the floor of poverty is key to action for social justice. Privilege is the problem, not poverty. It is not possible to achieve such high levels of consumption as those of the privileged, and to maintain the sustainability of the planet. The planet is able to sustain the needs of everyone, but not the wants of the greedy!

To Townsend, 'social justice should be understood and applied in terms of the equalisation of life chances' (Walker, Sinfield and Walker, 2011, p 276). His starting point on social justice was based on the moral unacceptability of inequality. The main part of his career was preoccupied with demonstrating the social and economic costs of inequality, but in his later years, he argued from a human rights perspective, that we need to abolish poverty and reduce inequality (Walker, Sinfield and Walker, 2011, p 277).

Child poverty in political context

The 'tighten your belts, make the rich richer', trickle-down politics of the Thatcher–Major years in Britain resulted in a massive rise in inequality as wealth transferred from the *poor* to the *rich*. At the same time, child poverty escalated from one in ten in 1979 at the start of Thatcherism to one in three at the end of its long rule in 1997. The Blair–Brown governments put child poverty on to the political agenda for the first time:

> Action on child poverty is the obligation that this generation owes to the next: to millions of children who should not be growing up in poverty: children who because of poverty, deprivation and the lack of opportunity have been destined to fail even before their life's journey has begun, children for whom we know – unless we act – life will never be fair. Children in deprived areas who need, deserve and must have a government on their side, a government committed to and fighting for social justice. (Brown, 2000)

Significantly, the Labour government turned this into what Stewart Lansley calls 'a remarkable political coup' by gaining cross-party support for the Child Poverty Act 2010, which legalised the pledge to end child poverty by 2020 (2013, pp 14-17). Finally, a political consensus on the unacceptability of relative poverty had been reached.

So what went wrong?

There was a failure to challenge thinking in two areas which left the ideology of 'the welfare scrounger' intact: those of powerful vested interests, and public consciousness on issues of fairness and a common good (Walker, Sinfield and Walker, 2011). The New Labour policy raft, *Every Child Matters*, was based on the assumption that if poor children try hard at school, they will get jobs as adults. Tess Ridge (2004) points out that a state interest in children as future workers leads to policies that are qualitatively different from those that are concerned with creating happy childhoods. The limitations of the 'work-hard-at-school-to-get-a-job-in-adulthood' approach to child poverty has also been exposed by research such as that of Lucinda Platt and her team, who provide evidence from the UK Millennium Cohort study that enduring poverty has already done damage to poor children's cognitive development by the pre-school years.

On 12 May 2010, Cameron launched Britain's coalition government. His pre-election campaign, 'sprinkled speeches and photo opportunities with new flavourings – green trees, social enterprise, the "big society", free schools, hug-a-hoodie, vote-blue-go-green, the-NHS-is-safe-with-me' that were distractions from the real business of the day: 'Deficit reduction takes precedence over any of the other measures in this agreement' (Toynbee and Walker, 2015a). Under the smokescreen of 'deficit reduction' Cameron was able to realise his intentions to shrink the state. After the election, the brutal reality hit home: 'Margaret Thatcher privatised state-run industries; Cameron's ambition was no less than to abolish the post-war welfare state itself' (Toynbee and Walker, 2015a). The coalition government ran with anti-welfare, dominance of the market and individualism, dismantling the public sector and much of what had been built to protect people in times of vulnerability, at the same time as increasing vulnerability with a resurrected campaign based on hatred of the poor, reviling the stereotype of the 'welfare scrounger'. Individual greed was elevated over collective need, and the aims to end child poverty by 2020 embedded in law in the Child Poverty Act 2010 became undermined: this was a government violating the policies it had a legal obligation to meet. On 7 May 2015, the Conservative Party under the leadership of David Cameron won an unexpected majority in the UK parliamentary elections to continue its neoliberal mission.

Without the brakes of critical action from those who are prepared to speak truth to power, this has taken us back to Thatcherism's campaign to sell the idea of the 'public burden of welfare' as a spurious truth that legitimises targeting the poor to benefit the wealthy. In fact, we hear a remarkable similarity of argument that justifies transference of wealth from the public to the private sector. In 2008 Killeen posed the question: is poverty in the UK a denial of people's human rights? Arguing that the refusal of successive governments to adopt the International Covenant of Economic, Social and Cultural Rights into UK law since the Thatcher division of deserving and undeserving poor has reinforced social attitudes that revile people in poverty and undermine anti-poverty policies, he claimed that 'povertyism' now sits alongside racism and sexism as a structural inequality, based on a belief that poor people are of less value (Killeen, 2008). In this respect, think also of Paulo Freire's comment on poverty as 'a crime against humanity' (Freire and Macedo, 1995).

> **Pause for thought...**
>
> Toryism is now in deep intellectual disarray. What is the party for, beyond cosseting corporate interests, the much-praised 'wealth-creators'? Shrinking the state is a reflex, not a vision.... Unpicking the values of the welfare state has meant undermining the idea that people should care for others beyond their own. (Toynbee and Walker, 2015a)
>
> Toynbee and Walker's idea of 'intellectual disarray' links to the theme of crisis threaded through this book. Henry Giroux (2009) talks about neoliberal narratives that define youth as *the* problem as an assault on children indicative of a deep moral and political crisis. Stuart Hall (in Davison, 2011) comments on conjuncture (a crisis of the current system) as an opportunity for change. If we overlook the need to set practice within its political times, we miss this opportunity to change the structures of discrimination that create injustice.
>
> Thompson (2006) identifies oppression as working on three levels in society: the personal, the cultural and the structural. All three levels interact in ways that mutually reinforce prejudice and discrimination. They can never be seen in isolation from one another simply because they form an interactive dynamic which constantly maintains social divisions and serves the power relations in society. This is why community development practice needs to be contextualised, not only in the community, but also in its political times.

In order to contextualise practice, we need to be aware not only of social and political trends, but of economic trends too. We have paid attention to how dominant ideologies create stories that set the mood for policy development. Neoliberal ideologies that elevate the market and profit above human wellbeing are founded on stories of the 'welfare scrounger' that pave the way for policies that dismantle the welfare state. These trends are not happening in national isolation, but need to be understood as world trends.

Poverty trends from Oxfam

The World Economic Forum gathering in Switzerland in January 2015 attracted the force of the anti-poverty charity Oxfam, which is calling for urgent action on narrowing the gap between the world's rich and poor. Oxfam's research shows that the share of the world's wealth owned by the wealthiest 1 per cent increased from 44 per cent in 2009 to 48 per cent in 2014, while the poorest 80 per cent currently own just 5.5 per cent. At this rate, in a year, 1 per cent of the world's population will own more wealth than the other 99 per cent (see www.oxfam. org/en/pressroom/pressreleases/2015-01-19/richest-1-will-own-more-all-rest-2016). Oxfam's message is that global wealth is increasingly in the pockets of a small privileged elite who are managing to generate wealth by focusing on a few economic sectors, such as finance and insurance, pharmaceuticals and healthcare, to lobby for policies that enhance their interests further: '85 billionaires have the same wealth as the bottom half of the world's population' (www.oxfam.org.uk/media-centre/press-releases/2014/10/number-of-billionaires-doubled-since-financial-crisis-as-inequality-spirals-out-of-control).

This is of immense concern as a human rights issue and for the future of the planet. Let's move our attention back to the UK now to explore specific evidence of poverty trends and their impact on children.

Child poverty: some facts and figures from the Child Poverty Action Group

CPAG, the organisation co-founded by Peter Townsend, is a leading watchdog and campaigning body on child poverty in the UK. For community development practitioners it offers current statistics on poverty trends, ideas about poverty and information on campaigns to end it. You will find all this information on its website at www.cpag.org.uk.

A summary based on their 2013/14 statistics reveals that:

- there are 3.7 million children – 28 per cent of all children – living in poverty in the UK;
- at a local level, there are serious concentrations of poverty: in 16 local wards the majority of children are poor;
- contrary to popular opinion, almost two thirds (64 per cent) of children growing up in poverty live in a family where at least one member works.

Explanations that put poverty down to drug and alcohol dependency, family breakdown, poor parenting or a culture of worklessness are not supported by the facts. On the other hand, it is important to understand how poverty affects children. According to CPAG:

- Growing up in poverty means being cold, going hungry and not being able to join in activities with friends. For example, 60 per cent of families in the bottom income quintile would like, but cannot afford, to take their children on holiday for one week a year.
- Child poverty has long-lasting effects. By the age of 16, there is a 28 per cent gap between children receiving free school meals and their wealthier peers in terms of numbers achieving at least 5 A*-C grades at GCSE. Leaving school with fewer qualifications translates into lower earnings over the course of a working life.
- The upward trend in child poverty is expected to continue, with 4.3 million children projected to be living in poverty by 2020 (according to Save the Children, this figure could be as high as 5 million; www.savethechildren.org.uk/).

Who lives in poverty?

CPAG's analyses reveal that while no one is exempt from poverty, some social groups face much higher risks than others:

- families with children are more likely to be poor than those without children;
- lone parents are more likely to be poor than couples;
- parents or children with disabilities are more likely to live in poverty, with workplace discrimination playing a part in reducing income;
- minority ethnic families also face workplace discrimination that depresses incomes;
- families with one or more workless parents are at much higher risk of poverty;
- a high cost of living and high housing costs can be location-specific, for example, London has some of the biggest concentrations of families at risk of income poverty.

Impact of poverty

CPAG's message is that poverty damages society and everyone in it: it damages childhoods, it damages life chances and it damages us all. Some of the specific evidence of its damage is in the following areas.

Education:

- Children from poorer backgrounds underachieve in education.
- By the age of three, poorer children are likely to be nine months behind children from richer homes.

Health:

- Poverty causes ill health and kills people prematurely, reducing life expectancy by an average of eight years.
- Children born in the poorest areas of the UK have lower birth weights than those born in the richest areas.
- Children from low-income families are more likely to die at birth or in infancy than children born into richer families.
- Poorer children are more likely to suffer chronic illness during childhood or to have a disability.

Communities:

- Children living in poverty are almost twice as likely to live in bad housing, which affects their physical and mental health and educational achievement.

- Fuel poverty sometimes forces families to choose between food and heating, affecting children adversely.
- Children from low-income families often miss school trips and other events, cannot invite friends round for tea, and cannot afford a week's holiday a year.
- Playgrounds in poor communities are prone to vandalism, misuse and present danger of injury.

Causes of poverty

CPAG highlights the complex range of factors that work together to create poverty risks.

Worklessness:

- In 2009/10, 42 per cent of all families below the UK poverty line had no working members.
- People are not able to work for many reasons – some have caring responsibilities, others have a health condition or disability, and some are discriminated against and find it hard to get a job.
- Structural reasons add to this: if the labour market does not provide enough jobs to match the skills and qualifications of unemployed people, or jobs are not close to people's homes, working is not a realistic option.
- Even when people do work, this is not always a route out of poverty. In 2009/10, 58 per cent of families below the UK poverty line had at least one working member.
- Low wages, part-time work and the high costs of childcare all conspire to reduce incomes.
- Many low-wage jobs are poverty traps, offering no prospects ('low pay, low prospects' or 'low pay, no pay').

Inadequate benefits:

If benefits are insufficient, there is no safety net to protect people. For example, it is estimated that a family with one child claiming Jobseeker's Allowance in 2009/10 received only 65 per cent of the amount they required to live above the poverty line.

Family breakdown:

- Lone parents are at a higher risk of living in poverty, but family breakdown provides an inadequate explanation of poverty in the UK.
- In 2009/10, 63 per cent of children in poverty lived in families with two parents.
- Factors such as lack of affordable childcare and flexible jobs are why many lone-parent families struggle to make ends meet.

Busting the myths of poverty

There is a lot of blame aimed at poor people for their own poverty.

Drug and alcohol misuse:

- Drug and alcohol misuse is often given as a reason why people live in poverty.
- While it is sensible to assume that people who do misuse drugs and alcohol find it challenging to function in the workplace and other areas of life, the statistics show that such behaviour is far from typical for low-income families.

Pause for thought...

A 2008 government study estimated that only 6.6 per cent of the total number of benefit claimants in England were problem drug users.

This group of people find it hard to escape poverty, but this clearly has no explanatory power for the other 93.4 per cent of claimants.

How do these facts sit alongside the dominant stories of poverty?

Benefit dependency:
- Some claim that the UK benefits system has created a culture of dependency and, as a result, claimants are reluctant to help themselves by looking for work.
- In fact, the inadequacy of benefits tells us much about the financial incentives that claimants have to look for work.
- Data also shows that many claimants rely on benefits for only short periods of time. For example, 67 per cent of Jobseeker's Allowance claimants find work within six months, while a further 22 per cent are no longer claiming benefits after 12 months.
- CPAG refer to recent Department for Work and Pensions (DWP) focus group research as an interesting insight into the job-seeking behaviour of claimants. It revealed that while 22 per cent of the group were not actively looking for work, half of these dedicated their energies instead to their families. This statistic speaks to other types of important work that claimants may undertake, but which has no monetary value (www.cpag.org.uk/content/child-poverty-myths).

Understanding the contradictions of child poverty

Richard Layard's research into happiness suggests that a society cannot flourish without some sense of shared purpose, that the self needs to be connected to something larger, a common good in which we pursue the greatest happiness for all (2005, p 234). Layard and Dunn (2009) highlight this in their work on

Figure 6.1: Oxfam's campaign, 'Make Poverty History', supported by the late Nelson Mandela

childhood, arguing that individualism has gone too far, and what we need instead is a society based on the law of love.

So let's look at what has led to the creation of a rich society that fails to feed its children. By the early 1970s, a rising welfare budget, together with the impact of a recession, created a niche for a changed way of thinking. As the decade went on, neoliberal ideology, previously little known or accepted, colonised this space and erupted on the world stage as Thatcherism in the UK, Reagonomics in the US, with Pinochet in Chile, the International Monetary Fund (IMF), the World Bank and others buying into this elevation of the free market, putting profit before people. Prior to this, ideas based on a notion of the market controlling people's lives would have been laughed out of existence. But this transformative moment was well anticipated, and a repressive state emerged based on 'privatisation, deregulation, outsourcing, and a marauding market fundamentalism' (Giroux, 2009, p 5). Going back to Gramsci, we need help in understanding how this could happen if we are to develop practice that is capable of change. To guide this process, read this extract from a talk given by Susan George. It is an excellent prod to our thinking.

Pause for thought...

Over 50 years ago Polanyi made this amazingly prophetic and modern statement: 'To allow the market mechanism to be sole director of the fate of human beings and their natural environment ... would result in the demolition of society'.

And just as Polanyi foresaw, this doctrine is leading us directly towards the 'demolition of society' ....

How did neoliberalism ever emerge from its ultra-minoritarian ghetto to become the dominant doctrine in the world today? Why can the IMF and the Bank intervene at will and force countries to participate in the world economy on basically unfavourable terms? Why is the Welfare State under threat in all the countries where it was established? Why is the environment on the edge of collapse and why are there so many poor people in both the rich and the poor countries at a time when there has never existed such great wealth? Those are the questions that need to be answered from an historical perspective....

[Neoliberals] have built this highly efficient ideological cadre because they understand what the Italian Marxist thinker Antonio Gramsci was talking about when he developed the concept of cultural hegemony. If you can occupy people's heads, their hearts and their hands will follow.... No matter how many disasters of all kinds the neoliberal system has visibly created, no matter what financial crises it may engender, no matter how many losers and outcasts it may create, it is still made to seem inevitable, like an act of God, the only possible economic and social order available to us. (George, 1999, pp 73 and 251)

Does Susan George's thinking link to Gramsci's concept of hegemony as outlined in Chapter Four? Can you see hegemony in action from this account? How does this help to identify action for change? How can you create spaces for critical dissent dialogue capable of developing counternarratives of change?

Child wellbeing in rich countries

In 2007, the UNICEF Innocenti Research Centre report on child wellbeing in rich countries (UNICEF, 2007) ranked the UK bottom out of 21 in creating unhappy childhoods, and raised many questions in the process. The new UNICEF study on child wellbeing in rich countries in 2013, ranking 29 economically developed countries on the wellbeing of their children, put the UK in 16th place. Any comparison with their 2007 report is limited by changes in measures and methods, but a 'limited overview', based on four dimensions common to the 2007 and 2013 reports – material wellbeing, health, education and behaviours/risks – indicates that while the UK appears to have made a significant stride forward, this is largely based on improvements in some health and material conditions. The UK still has high infant mortality, the lowest further education rate in the developed world, is one of only three countries in which the teenage birth rate has not fallen, and has one of the highest alcohol abuse rates by young people. This is despite the fact that UNICEF UK called a conference at Ditchley Park to discuss the findings of the 2007 report. This led to the Ditchley Declaration, with all-round party support for the Child Poverty Act 2010 (Nastic, 2013).

> Protecting the years of childhood is ... essential, both for the wellbeing of those who are children today and of the UK society of tomorrow. The commitment in the coalition government's programme to eradicate child poverty by 2020 and to introduce various measures to support families should not be set aside, even temporarily, because other problems appear more pressing. This commitment should have first call on the UK's capacities; it is a commitment to be maintained in good times and bad. There will always be something more immediate than protecting the wellbeing of children. There will never be anything more important. (Nastic, 2013, p 13)

Poverty works in the self-interests of individualism and against the collective good: inequality is divisive and socially corrosive, reducing the quality of life for all (Wilkinson and Pickett, 2010). Yet, since the election of the coalition government in 2010, there has been a change of heart on the redistribution of wealth from rich to poor, accompanied by a rise in pathologising people in poverty as inadequate and delinquent. The Conservative government elected in 2015 continues this neoliberal ideology.

An online poll by the DWP was set up in 2012 to gauge public feeling on the key factors underlying poverty (HM Government, 2012). Cleverly added to the items assessing whether a child is growing up in poverty came reference to having parents who are addicts alongside questions on low income and family breakdown. Unsurprisingly, 90 per cent of respondents chose the key issue as drug and alcohol addiction, with only 79 per cent choosing lack of income. Seized by the government as 'truth', this was then echoed in a speech given by Iain Duncan Smith, Work and Pensions Secretary, to the Kids Company on 31 January 2013, cleverly reflecting this changed thinking on behalf of the government.

Pause for thought ...

How would you critique this outline of Iain Duncan Smith's speech to Kids Company?

On disadvantage:

- "Listening to your stories, it is clear that the children who come here – like too many others across the country – face profound disadvantages."
- "Growing up in very dysfunctional or violent families ... often with emotional and mental health difficulties ... or facing problems around substance misuse ... their need for Kids Company could not be more pressing."

On the carefully constructed DWP poll:

- "A recent poll conducted as part of the consultation process shows that while not having enough income is thought to be one important factor ... having a parent addicted to

---

drugs or alcohol was thought to be the most important factor of all ... above and beyond other dimensions such as going to a failing school, living in a cold damp home, or having to care for a parent."

- "Of course, not every child in poverty will have drug or alcohol-addicted parents. Nor have we made a decision on which factors should be included in the new measure. But it is striking that so many people pick out as central to a child's experience of poverty, a factor that so rarely features in the poverty debate. Nothing illustrates more clearly how far off course the current measure has taken us *and* why we need a new measure ... one which both identifies those most in need and entrenched in disadvantage and is widely accepted by as being meaningful and accurate."

On action on poverty:

- "For a poor family where the parents are suffering from addiction, giving them an extra pound in benefits might officially move them over the poverty line. But increased income from welfare transfers will not address the reason they find themselves in difficulty in the first place. Worse still, if it does little more than feed the parents' addiction, it may leave the family more dependent not less ... resulting in poor social outcomes and still deeper entrenchment."
- "What such a family needs is that we treat the cause of their hardship – the drug addiction itself. Rather than simply tracking income levels, this surely is what a measure of child poverty should capture ... measuring whether the family has an opportunity to break the cycle of disadvantage ... so that parents can take responsibility for their own lives and improve the life chances of their children." (Duncan Smith, 2013)

It is very important to critique the arguments that are influencing public consciousness. As Lansley (2013) says, there has been a shift from anti-poverty to anti-poor and this paves the way for policies that pathologise and punish poor people.

Pause for thought ...
Read the following facts, and refine your critique based on the evidence:

- When policies boosted low incomes up to 2005, low-income families increased spending on children's shoes, books and fruit and vegetables, relative to other families with children, and reduced spending on alcohol and tobacco (Gregg et al, 2005).
- Drug addiction, bad parenting and welfare dependency are only minor explanations of poverty – for example, 0.9 per cent are problem drug users and 3.8 per cent are alcohol dependent (Harkness et al, 2012).
- The proportion of poor children in *working* families has risen in 30 years from about 33 per cent to 60 per cent:
  - one in five workers are low paid – double the mid-1980s rate;
  - 45 people apply for every unskilled vacancy;

- transferring money away from benefits to services raises short-term poverty and reduces life chances;
- welfare cuts make short-term savings, but bring long-term social and economic costs;
- current benefit cuts will remove £20 billion from welfare to mend the economic deficit;
- the ideology of the 'welfare scrounger' has been resurrected by a harsh media campaign: 'scrounger' was used in national newspapers on average 250 times annually from 1994 to 2009; this rose to a massive 2,500 in 2012;
- at the same time, the top 1 per cent now have about 14 per cent of the national income compared with just over 5 per cent in the 1970s – it is vital to reduce this upper level concentration of wealth if child poverty is to be reduced (Lansley, 2013).

The most significant point to take from this chapter is that social change rests on a critical analysis of not *who* is poor, but *why* they are poor. Rich people have power over the lives of poor people: rich nations have power over the policies of poor nations. Social and economic structures support inequalities between rich and poor so that the rich get even richer (and more powerful) and the poor get even poorer (and less powerful) (Gunn, 1978).

Figure 6.2: End Child Poverty

Theory in action 6

Ending child poverty

Figure 6.3: Children's experiences of poverty

© Photo by Jeff J Mitchell/Getty Images

Issue
What can you see in this photograph?

What's going on?

Do you recognise where it is?

Who is this?

Why is he there?

What is he doing?

What's happening?

How do you think he is feeling?

Evidence
The government-sponsored Millennium Cohort Study (www.cls.ioe.ac.uk) has tracked 14,000 children born at the start of the century to build a picture of how family circumstances

determine a young person's education, health and happiness in Britain. These findings are from 2009, when the children were seven years old. According to the study:

- Almost one fifth of seven-year-olds live in severe poverty.
- Almost three quarters of children whose parents are of Pakistani or Bangladeshi origin live in poverty.
- Just over half (51 per cent) of Black seven-year-olds and just over a quarter of White seven-year-olds live in poverty, with three fifths from these groups in single-parent families.
- Seven-year-olds are most likely to live in poverty in the North East (40 per cent), and least likely in the South West (22 per cent). The figure for London was 36 per cent.
- Just under 7 per cent of seven-year-olds living in poverty do not have two pairs of all-weather shoes, and just under 50 per cent do not get pocket money.

The researchers focused on the UK's most deprived neighbourhoods, but adjusted the weighting of their findings to reflect all parts of Britain.

Go to the *Millennium Cohort Study: Initial findings from the Age 11 survey* (available at www. cls.ioe.ac.uk) to see the latest research results.

Go to the Breadline Kids website (www.channel4.com/programmes/dispatches/videos/all/breadline-kids) and hear testimonies of child poverty from Rosie and Becky.

Analysis
PEN (Poverty Ends Now): a children's manifesto on poverty

Children North East and Rys Farthing from the University of Oxford have taken on a piece of work for the All-Party Parliamentary Group on Poverty to produce a children's manifesto and action plan on poverty. This links to the understanding that until people in poverty are involved in action against poverty, nothing will change.

Young people from the North East, London, Manchester and Liverpool, who were already actively involved in tackling child poverty, came together to form a national group which they named PEN – Poverty Ends Now.

The group met over several residentials to produce a six-point children's manifesto on poverty:

- Every family in Britain should meet a minimum standard of living, and not just be surviving.
- An equal school experience for all.
- Affordable, decent homes for everyone.
- Every young person should have access to three affordable, healthy meals a day.
- All should feel and be safe within their communities and at home.
- All young people should have affordable transport everywhere.

Action
PEN worked on three national actions throughout 2014:

- Launching their manifesto in Parliament on 15 October 2014.
- Tabling Parliamentary Questions (PQs) and writing evidence submissions to select committees.
- Undertaking a national media campaign.

PEN members are also working on taking action at a local level within their own cities:

- Decent Incomes – Liverpool: play and community discussion during National Living Wage Week.
- Equal Schools – North East: local evidence session in Darlington, 28 November 2014.
- Housing – London: parliamentary evidence session.
- Food – Gateshead Youth Assembly: holiday hunger activities.
- Feel Safe – Manchester: walking tour and Question Time with decision-makers.
- Transport – Newcastle Youth Council: distributing discount cards across secondary schools (for more, see www.children-ne.org.uk/pen-poverty-ends-now-%E2%80%93-children%E2%80%99s-manifesto-poverty#sthash.b2hxHpI7.dpuf).

Find out about patterns of poverty and employment in your community from local authority data, internet sources and watchdog bodies like CPAG. Make sure that the data for your community is not skewed by the inclusion of wealthier neighbouring communities.

Who is likely to be poor? Does this have a gendered, age-related, 'dis'abled, 'race', culture or religion, or any other connection? How does this fit with national, international and global patterns of child poverty?

Knock on doors, talk to people wherever they gather in the community, listen to their concerns, identify generative words/themes that get repeated. What do people feel passionately about, what creates emotional responses in them? How do people see the community, its history, its people, its problems, its assets, its resources …? Set up an End Child Poverty group locally and make links with other campaigning groups nationally. Visit politicians, employers, residents groups, shops and schools.

Set this work within a longer-term aim: what needs to be done to end child poverty?

Four million children – one in three – are currently living in poverty in the UK, one of the highest rates in the industrialised world and this could rise to five million by 2020 (savethechildren.org.uk). This is a shocking fact for the seventh richest country in the world to face.

Go to CPAG's website at cpag.org.uk to find out child poverty levels in your area. Poverty has a profound effect on children, their families, communities and the whole of society. It often sets in motion a deepening spiral of social exclusion, destroying life chances and creating low self-esteem and poor health.

Most people do not realise the unacceptable levels of child poverty in Britain, so there needs to be greater public consciousness to grasp the extent of the problem and to understand its consequences. CPAG has information that you can use to help you with this. It is important to translate the issue into action for change, so visit CPAG's policy and campaign webpages to see what your community could do to swell collective action for ending child poverty. For example, CPAG is now hosting the End Child Poverty campaign.

Effective action must be informed by an analysis of the current political context, and this is what I will move on to in the next chapter, with particular focus on how the story of the 'welfare scrounger' has been developed and extended to target specific social groups as disgusting and disposable. The image gives rise to fear and hatred in the minds of the population at large, and, as a result, poor people become seen as unworthy Objects, occupying the borderlands of society.

SEVEN

Power and political times

I have attempted to story this book from all angles: stories of people and power, stories about ideas as well as stories about the theorists who had the ideas, and stories of action that begin the counternarratives of change. The theme of this book is theory in action, with Freire as the foundation for an eclectic range of ideas that take a Freirean approach into current political times. I have woven together changes in the political context that have evolved since the welfare state consensus was subsumed under the sudden tide of neoliberal ideology that erupted in the 1980s, elevating profit over people and the planet. Freire, complemented by Gramsci, Foucault, feminism and anti-racism, has served community development well, but they are no longer enough to make sense of these current times of crisis, a historical conjuncture that opens an opportunity for change. Action for change must be predicated on an analysis of power that is capable of identifying what needs to be changed. This chapter therefore introduces Imogen Tyler's social **abjection** theory as a significant theoretical advance to add to our Freirean toolkit.

Critique and dissent

Critique and dissent are important processes in deepening democracy: as I have already emphasised, a society that 'neither questions itself nor can imagine any alternative to itself' is dangerous (Foucault, quoted in Giroux, 2009, p 177). Kothari (2001), Craig (2008) and Darder (2009) warn of the dangers of simplifying the nature of power. Kothari says that while we fail to see knowledge as an accumulation of norms, rituals and practices that are embedded in power relations, we fall back on simplistic dichotomies of power that are not capable of changing the way that discrimination is structured into society. We can think about this in relation to the way that feminists challenged Freire's oppressor/oppressed dichotomy as hiding more than it revealed in relation to women's lives. Dealing with class discrimination does not expose the hegemonic function embedded in male/female relations, and the 'norms, rituals and practices' that fill people's minds with images of what is normal and natural. Gary Craig (2008) warns that an inability to analyse power at policy and personal levels has created an inability to understand racism, so that issues of social justice, culture and identity constantly get swept under the carpet.

Darder (2009) reminds us of the danger that postmodernism posed to critical theory by fragmenting understanding of major power structures. This suggestion, that there are no collective ways of understanding power, came at a time when globalisation was accelerating round the world, reasserting forces of domination and exploitation. Postmodernism offered a smokescreen for the forces of power by suggesting that we can only understand the world in fragmented ways. Critical thinkers rose: 'postmodernism is an obstacle to the formation of open and radical perspectives which challenge inequalities and the deepening of the rule of capital in all areas of social life' (Rikowski and McLaren, 1999, p 1). Their concern is that 'for postmodernists, all concepts are decentred (fragmented, splattered) and all dualisms (such as the Marxist notion of two major social classes) deconstructed' (Rikowski and McLaren, 1999, p 2). Their driving preoccupation is that postmodernism, in attempting to dismantle the dominant hegemonic emphasis on a single truth as the real truth, created an alternative so hopelessly fragmented that it offered a smokescreen for the radical right (Hill, 2000). This radical group of critical thinkers reasserted the importance of 'race', class and gender as three overriding discriminatory forces of discrimination in the world today that need to be understood and acted on.

Community development is in the business of questioning everything about life in order to discover the nature of discrimination, subordination and oppression, and to act to bring about change.

The story so far...

Paulo Freire put community at the heart of social change. He is clear that *praxis*, or *theory in action*, is vital to this process, and that in dialogue with local people, popular educators will coordinate communities of learners, building theory in action that is capable of informed action for change. An altered way of seeing the world emerges from critical consciousness, awareness that creates an *epistemological* shift, a new way of making sense of the world that seeks the root causes of inequalities. Rather than passive Objects, the Others of a society based on status and privilege, this process locates people as thinking, active Subjects capable of transforming the world. Part of our conceptual toolkit, in this sense, is to ensure that community development keeps abreast of new thinking in order to develop the critical approach to practice necessary to analyse power and to inform action.

In Chapter Four, we considered Gramsci's concept of hegemony as a system of power based on *coercion* and *consent*, and we also looked at Foucault who concentrates on power not only from above, but as a web-like system that weaves its way across the ground through every interaction. Patricia Hill Collins' immense contribution based on intersectionality extended analyses of power in Chapter Five, locating power as a system of overlapping, intersecting oppressions, rather than separated out into single dichotomies of oppressor/oppressed, Black/White, male/female.... This struggle with ideas is part of our everyday practice; without them we are not equipped to engage with social injustice.

Dominant ideology

Telling stories of inferiority and superiority have been central to forces of domination/subordination in the British class system over the ages, and lie at the heart of inequality. We are now discovering new ideas that explain the ways in which hegemonic stories that demonise people at the bottom of the pecking order work to maintain privilege for those at the top. Jones suggests that the class war, raged by Margaret Thatcher from her ascent to power in 1979, used demonisation of the working class as an:

> … all-out assault on the pillars of working-class Britain. Its institutions, like trade unions and council housing, were dismantled; its industries, from manufacturing to mining, were trashed; its communities were, in some cases, shattered, never to recover; and its values, like solidarity and collective aspiration, were swept away in favour of rugged individualism. Stripped of their power and no longer seen as a proud identity, the working class was increasingly sneered at, belittled and scapegoated. (Jones, 2011, p 10)

The Blair government, no longer seeing itself as the party of the working class, misguidedly believed that neoliberalism could bring about a new-style, market-driven, classless society. But an overt commitment to ending child poverty sat uncomfortably alongside a reluctance to tax the rich in order to pay back the wealth siphoned from the poor during the Thatcher years!

The story of the 'welfare scrounger' has now taken hold so powerfully in the public imagination that it remains an unquestionable 'truth'. The media has played a key role in maintaining this truth, but the Blair–Brown years did nothing to challenge it, choosing instead to default on Labour's traditional working-class roots by playing into the idea of the end of class. All those capable were to 'aspire' to join the ranks of a swelling middle class, but this idea left the most disadvantaged of all vulnerable and without protection.

It is this politics of aspiration that led to *Every Child Matters* as a policy raft that saw children as future workers, that is, work hard at school if you want a job. This was fundamentally flawed thinking: poverty damages children's lives before they start school, so the responsibility is to create happy childhoods while they are growing up. Labour at this point shifted from its traditional class analysis to fall captive to neoliberalism by pathologising an underclass that lacks ambition, talent and determination to do better for themselves. In this way, the finger of blame is pointed at the most disadvantaged in society, diverting attention away from privilege as the real problem.

The reality is that life chances in the UK today are more prescribed by where and to whom we are born than at any time since the Middle Ages (Dorling, 2007, p 5). So the context is one of rising inequalities and a downturn in social mobility at the same time as human rights, civil liberties, trade unions, democratic protests and social movements have been eroded, effectively removing critique and dissent from the agenda. At the same time, we are living through a massive transference of wealth from the public purse to private pockets in just the same way as under Thatcherism, with one in seven of our children going to school without breakfast as families struggle with decisions about whether to pay the rent or feed the family, and food banks become the order of the day.

The question is, why does child poverty exist in the UK, the seventh richest country in the world? The anti-poverty consensus, embedded in law in the Child Poverty Act 2010, came with all three major political parties behind the aim to end child poverty by 2020. This has turned. Indeed, Stewart Lansley sees a shift in ideology:

> ... the rhetoric has become more 'anti-poor' than 'anti-poverty', with policy priorities redirected away from maintaining the income floor (and existing benefit levels) to tackling a narrow range of 'causes' associated with behavioural weakness. Underlying its approach has been a sharp shift in philosophy towards poverty, one that has shifted sharply away from Labour's 'welfarist' approach to a much more 'individualistic' model, one more in tune with the views of the 1980s. (Lansley, 2013, p 15)

Foucault argues that the rise of neoliberalism in Europe and North America was a result of the horrors of Nazism and, together with the dismantling of former communist states, a 'state' phobia reaction from the political left and right, placed 'the big state' as the enemy of freedom (Foucault, 2008, p 116). Deceptively, the power of 'the small state' was not shrunk: it was set to govern for the market, invading every nook and cranny of social life to remove any resistance to profit generation for the benefit of 'the new global class of the super-rich. As governments have come to govern for the market they have also come to govern *against* the people' (Tyler, 2013, p 6; emphasis in original). This is not a laissez-faire free-market 'small state', but a vigilant, active, interventionist state (Foucault, 2008), which creates rising social inequality at the same time as eroding workers' rights, civil liberties and human rights as perceived threats to market competition. At the same time, dissent has been undermined, and political protests that forged change in the 1970s and 1980s have been weakened and even criminalised, thus damaging democracy (Tyler, 2013). Think about the invasion of Iraq: despite some of the biggest street protests ever known expressing dissent, no impact was made on the UK government's decision to invade. And so, as the political right and left merged, leaving no opposition to the march of neoliberalism, democratic freedoms have been curbed, communities have been fractured, and social life has been reduced to Victorian levels of inequality.

Neoliberalism is a canny class project that flies the banner of individualism, choice, freedom, social mobility and the security of the nation by creating its own human detritus, abandoned lives that are violently targeted, stigmatised and assigned to a human waste heap. Imogen Tyler develops this idea of stigmatisation as a form of legitimising increasing inequalities and injustices. She does this by revisiting class within the complex ideas presented by *intersectionality*. In other words, her intention is:

… in focusing on not one but several different categories and groups of people 'laid to waste' by neoliberal economic, political and social polices (including asylum seekers and other unwanted irregular migrants, politically and economically disenfranchised young people, Gypsies and Travellers, people with disabilities), my intention is to produce an intersectional account of marginality and resistance that will deepen critical understandings of the *common* processes and practices of neoliberal governmentality both within Britain and beyond. (Tyler, 2013, p 8; emphasis in original)

At this point, I would like to explore the usefulness of Tyler's ideas on social abjection theory as a theoretical extension of Freirean thought for neoliberal times.

Social abjection theory

Social abjection is a theory of 'power, subjugation and resistance'. In other words, it offers analyses of the way power works to subordinate some social groups, but it also offers ideas for action. We can explore it as an addition to a critical living praxis. Tyler develops the concept of *abjection* as a lived social process that targets certain social groups as the butt of violent disgust, unworthy Objects on the margins of society. As a hegemonic strategy for maintaining power, stories that dehumanise people as Objects, occupying the dark and dangerous borderlands of society, pour fear and hatred into the minds of the population at large.

This links to Gramsci's concept of hegemony as power through both *coercion* and *persuasion*: stories of disgust seep into the minds of the majority as common sense, reinforced through everyday conversations and echoed in the media to reinforce the process of exclusion by *consent*. Social abjection theory, in these ways, reveals the need for state power to constantly reproduce relations of the powerful, worthy Subject and the disempowered, unworthy Object, a dialectical contradiction in which one reinforces the other. Without one, the other would not exist. Hegemony is that fragile, relying on the strength of the stories it tells to maintain its power and legitimacy.

Pause for thought…

This analysis of the violence of the state in using exclusion as a power that strips every bit of human dignity from the poorest and most vulnerable to hold them up as dehumanised, social detritus – undesirable, unworthy, disgusting and disposable – helps to identify the process of discrimination and the role of the outcast. To do this in a fully coherent way, we need to think about the way that state violence and social exclusion get acted out on diverse levels and from multiple perspectives. Importantly, to use this as a *critical living praxis*, we need to think how we can use the contradictions of abjection, that is, the way that dominant hegemony, while holding vulnerable social groups up as Objects of ridicule in order to destroy their power, paradoxically relies on their presence in that form to maintain dominant power. This opens up a political crack for us to contest, challenge and change *the state we are in*.

So let's begin by exploring the concept of disgust within the project of neoliberalism.

The neoliberalisation of disgust

Tyler picks up power and disgust as crucial to understanding power relations. 'All political ideologies – but perhaps particularly those preoccupied with social hygiene, such as racism, xenophobia, eugenics, homophobia and misogyny – are mediated through revolting aesthetics' (Tyler, 2013, p 25). She says that the dehumanising violence embodied in the image of the 'welfare scrounger' paved the way for material violence in the form of benefit cuts. Take, for instance, the political stories about 'dis'ability claimants, picked up by media stories that reinforced disability benefit fraud, which then gave rise to 'dis'ability hatred expressed as violence on the streets.

Pause for thought...

Tyler takes our gaze immaculately from an over-concentration on neoliberalism as solely free-market rule to a deeper understanding of the way that neoliberalism gains powerful public consent for policies that increase inequalities. Consider policies that dismantle public sector provision to privatise in the name of profit, threatening the very fabric of democracy.

Rather than neoliberalism as market rule in a classless society, Tyler argues that *neoliberalism is a class project in its own right*. The political left and right now occupy a neoliberal consensus where there is no voice remaining to act in opposition to defend democratic freedom, fractured communities, the eroded fabric of social life and the economic inequalities that destroy social progress made since the industrial revolution.

Foucault's *The birth of biopolitics* (2008) is drawn on by Tyler to explain neoliberalism's elevation of the market over the state, 'a state under the supervision of the market rather than a market supervised by the state' (Foucault, quoted in Tyler, 2013, p 6). As I repeatedly emphasise, the 'small state' paradox is that 'as governments have come to govern for the markets they have also come to govern *against* the people'. So, the small state becomes an interventionist state dismantling impediments to profit by dismantling public sector protection at the same time as organised labour, democratic protest and social movements have been 'fatally undermined' (Tyler, 2013, pp 6 and 7).

Individualism has served neoliberalism well: it not only undermines the ideas of a common good, but it fragments collective organising, collective action for the wellbeing of all.

Being made abject

Tyler's comment that successive governments have focused on governing for the market, and in doing so 'they have also come to govern *against* the people' emphasises that in the name of a 'free' market we are manipulated and controlled by the state. Far from being the classless, meritocratic society that Blair aspired to, she offers critical analysis of precisely how right-wing governments are using stigmatisation to operate a form of governance that legitimises social inequalities and injustices as individual pathologies. She uses *intersectionality* as a way of understanding difference and resistance.

British citizenship has been redesigned to abjectify specific groups and populations, producing paralysed, dejected and deportable populations of non-citizens within the borders of the nation state. The aim is to target certain social groups and to disqualify them from belonging, abjectifying them outside of the realms of citizenship.

The death of class

Margaret Thatcher told us that 'there is no such thing as society, only individuals and their families'. I was a community worker in Hattersley at the time, a White, traditional working-class community 'invented' as part of the 'slum clearance' initiatives of the 1950s and early 1960s. Families from urban Manchester who had been united in the Blitz were relocated to peripheral, isolated, rural land over the city boundary in Tameside. Although old Manchester neighbourhoods were fragmented by the move, working-class solidarity survived until 1987, when Thatcher's 'no such thing as society' interview in *Woman's Own* had an immediate impact. There was an unwritten law that you never robbed your own people, but within a short space of time, the language of the streets was 'if you've got any sense, you just take care of yourself and your family', and crime turned in on the community in ways that had not been seen before.

In 1999, Tony Blair announced that the class war was over in an attempt to disengage inequalities from the political class struggle, continuing the process of class abjection entrenched by Thatcher. Class is dead is an idea that emerged from the partnership between New Labour and Anthony Giddens, the sociologist who argued that globalisation had transformed class into 'selfhood' in which life chances relate less to birth and more to us seizing opportunities – the redistribution of possibilities rather than resources. The reality is that this attitude has led to birth being a bigger determinant of life chances than ever as social mobility decreases with the widening of the class divide. Giddens was extremely influential in shaping New Labour policies, and therefore instrumental in changed attitudes to a new individualism, which led to "an underclass of people cut off from society's mainstream, without any sense of shared purpose ... the decline of old industries and the shift to an economy based on knowledge and skills [have] given rise to a new class: a workless class" (Tony Blair, 1997, speech at the Aylesbury Estate, Southwark, available at www.parliament.uk/business/ publications/business-paper/commons/deposited-papers/?page=1251&sort=1). New Labour constructed citizenship around inclusion/exclusion and work/ worklessness, staking the poorest out as Other than citizens, with work as the only route to social inclusion. Those who are classed as unemployable or who are barred from the labour market, like asylum-seekers, as well as those who fall into the 'underclass' racialising category of unemployed, or Gypsies and Travellers who have always been in a struggle against capitalism, face punitive policing and policies, and have now moved from demonisation in the press to BAFTA-nominated celebrity status through Channel 4's *Big Fat Gypsy Weddings*, in what Tyler sees as the depoliticisation of social conflicts and struggles:

> … pretending to enrich democracy by extending visibility to marginal communities, cultural enterprises such as reality TV not only profit from the free labour of participants, but function to elide the political struggles of minority subjects and incite further social antagonisms. (Tyler, 2013, p 145)

Take another look at the 2011 English riots as a political event. The rioters temporarily reconstituted themselves as a new class, bridging differences in order to claim a public space:

> … enemies next to each other rioting … everybody knew they was fighting for a cause … I couldn't believe and I was happy that there was actually standing together and I was thinking, why would it cause something like this for these people to get together?...
>
> Everyone's aiming for the government today. Everyone's voices need to get heard. And that's what it was. (Fenn and Owen, 2011, in Tyler, 2013, p 203)

The LSE/*Guardian* survey (Lewis et al, 2011) revealed, rather than Cameron's tub-thumping claim of 'criminality pure and simple', a new form of collective unity, a space seized in the moment which was seen by many young people as a 'negative freedom' to express their rage against power – the police, the government, the rich – for their powerlessness: 'people who have got nothing wanted to show that they had nothing' (Tyler, 2013, p 204).

The riots came after the banking crisis, the MPs' expenses scandal, and a series of public outrages over pay incentives awarded to the already rich as the neoliberal state was seen as increasingly acting in the interests of the minority against the majority. However, as the rioters took on the role of the abjects in the dominant story of power, this legitimised the story of an underclass, a wasted population in which Whites became Black, criminalised on TV screens the country over, with savage punishments justified, yet, ask Revel and Negri (2011), where are the mugshots of the criminal bankers and corporate bosses who keep fattening their profits out of this crisis? As Keith Popple points out, 80 per cent of the deficit is being paid for by the poorest, when the debt could be written off by taxing the excessively rich without them even noticing the loss (Popple, 2013).

Chavs

Tyler's fundamental tenet proposes class politics as central to the neoliberal project, and reformulated in the caricature of the 'chav'. By 2002, 'chav' had become the common term in use for disadvantaged, particularly young, White people.

In order to understand the role that dominant ideology plays in achieving popular consent, I want to introduce Imogen Tyler's interpretation of abjection theory. Her argument is based on identifying the way that neoliberal 'democracies' use fear and anxiety to generate consent, using stigmatisation to harden public opinion against some social groups as undeserving, undesirable and disposable.

Let's take a look at abjection theory as a way of aiding our understanding on how the dismantling of class struggle has been a smokescreen for the centrality of class, 'race' and gender relations in the epochal shift from industrial to neoliberal capitalism (Tyler, 2013, p 57). This builds on our consideration of the demonisation of the poor through Thatcherism, subsequently picked up by the Cameron–Clegg coalition government of 2010, with a preponderance of millionaires in office, which developed a more savage raft of cuts aimed at the poorest in society than had been known since the 1920s (Jones, 2011).

Jones critiques the Shannon Matthews case in 2008, the period leading up to the general election, as just one example of objectification serving political interests. Nine-year-old Shannon Matthews disappeared from Dewsbury Moor, a council estate in Yorkshire, and it was subsequently discovered that her mother had played a part in the kidnap for financial reward. Despite the fact that the community came together in solidarity, concerned about the safety of a missing child, it was the dysfunctional image of the mother, Karen Matthews, that was held up to dehumanise the entire community, and all those like it, as amoral, work-shy spongers, a theme reinforced by the media and internalised in popular consciousness:

> To the Conservatives, Karen Matthews had become a convenient political prop. The Tory leader, David Cameron, himself used the affair to call for a drastic overhaul of the welfare state. 'The verdict last week on Karen Matthews and her vile accomplice is also a verdict on our broken society', he argued in the *Daily Mail*. 'If only this was a one-off story.' As part of the reforms offered in response, Cameron pledged to 'end the something-for-nothing culture. If you don't take a reasonable offer of a job, you will lose benefits. No ifs, no buts.' Here it was again: a link between Karen Matthews and much larger groups of working-class people. It was a clever political tactic. If the wider British public were led to believe that people who shared her background were

capable of the same monstrous behaviour, they would be more likely to support policies directed against them. (Jones, 2011, p 25)

Pause for thought...

Reflect on your reaction to the Shannon Matthews case. Can you see dominant hegemony at work here?

Investigate it further by finding related newspaper articles. Extend your analysis by summarising Tyler's and Jones' critiques to present to your dialogue group.

Becoming critical

Tyler's argument, in line with what we have been discussing, is that if dominant hegemonic power relies on the creation of an abject Subject, then we need the analytic tools to stop this demonisation of humanity to inform action and resistance. She goes beyond neoliberalism as market rule, to offer insight into neoliberalism as a form of social and cultural control that gains public consent for policies and practices to entrench inequalities and dismantle democracy.

> Making education central to any viable notion of politics as well as making the political more pedagogical suggests that intellectuals, artists, community workers, parents, and others need to connect with young people in those public and virtual sites and spheres that not only enable new modes of dialogue to take place but also work to move beyond such exchanges to the much more difficult task of building organised and sustainable social movements. In other words, we need a politics that reinvents the concept of the social while providing a language of critique and hope forged not in isolation but in a collective struggle that takes social responsibility, commitment and justice seriously. (Giroux, 2009, p 66)

It seems clear to me that we cannot change anything without challenging the ideas underpinning the distorted reality that has so powerfully taken hold. The current failures of neoliberalism open cracks for challenge and change, and our thinking has to be sharp enough to argue for democracy and community, reducing the market to a place where it supports, not destroys, human potential.

Jones (2011, p 268) proposes that it is only through a global movement of working-class people, the solidarity of an international labour force, that we can overcome the way that the neoliberal tidal wave can be stemmed, this global 'race to the bottom'. Without this, he warns that the working class will:

> ... remain weak and voiceless ... the butt of jokes at middle-class dinner parties, detested in angry right-wing newspaper columns, and ridiculed

in TV sitcoms. Entire communities will remain without secure, well-paid work, and the people that comprise them will continue to be demonised for it. Living standards will go on stagnating and declining, even while the richest rake it in like never before.… At its heart, the demonization of the working class is the flagrant triumphalism of the rich who, no longer challenged by those below them, instead point and laugh at them. (Jones, 2011, p 269)

Figure 7.1: Stereotypical 'chavs'

Theory in action 7

Social abjection theory and a politics of disposability

Issue
Why are so many children growing up in poverty in rich countries?

Evidence
Jack Monroe is a 25-year-old single mother from Southend-on-Sea, who started writing an online blog (see www.agirlcalledjack.com) when she was unemployed and looking for work. She charted the realities of life on the breadline, and the difficulty of finding work as a single parent in an economic downturn.

'Breadline Britain', I live in the seventh richest country in the world

I live in the seventh richest country in the world, where a reported half a million people are dependent on free, charity food handouts from food banks.

I was one of those people, for six months of unemployment. But there was almost a year before that, that I struggled alone, in silence, putting a brave face on a truly desperate situation before I finally accepted help. I had no heating, no TV, I'd sold my car and unscrewed my light bulbs. I was missing meals, feeding just my son every night, and still applying for jobs every single day. I stopped counting after 300 applications went in, and nothing came back.

As I said in Parliament last Monday where I was invited to speak as part of a Just Fair event:

"When anyone asked, I lied and said that I was fine. Because that's the trouble, when you have holes in your socks and holes in your jeans, and your collarbones are jutting out of the two jumpers you wear to keep yourself warm. You tell everyone that everything is okay.

You tell everyone that everything is okay, because you think that if you admit to skipping meals, or to feeding your child the same cold pasta with tomatoes for four nights in a row, you worry that you might lose him, or that he might be taken into care.

And in the cold, the despair and the desolation, sometimes your son is the only thing that stops you from stepping off that busy flyover that you walk across every day. So you lie, and you say that you are fine."

I've been told that I don't look like a poor person. But what does a poor person look like? Standing in that queue outside a community centre, sixty deep, waiting for an hour for five tins of food and a packet of nappies, I find myself standing in front of a woman in a hospital uniform, and behind a man with a shirt on emblazoned with the logo of a supermarket seven miles away. People in work uniforms, do they look like poor people? Or me, in my smart winter coat that my grandmother bought for me for the Christmas just gone, do I look like a poor person?

Food banks are only dealing with the injuries, the deep gaping wounds left by fundamental flaws in the running of this country. They are not a solution. Children are starving, their parents are freezing. Something is wrong.

To paraphrase Desmond Tutu, there comes a point where you need to stop simply pulling people out of the river, and you need to go upstream, and find out why they're falling in. (Monroe, 2015)

Analysis

Why is there a current trend for rich countries to commit so many children to growing up in poverty? Imogen Tyler's development of social abjection theory suggests that:

- neoliberalism is more than a laissez-faire free-market ideology; it is a form of social and cultural control ...
- ... in which state power is constantly producing a dialectic of Subject/Object in relations of power and disgust.
- This maintains power in the hands of the privileged by hardening public opinion against poor people as unworthy, undeserving, undesirable and disposable ...
- ... reinforced by stigmatisation through the media ...
- ... to present escalating inequalities as a consequence of personal pathologies ...
- ... blaming the victims of injustice for the structural discrimination that creates their reality.
- In Gramscian terms, dominant hegemony internalised as common sense gains public consent ...
- ... and neoliberal policies continue to govern for the market against the people!

Action

Problematising Katrina

Let's start this process by problematising the case of Hurricane Katrina in 2005 as a way of developing critique. Use this approach in your own reflexivity or with participants in a dialogue group. Look at the photograph below, and explore your initial reactions to it. Then introduce each question, one at a time.

Figure 7.2: The aftermath of Hurricane Katrina

Source: Thomas Dworkin/Magnum

This scene is taken from the aftermath of Hurricane Katrina, when the rising sea levels burst through the poorly maintained levees in New Orleans and hit the unprepared Black communities. Those who had the means to get out, got out. Those who were left struggled to survive. The rest of the world looked on in horror, as images of largely Black, often very old or very young, female, ill or 'dis'abled, some dead in the floodwaters, others clinging to submerging rooftops appealed for help, while the rest of the US, the most powerful country in the world, carried on with business as usual. It was not for several days, when the outrage of the world forced a reaction, that President Bush acted on this national emergency.

Codifying Katrina

Now explore ways of using this photograph as a way of capturing neoliberalism's dehumanisation of people's lives.

Decodifying Katrina

In a dialogue group, project the photograph and stimulate dialogue by asking:

Do you recognise this place?

Who is this?

Where is it?

What is happening?

Who is affected?

Why is it happening?

Is it happening to other people?

What can be done about it?

Analysing Katrina: Henry Giroux

> A year later, and the victims of Katrina are not only deemed unworthy of state protections, but also dangerous and disposable. What does it mean, for example, when CNN's Anderson Cooper returns to the scene of the crime named Katrina and, rather than connecting the Bush's administration contempt for social programs to the subsequent catastrophe, focuses instead on the rumors of crime and lawlessness that allegedly spread over New Orleans after the hurricane hit? What are we to think when Juan Williams, a senior correspondent for NPR, writes in a *New York Times* op-ed that the real lesson of Katrina is that the poor 'cause problems for themselves', and that they should be condemned for not 'confronting the poverty of spirit'? Williams invokes the ghost of self-reliance and self-responsibility to demonize those populations for whom the very economic, educational, political and social conditions that make agency possible barely exist.

A new politics now governs American policy, one that I call the politics of disposability. It is a politics in which the unproductive (the poor, weak and racially marginalized) are considered useless and therefore expendable; a politics in which entire populations are considered disposable, unnecessary burdens on state coffers, and consigned to fend for themselves. Katrina laid bare what many people in the United States do not want to see. (Extract from newspaper article by Giroux, 2006b)

Use Giroux's analysis to broaden and deepen discussion.

In 2005, Hurricane Katrina hit the Black communities of New Orleans. The images projected by the world's media still remain vividly imprinted in my mind. Dead and abandoned, mostly Black, female, poor and often young or elderly citizens in the floodwaters or clinging to rooftops as the ill-maintained levees gave way. The rest of the USA, the most powerful country in the world, carried on with business as usual. The following year, Henry Giroux challenged us for failing to critique President Bush's non-response to the emergency (Giroux, 2006a, 2006b).

These dehumanising principles of neoliberalism have crept up on us imperceptibly in our failure to be vigilant, and have become accepted as a way of life, a strange human profit and loss account, measuring our market worth according to our relevance as consumers and producers in this politics of disposability. Those who are not central to the processes of production or consumption are dispensable to the generation of profit in this world of individual greed. 'Many now argue that this new form of biopolitics – the politics that determine the life and death of human beings – is conditioned by a permanent state of class and racial exception' (Giroux, 2009, p 9).

Imogen Tyler takes this thinking a stage further with social abjection theory, helping to identify the way the processes of discrimination are specifically targeted and actively filtered into the public imagination. Think about ways in which these ideas can be used in your own practice to develop a conceptual toolkit for problematising power.

When you combine these theories with the evidence on growing up poor statistically presented by CPAG, it is clear that risks of child poverty are not equally distributed; they are linked to forces of power and disempowerment. Building on new ideas, like those of Imogen Tyler and Henry Giroux, extends a Freirean approach to practice, giving us the tools to 'see' power in action in the context of current political times. It is only by contextualising practice in its times that we can develop action capable of challenge and change for a social justice outcome. The next chapter takes this thinking forward in search of a critical living praxis for community development.

EIGHT

Emancipatory action research as a critical living praxis

Stories interest me. They hold the answers to the way we see the world, and therefore the way we act in the world. Dominant narratives tell convincing stories based on the interests of the powerful, persuading us to act for the benefit of privilege. But when we start to question these stories, asking in whose interests they are told, we see different possibilities for changing the story, and therefore for changing the world.

Throughout this book, I have talked about the need to be critical, to question power and its changing form as political times change. As a result, we see the world through a different lens that exposes the contradictions we live by, and the dominant stories that persuade us to act in the interests of the powerful against the interests of the powerless. I have related this particularly to the rise of neoliberalism, not only as an ideology of the free market which is driven by profit, but as a class project that works on a politics of disposability. Profit generation concentrates on consumers and producers, with the most vulnerable, those who are dispensable to the profit game, getting stereotyped as unworthy and undesirable. This justifies dismantling public sector protection for the most vulnerable groups in society, and social inequalities escalate, the rich get excessively rich and the poor become dehumanised.

Neoliberalism erupted around the world as capitalism went global; in the UK it became known as Thatcherism from 1979 onwards. The story changed from welfare as a human right, implicit in the welfare state, to a powerful story of 'the welfare scrounger', one that has stuck in the public consciousness because nobody changed the story to a counternarrative based on freedom from discrimination. As individualism took hold, action was taken to eliminate collective forms of protest that might get in the way of profit. The Miners' Strike of 1984–85 was a pivotal point in British history as the Thatcher government targeted the National Union of Mineworkers (NUM), determined to dismantle the largest force of organised labour in Britain. This marked the end of working-class solidarity. As a community worker at the time, I was at the front line of a system that used divide-and-rule politics to turn people against each other. The image of 'the welfare scrounger' turned working people against unemployed people, and within communities images of 'rip-off lone parents' divided poor communities into worthy and unworthy. The poor got poorer as the rich got richer, and children replaced retired people as the biggest single group at risk of poverty.

Despite the attempts of the Blair–Brown government to put child poverty onto the political agenda, even achieving cross-party consensus for the Child Poverty

Act 2010, no progress was made to end child poverty because the images of 'welfare scroungers' were not challenged. This left the way open for the Cameron–Clegg coalition to build on this image from 2010, and now the Conservative government under Cameron, elected in 2015, is neoliberalism unfettered. In the last chapter I introduced Imogen Tyler's ideas on social abjection as a story of revulsion and disgust of the poor, an analysis of the relationship of power and subordination. The story of the 'chav' has taken us from the welfare scrounger to a dominant narrative of human detritus.

Without sufficient strength of numbers standing up to demand change, escalating social divisions are taking us headlong into a crisis of social justice. Grassroots collective action offers a transformative moment for social change, which is why community development needs to be part of social movements. There are signs that new ways of protesting are emerging. Here, by way of example, I want to link the international social and economic movement, Occupy, with the Dale Farm eviction of Travellers as a significant story of new alliances across difference in the struggle against injustices that continue to undermine British democracy. I have talked about dominant stories that act in the interests of power relations, and the little stories in the media and on the streets that repeat the message. Here we explore social abjection as a theory of resistance, a counternarrative for change. Tyler refers to a comment posted on the Dale Farm website on 19 October 2011:

> The time has come for a final reckoning with the scum [Gypsies and Travellers] and their bedfellows, the Chavs. We will NOT allow our country to be held to ransom by these parasites and their idiotic supporters.... Well, my friends, that final reckoning is near. It is up to every decent, law-abiding, moral citizen to rid this pestilence and filth from our land and reclaim this country.

Following this incitement of prejudice, bailiffs arrived and scenes of terror were witnessed in the world media as caravans burned and children screamed, two days of fear and intimidation as their homes and community were destroyed. The story of scum justified the dehumanising action.

At the same time, there were new alliances forming at Dale Farm:

> 'Camp Constant' the activist camp built alongside and in solidarity with the Travellers at Dale Farm ... attracted activists from across Europe from different political affiliations and groups, many of whom had little or no knowledge of, or previous relationship with, the struggles of Gypsies and Travellers. Indeed, given the long histories of stigma, prejudice, distrust and fear, Gypsies and Travellers have historically had notably few political allies among the settled community. Among the activists who gathered at Camp Constant were members of the NoBorders and No One is Illegal networks, which campaign for migrant rights and freedom of movement across Europe and

international border zones, activists from the Occupy movement [camped outside St Paul's Cathedral at the time], Climate Camp, trade union representatives and human rights monitors ... to create a Traveller Solidarity Network, which today describes itself 'as part of the antifascist movement and the wider struggle against racism and class oppression' (Traveller Solidarity Network, 2011). (Tyler, 2013, p 152)

Tyler underlines the way that this is one of the best examples of grassroots action forging new and unexpected forms of alliance to challenge the neoliberal consensus, marking a significant moment of political revolt in Britain to voice resistance against the dehumanisation central to the neoliberal government. Paul Gilroy (2011, quoted in Tyler, 2013, p 149) called for new media images that offer alternatives to the stories of stigmatisation in the aftermath of the English riots: 'one of the worst forms of poverty that's shaped our situation is poverty of the imagination'. Tyler links this idea of *poverty of the imagination* to the role of news agencies and entertainment programmes in reinforcing perceptions of poor people that play to the power of the neoliberal state. We need to tell stories of hope and possibility, counternarratives that challenge this story of human waste, with alternatives based on respect, dignity and human worth.

Pause for thought...

Reflect again on Foucault's comment: a society that 'neither questions itself nor can imagine any alternative to itself ... [feeds] ... the growing ineptitude, if not irrelevance, of (in)organic and traditional intellectuals whose cynicism often translates into complicit with the forms of power they condemn.' (Foucault, cited in Giroux, 2009, p 177)

If we fail to come up with counternarratives of possibility, alternatives that challenge and change the injustices of life as it is, there is no means of keeping power in check. The theory/practice divide is symptomatic of Foucault's warning: if we fail to question, then we are in danger of becoming complicit with the power we condemn. This sets the scene for exploring a *critical living praxis* for community development to take its stand as a practice for social justice into a simple practical process.

hooks reminds us that '... many of the people who are writing about domination and oppression are distanced from the pain, the woundedness, the ugliness' (hooks, 2015, p 215). It is this pain that comes alive in Frantz Fanon's thinking on oppression and racism as the internalisation of inferiority, that is, how the experience of being Black is created by a White Other (Fanon, 2008). The argument Fanon is putting forward is that it is not just about being Black, but also about being Black in relation to being White. His thrust is that power operates not just by being treated as a 'thing', but most importantly because this is taken on as a self-belief, that is, our minds are so colonised by this idea that we become that 'thing' to ourselves. It is this erosion of self-worth that makes us so vulnerable to oppression, a dehumanisation that wounds the soul to create hopelessness, depression, suicide and other mental health vulnerabilities (Fanon, 2004).

As with Freire, Fanon's important contribution is *praxis*, a unity of action and reflection. Critical consciousness creates a crack to let the light shine in for collective action. Dehumanisation eliminates targeted groups from society, but to explore 'who am I?' bridges absence to claim presence and power. This is why work with identity is so important to community development. Critique, reflection and dialogue lead to action for change that challenges this dehumanising reality to create a better society for all. Everyday life is full of contradictions that we take for granted because we have been raised to accept the way things are. Freire believes that if we expose the contradictions we live by, we change the way we see the world. And by changing the way we see the world, we engage with it differently. We are less likely to be passive and apathetic, and more likely to get actively involved in wanting to bring about change. This process is *conscientisation*. It involves becoming critically aware of the structural causes of social problems, and this process starts by simply questioning the way things are from our experience of everyday life.

A pedagogy of love and a politics of hatred

Our work is captured by Freire: we are working for a 'democracy that does not fear the people', 'a politics of love for the world and its people rather than hatred' (Freire, 2005, p 49). He talks about love as an act of courage and a commitment to others. In Darder's words, Freire offers 'a way of living, loving and interpreting the world', and in taking a Freirean approach to practice we experience 'a profound transformation of ourselves as human beings in our work with others' (Darder, 2002, pp 205-7). In transforming the world, we transform ourselves.

> Dialogue ... is nourished by love, humility, hope, faith and trust. When two 'poles' of the dialogue are thus linked by love, hope and mutual trust, they can join in a critical search for something. (Freire, 2005, pp 45-6)

Practising critical reflection

In order to develop a critical approach to practice, it is necessary to become self-critical. I say this because we are all products of a system of domination/subordination that has fed us with stories of superiority/inferiority that lurk in the inner recesses of our minds. In order to work in this way, we must become fully aware of the attitudes that have gone deep inside to embed discrimination in cultural reproductions of privilege. Peggy McIntosh (2004) found a way of identifying moments in everyday life that contain the unconscious privilege of Whiteness, although this process can be equally applied to other assumed superiorities, say, class, gender, age, ability.... The idea here is to concentrate on power rather than powerlessness. This focuses our thoughts on the invisibility of privilege, and calls on those with power to examine what is assumed as 'normal'. McIntosh calls this an 'invisible knapsack' of unearned privileges that can be unpacked and examined. We need to unearth them in our consciousness and understand how they stay so invisible that we do not even know we are assuming their power in everyday encounters.

Mekada Graham talks about this long silence on the part of White power as essentially racist: 'Whiteness carries a positive identity and without racial others it could not exist' (Graham, 2007, p 61). Frantz Fanon talks about a society that fails to question itself as a society in which it is not good to be alive. He talks about the internalisation of inferiority, the politics of experiencing oneself as Black by a White Other through the barrage of everyday images that come out of books, newspapers, education, posters, cinema, radio … to 'work their way into one's mind and shape one's view of the world and of the group to which one belongs … I am battered down by tom–toms, cannibalism, intellectual deficiency, fetishism, racial defects, slave ships' (Fanon, 2008, pp 83-5). Bhavani et al (2005) discuss Whiteness as avoiding a label because it does not define its ethnicity; it just assumes its superiority.

McIntosh (2004) gives a simple way to start identifying power in the ordinary, everyday encounters of daily life. In a process of self-reflection, she discovered and named 46 daily privileges that she took for granted, and here are just some of them to give you an idea of how to go about it:

- I can, if I wish, arrange to be in the company of people of my race most of the time.
- I can be pretty sure that my neighbours will be neutral or pleasant to me.
- I can go shopping alone most of the time, pretty well assured that I will not be followed or harassed.
- I can turn on the television or open the front page of the paper and see people of my race widely and positively represented.
- Whether I use cheques, credit cards or cash, I can count on my skin colour not to work against the appearance of financial reliability.
- I can remain oblivious of the language and customs of persons of colour who constitute the world's majority without feeling in my culture any penalty for such oblivion.
- I can go home from most meetings of organisations I belong to feeling somewhat tied in, rather than isolated, out of place, outnumbered, unheard, held at a distance or feared.

Pause for thought…

Read Peggy McIntosh's reflections above, then spend some uninterrupted time reflecting on your week, and think about the way that power has worked for you. List the unearned freedoms that have given you privileges in your life that you take for granted. What form of discrimination are they related to? Get together with someone else, and discuss the

> similarities and differences between your reflections, and take your understanding of them
> deeper into how these are both invisible and hegemonic, linked to personal identities that
> mutually reinforce structural discrimination.

If, as Bhavani et al (2005) suggest, racism is reproduced in the everyday discriminatory practices acted out at micro level (as well as in the structures of society), then White people need to be accountable for the role they play in reinforcing the structures that privilege Whiteness.

Exposing the collective lie

Michelle Fine (2008, p 216) introduces the Jesuit priest and activist thinker Ignacio Martin-Baró's (1994, p 189) argument that our challenge is to uncover the *collective lie* that persuades us to go along with a way of life based on the interests of the privileged. This lie is played out in the dominant story of feckless wasters, holding the privileged up as deserving and the poor as undeserving. It is a lie that distracts attention from discrimination and injustice to present such a convincing story of scum and scoundrels that it is accepted unquestioningly as *common sense*, and internalised under the surface of our skins as a truth, persuading us to act in the interests of the few against the interests of the many.

In order to play our part in exposing this collective lie, the most powerful force of power that we face in the struggle for social justice, we need to bridge the theory–practice gap, and develop a simple structure to build *theory in action*. So let me first introduce participatory action research (PAR) and the reasons that it presents an enhanced approach to practice that builds theory in action and, in turn, action as theory. PAR challenges traditional approaches to research in relation to top-down power and knowledge that reinforce a single truth that favours privilege. It is based on an understanding that there are many truths, based on identities formed out of social differences, and that there is a wisdom that is contained in the lived experience of those who are most oppressed that provides the foundation for co-creating new knowledge as the basis of action for change. Exploring who we are helps us to see the way that forces of subordination and domination work on identities to privilege some and marginalise others.

> **Pause for thought...**
>
> Re-read the story of critical reflections on my life with Paula in Chapter Five. Think about the way that, despite our strong friendship as two women with similar backgrounds as community workers and similar roles as colleagues in university, her Blackness and my Whiteness differentiated us visibly in everyday life. We stood beside each other in stark contrast, my everyday assumed privileges separating me from her everyday discrimination. Her life experience was punctuated with negative images of herself and her culture that diminished her, whereas mine was often negative because of my gender, but powerful because of my Whiteness.

Insights such as this change the way we see the world, and once we see power in action, we can create new possibilities for a better world, a future built on greater equality, respect and compassion. But first, it is vital to understand the way that our thinking is distorted by the stories we hear. Gramsci talked about *rearticulation* as the dismantling of hegemonic stories in order to create counternarratives that capture new possibilities for a more just and equal future. Imagining a better way forward needs to be built on an understanding of what is going on in the present, and what led up to that in the past.

PAR recognises the need to create critical spaces to understand the issues, to develop the methods and to build this on praxis. In this respect, Paulo Freire's emphasis on praxis is central to PAR, and his emphasis on critical consciousness through dialogue is the key to exposing the collective lie. Problematising the stories of everyday reality by lifting them out of the taken-for-grantedness of daily life helps to develop a more critical perspective on what is going on. In turn, developing theory in action and applying that theory to a further cycle of action builds the process of change in cycles. As Giroux et al (1996) say, counternarratives not only counter grand narratives, but they also challenge the hegemonic narratives of everyday life that manipulate people to think and behave according to a dominant set of cultural beliefs.

Freire and participatory action research

I have talked about the impact of Paulo Freire's thought on community development in the early 1970s, when *Pedagogy of the oppressed* was first published in English and available widely in the UK. Freire's ideas also had a big impact on the PAR movement, which challenged the dominant assumptions of traditional research, identifying power by asking, (a) whose ideas are informing the research questions and in whose interests is it taking place, (b) who is controlling the research process, and (c) who decides on the results and outcomes of the research for whose benefit? Participatory action researchers increasingly called for a new worldview, suggesting that 'the modernist worldview or paradigm of Western civilisation is reaching the end of its useful life … that there is a fundamental shift occurring in our understanding of the universe and our place in it, that new patterns of thought and belief are emerging that will transform our experience, and our action' (Reason and Bradbury, 2001, p 4). A participatory paradigm for research, one based on true democracy, aims to give autonomy to the voices of subordinated groups. It elevates the diversity of human experience over the imperative of economic 'progress', and locates social and environmental justice at its heart.

How participatory action research changed me

My own story captures the elusive nature of power. I spent three years training to be a teacher being told that there is nothing political about the classroom. This is, of course, an untruth: the classroom is a profoundly political space, where power relations get acted out in every moment. As a young teacher, I knew that something was not right, but I did not have the tools to give me any understanding of power. I found the culture of the staffroom disturbing: "Well, that's sorted that lot out; there are some that'll make it, some that don't stand a chance, and a few in the middle." I moved to adult literacy. Then I began to think that the answer lay in educational psychology. Without an analysis of power, I had no idea that I might be putting the blame on the victims of injustice rather than on the system.

It was Vietnamese refugees who gave me my first glimpses of injustice and global discrimination, escaping from one form of tyranny only to face another. I realised that their hopes in democracy would be dashed when they came up

Figure 8.1: A culture of silence

against structural discrimination in British society. As they unfolded their stories of the indignity of giving birth on rusty old landing craft adrift on the South China Sea, without food and water, while ships from the West sailed past, I turned my back on classroom teaching and educational psychology in favour of community development and its political commitment to social justice. At the University of Edinburgh, I met David Alexander who introduced me to the thinking of Freire, Gramsci, feminism and anti-racism, and in doing so he changed my life. Equipped with a critical approach to practice, I could see power in action: Freire's concepts came alive in everyday life, *naïve consciousness*, *a culture of silence*, *horizontal violence*, and so on. Yet, when I decided to do a PhD to provide a structure for my practice, keeping me critical, focused and analytical, I fell into a further trap. With a research hat on, I found that there were expectations from the university to do research in a particular way. Fortunately, I had the support of a progressive supervisor in the form of Ralph Ruddock, the celebrated adult educator, who believed in my determination to forge through the gatekeepers to legitimise new ways of creating knowledge. Nevertheless, there was a jarring dissonance as I searched for research methods. I did not realise that these were warning bells to alert me to a disconnect between my community development values and my role as a researcher: I felt obliged to work *on* people rather than *with* them.

Then one day, my friend and colleague Paul Jones, put Reason and Rowan's *Human inquiry* into my hands. This was another critical moment in my politicisation. I read: 'this book is about human inquiry ... about people exploring and making sense of human action and experience ... ways of going about research which [offer] *alternatives* to orthodox approaches, alternatives which [would] do justice to the humanness of all those involved in the research endeavour' (Reason and Rowan, 1981, p xi), and my eyes lit up. Reason and Rowan's gathering together, in one large tome, of an eclectic range of methods within an action research approach gave me confidence in participatory action research as consonant with the value base of community development. It offered me an *integrated praxis*, a way of building knowledge in action and acting on that knowledge in iterative cycles that go ever deeper and broader into understanding and change.

Influenced by Paulo Freire, here was research based on working *with* people in reciprocal, mutual relationships to co-create knowledge in cycles of action and reflection, and acting together on that knowledge to transform situations by:

- rejecting the alienating methods of scientific research;
- emphasising connection, wholeness and healing injustices;
- countering fragmentation of thought and action;
- committing to critical pedagogy as action for change;
- developing language and methods to discover new knowledge and new truths.

Values of community development and participatory action research

It is vital to use an approach to research that shares the same value base as community development. Let's remind ourselves that community development is committed to:

- principles of social justice and environmental justice;
- a vision of a just and sustainable world;
- values of equality, respect, dignity, trust, mutuality and reciprocity;
- a process of critical consciousness through popular education (critical pedagogy), practical projects and collective action for change;
- a theory base that helps to analyse power and discrimination;
- contextualising practice in its political context.

Participatory action research is committed to:

- social justice and environmental justice;
- values of equality, respect dignity, trust, mutuality and reciprocity;
- working *with* and not *on* people;
- using non–controlling methods;
- working mutually as co-researchers and not controlling researchers;
- different ways of knowing the world.

These two approaches fit together to provide a process of education-research-action, weaving theory and practice into a unity of praxis.

Emancipatory action research

In order to practise social justice, community development urgently needs to bridge the divide that exists between theory and practice. For too long, we have allowed ourselves to be seen as a 'doing' rather than a 'thinking and doing' occupation. Doing without thinking results in 'thoughtless action' (Rennie Johnston, quoted in Shaw, 2004), and this is dangerous. It has left us wide open to being hijacked as deliverers of top-down policies that act against the principles and values we claim to stand for. Developing a *critical living praxis* that is capable of weaving our theory and practice together is my purpose here, one that shares community development's value base, that co-creates knowledge in action in partnership with marginalised people, and that is relevant to the changing political context. I choose to use the term *emancipatory action research* (EAR) because it overtly states its purpose to bring about social change as part of its process.

Stephen Kemmis (2010) talks about a *unitary praxis* as an approach to life in which we 'aim to live well by speaking and thinking well, and relating well to others in the world.... If we accept this view, then we might say that action research should aim not just at achieving knowledge of the world, but achieving a better world.' If, as Stephen Kemmis says, we really want to set the bar high and achieve a better world by being better in the world, it suggests that, like community development, EAR is a way of life, and not just a job. We are part of the process of change for a fair and just future; we are not detached from the process. This comes with responsibility! We have to be able to evidence that we are doing what we say we intend to do.

So let's explore what that involves. First, EAR is about participation: all people involved come together as co-participants in a process of education for critical consciousness that informs action for social change. Co-participants are equals, and this fits well with Freire's notion of co-learners and co-teachers, a spirit of mutuality in which everyone is prepared to teach, listen and learn. Creating critical spaces for dialogue is important, involving all co-participants in co-creating knowledge for our times. These are counter-hegemonic critical spaces where power relationships are investigated and deconstructed in order to act to reconstruct democratic relations with new possibilities for a world that is fair and just. This concept of a democratic public space is an essential context for community development as a site for critical dialogue and participation in the process of participatory democracy (Habermas, 1989). Public space is not only a place where people who identify with a group can participate and interact, even as strangers, but also the space where there is a connection between groups that provides the glue that binds people together in a community. As globalisation has accelerated, so there has been increased privatisation of public spaces. We need to find new ideas for spaces where we can get involved in critique and dissent, identifying new truths, and developing the courage to 'tell unwelcome truths' (Kemmis, 2006) in the wider world as part of our action.

Pause for thought...
Go to Chapter Five (p 97) and look at the Coffeehouse Challenges, then go to Chapter Nine (p 168) and look at NatCAN. How can you use either of these approaches to creating critical spaces in your work?

Critique and dissent are the processes that Freire had in mind when he talked about denunciation and annunciation: critiquing the status quo opens the space to transform the present into a better future. In these ways, EAR contextualises personal lives within the political, social and economic structures of our times (Kemmis, 2006). And to have a sustainable impact on social change, it needs to extend beyond individuals and groups 'to build systemic pictures of what is going on, and systemic intervention strategies, developing multiple inquiries that engage whole systems in ongoing cycles of inquiry' (Burns, 2007, p 18).

Emancipatory action research is an approach to research committed to change for social and environmental justice by:

- equalising power in its process by working *with* and not *on* people;
- using methods that liberate, not control, so the traditional 'Objects' of research become 'Subjects' co-creating new knowledge from lived experience as a valuable truth;
- co-creating new knowledge that is beyond the written word through story, dialogue, photographs, music, poetry, drama and drawings;
- contextualising personal lives within the political, social and economic structures that discriminate;
- demonstrating an ideology of equality in action using demonstrable skills of mutual respect, dignity, trust and reciprocity;
- dislocating the researcher as external expert to become a co-participant;
- supporting co-participants to become co-researchers in mutual inquiry;
- creating the research process as a participatory experience for all involved so that the research process becomes empowering in its own right, as well as achieving a social/environmental justice outcome through collective action for change based on new understandings of the world.

Stephen Kemmis (2010) proposed sustainability criteria against which to judge the contribution of emancipatory action research initiatives if they are to *change history and not just theory*!

Kemmis's sustainability factors

Practice should not be:

1   *Discursively unsustainable:* based on false, misleading or contradictory ideas.
2   *Morally/socially unsustainable:* aspects of the process or outcome are excluding, unjust, oppressive or dominating.
3   *Ecologically/materially unsustainable:* aspects of the process or outcome involve either excess consumption of natural resources or degradation of the environment.
4   *Economically unsustainable:* aspects of the process or outcome fail to address costs and benefits to people or expose power relations between privilege and poverty.
5   *Personally unsustainable:* physical, intellectual or emotional harm or suffering is a consequence of the process or outcome.

Here you have a structure from which to develop evidence of practice that leads to social change. Building this level of critique into your practice opens the space to transform the present into a better future. Problematise the unsustainable by taking photographs of the consequences of poverty in your community, and relate them to Kemmis's five sustainability factors.

Developing critical consciousness is a process of empowerment: colonised identities are liberated, leading to personal autonomy, and this, in turn, leads to collective autonomy and the energy to act together for change for a better world.

Becoming critical through a reflexive journal

Practitioners need to be open to this process of becoming self-critical in order to take a critical approach to practice. In busy lives, it is important to have structures to aid the discipline of developing theory in action, and one aid to this is a reflexive journal. This can clarify thinking and develop noticing skills in the process of becoming critical. By questioning, contradictions are exposed that interrupt the taken-for-grantedness of life. This helps the process of making links between knowledge and experience, theory and action, and values as skills. Future action becomes more informed, connections are made with the bigger political picture, and a social justice purpose is maintained. For instance, each week, on the left-hand page of the journal, record critical incidents, and on the right-hand side, link thoughts that connect to Stephen Kemmis's sustainability factors above.

I call this a reflexive journal because it suggests going ever deeper by reflecting on your reflections. Use your reflexive journal to become critical in the following ways:

- to clarify thinking
- to develop noticing
- to become/stay critical
- to question
- to expose contradictions
- to interrupt taken-for-grantedness
- to identify issues
- to make links between knowledge and experience
- to understand values in practice
- to inform action
- to make connections
- to become focused
- to maintain purpose
- to plan action
- to stimulate dialogue.

Doing emancipatory action research with the help of the cycle model

The cycle model (illustrated in Figure 8.2) captures the key stages of emancipatory action research in circular movement, in inner and outer stages of development.

Figure 8.2: The cycle model

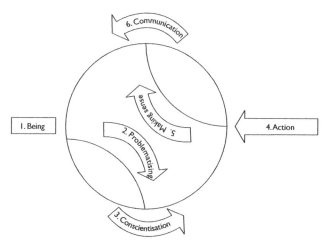

Source: Adapted from Rowan (1981)

Stage 1: Being

This is a point in everyday practice where you notice an issue or a situation that needs attention. It might be a new insight into a regular event in your practice, such as noticing children playing in dangerous conditions, or it may be that something new has erupted, such as changes in policy that have reduced benefits for the poorest in the community.

Stage 2: Problematising

Capture the situation in a photograph or any other medium that is relevant to local people. If the scene is familiar to local people, it will generate interest and evoke feelings, a *generative theme*. This is a *codification*. For the process of *decoding*, invite a group of people to join you. Project the photograph onto the wall, and encourage dialogue by asking people what they notice about it: who is this? Where is it? What's going on? Why is it happening? Attention eventually turns away from the photograph and to the group, as questions open up new awareness. Further information is needed. Perhaps national data on social trends and poverty statistics would deepen understanding on why child poverty is getting worse in the community. It could be that going to the local authority to get a breakdown of current ward statistics might be useful, or checking CPAG or the Joseph Rowntree Foundation's websites for latest poverty trends. Different people may volunteer to find out information, from talking to local schools or surveys of local people, and they could bring the information back to the next group meeting.

Stage 3: Conscientisation

As the process develops, the local issue will be seen in its political context, and questions will concentrate on 'What shall we do about it?'. An outer stage, where critical awareness of structural implications exposes the contradictions inherent in local lives, calls for a plan of action capable of change.

Stage 4: Action

This is the stage of engaging in action with the wider community. It could be that a group of local residents want to form a local child poverty action group to help more local residents make connections with the injustices of child poverty. Wider action could take the shape of making links with the End Child Poverty campaign to be part of an alliance of local groups in a movement for change.

Stage 5: Making sense

This is the stage at which 'experience turns into meaning and knowledge' (Rowan, 1981, p 100). Find ways to support those involved to deepen understanding of the experience in order to identify another cycle of development. Use Stephen Kemmis's sustainability factors listed earlier to analyse the experience and to plan the next stage. Consider it in conjunction with the following questions that help to check the quality and validity of the process, making sure that we are doing what we claim to be doing. This is a collaborative process, and these questions should be decided on by all those involved.

Quality and validity questions

1. *Methodology and methods:* What is the approach to this research? How is information gathered? How does it fit with the value base of community development?
2. *Process questions:* Who has initiated the research? Who has defined the problem? Who is involved? How is the power and decision-making shared?
3. *Power questions:* Is the social/political/economic context being taken into account? How is this research representative of the diversity of the community?
4. *Dialectical questions:* Is just one answer being sought? Is the situation being explored from more than one angle?
5. *Legitimacy questions:* Is there pressure to avoid certain problems? Who is funding the research? Are there preconceived outcomes?
6. *Relevance questions:* How will this research benefit people? Will it benefit some people more than others? Is it relevant to the people who took part? How does it contribute to social and environmental justice? How does it address

'race', class, gender, age, 'dis'ability, faith, culture, religion, sexual preference ... issues?

(The questions are influenced by Rowan, 1981, and Reason and Bradbury, 2001.)

Stage 6: Communication

The final stage of the current cycle is that of communicating the new knowledge that has been co-created by the participants so that others can learn from the experience. You may want to use the following evidence questions to prompt your thinking.

Evidence questions

1. How is practice working towards social and environmental justice?
2. What evidence is there that values of trust, dignity, mutuality and respect are operating at every level of practice?
3. How is the process empowering to all those involved?
4. What evidence is there that the outcome is contributing to change?
5. What evidence is there of greater equality in the process or outcome?
6. What evidence is there that people are working together for a common good?

Inside the community, the findings could take the form of a photograph display in the library or community centre with captions, or a public meeting run by the participants to get more support for the next stage. There could be coverage by local or national media, or an article written in a journal. A local group could go to a national conference to present their work, there could be a regional roadshow, other communities might invite you to visit and share the experience, or councillors and MPs could be invited to come to hear the findings. In doing so, we contribute to an increasing body of community development knowledge. This keeps community development critical and at the forefront of social justice practice.

Theory in action 9: Emancipatory action research for changing history

Issue

Lasting solutions to poverty will require the effective participation by those who experience poverty. Those are the voices that are usually silenced; they are the voices that provide a powerful alternative to distorted stereotypes of people in poverty.

Figure 8.3: Benwell, North East England, children playing

Source: Ted Ditchburn/North News & Pictures Ltd

Evidence

Figure 8.3 is a photograph of children playing on a burned-out car in Benwell, Tyneside, North East England, where 40 per cent of seven-year-olds live in poverty. This could be a codification of a familiar scene for local people. In the process of decoding, simply generate dialogue by asking questions: Where is this? Who do you see? What is happening? Why is it happening? In whose interests? If the focus is relevant to the participants, it generates a passionate response to the situation. This is the point at which critical consciousness deepens and people want to find out more about why this should be the reality of life in the community. In these ways, emancipatory action research contextualises personal lives within the political, social and economic structures of our times (Kemmis, 2006).

Analysis

Sustainability factors for changing history (Kemmis, 2010): refer to **p 150** and apply the criteria as a framework for your analysis:

Action

The Fed-up Honeys, a story of EAR in action

In their community in Lower East Side, seven young Black women aged between 16 and 22 joined Caitlin, a researcher, to do a participatory action research (PAR) project in their neighbourhood. They agreed, with pride, that it was a diverse, safe and tolerant place to live. In a dialogue group they started asking questions to explore what they cared about, what they knew ... and what they did not know. At the same time, they were learning about PAR as an emancipatory process with potential for 'opening eyes'. Ruby said, "I just see with different eyes now. Open eyes...!" They were given an 'official' report on their neighbourhood that made judgements based on assumptions about common stereotypes. For instance, a case study in the report used this stereotype: 'Taneisha, whose single mother is a high school dropout on welfare, has little supervision. She drops out of high school herself, shoplifts, and by age 16 finds herself with a police record, pregnant and with HIV.' After reading the report, they decided to develop a response research project to speak back to the report. Identifying the dehumanising impact of such stereotyping they drew on a complex range of other connections, from lack of resources to misrepresentations of Black women. Reading the report was a turning point for the Fed-up Honeys. They said it forced them to confront what Freire calls 'the roots of oppression', the social, political and economic contradictions of daily life. But most disturbing to them was the awareness that they had internalised this discrimination by blaming themselves for what they saw as failure. The Fed-up Honeys, in a room overflowing with young women just like them, but in Chicago, shared their questions and their findings.

In these simple ways, EAR contributes to a movement for change for a better world based on:

- creating critical spaces to question lived experience;
- exposing the taken-for-granted contradictions we live by;
- critical consciousness – seeing the world differently;
- telling a new story of hope and possibility that leads to social change.

Summarising Stephen Kemmis on emancipatory action research
- Action research should aim to achieve a better world.
- Inadequate action research is decontextualised from social, economic and political structures.
- Unitary praxis is about a coherent way of life that aims for the good of humankind, consciously and collectively.
- Action research makes a direct contribution to transformative action and to changing history.
- The first concern of action researchers should be the contribution of their action to history, not so much to theory.
- In times of global warming and human threat to life on earth, a huge task is required of action research for sustainability.

At this point, we move into the final chapter to summarise the key critical ideas woven throughout the book, and to focus on collective action in particular.

NINE

Staying critical: organising collectively

Here I start with a summary of many of the ideas covered in this book so far. It is based on a talk I gave at the National University of Ireland at Maynooth in 2013 to a gathering of community workers from all over Eire. It seems to me a very useful way of seeing how the ideas in this book weave together.

Reclaiming the radical agenda

When I received the invitation to come over and share some ideas, it occurred to me that the first time I trod on Maynooth soil, in 2006, was to talk about this very same subject, 'Reclaiming the radical agenda'. I arrived on a dark, cold and uninviting winter's night. Imagine my surprise, the next day, when I found a hotbed of fire-in-the-belly radicalism in the heart of the Irish countryside! Perplexingly, however, the issues are the same today as they were then. The worrying difference is that the political context has dramatically changed, and the global crises of our times have accelerated. We urgently need to become more critical. If community development is to aspire to what it claims to do, and by this I mean practising social justice, it is not just about improving service delivery, about delivering top-down policies unquestioningly. We have to resist this attempt to colonise our minds and become diverted from our purpose. Community development is about radical, transformative change for social justice and sustainability, and this calls for us to situate our practice in its political context. Otherwise, we are easily distracted by the symptoms, rather than focusing on the root causes of discrimination. We drift along the surface of life, patting people on the head, making life a little bit better around the edges, but not lifting the lid off and going deep enough to find the root causes of what's creating an unjust reality. Practice becomes placatory, ameliorative rather than transformative, and we stand accused of being duplicitous; in other words, we say we are working for social justice, but there is little evidence to suggest that we are doing this in reality. In fact, such placatory practice can end up delivering the very policies that are contributing to the problems, rather than addressing solutions. We become part of the problem.

Never before has community development been more important. Our role is vital in these times. By 'reclaiming the radical agenda', I mean that we should get to grips with a critical approach that analyses the political context we are in, in order to make a difference to social justice outcomes. Social justice is our driving principle, and a social justice outcome that has a transformative potential demands that we challenge power relations. We can't aspire to a social justice outcome without changing power relations. We have to work towards collective action for change, and that action has to be towards redistributing wealth. For these reasons community development is a political activity that calls for an analysis of power in order to see how the forces of power are acted out in everyday lives in relations of poverty and privilege.

Critique and dissent are central to deepening democracy. Social justice critique involves questioning attitudes, policies and practices from a perspective of fairness and equality. Social justice dissent involves objecting to policies and practices that lead to prejudicial outcomes. Dissent has effectively been excluded from the political agenda, as dissenting voices are eliminated from public debate. As social divisions have widened, community development has internally critiqued itself for allowing its theory to become disengaged from its practice, resulting in a void between our thinking and our doing. If we became more critical and really opened our minds to see what's going on, we would understand that:

- our local projects are staying local, not linking to global movements for change;
- our radical concepts have been hijacked, diluted and imported into policies that have persuaded us to accept improved service delivery as social justice, with participation, empowerment, social inclusion, and so on liberally scattered over the policy agenda;
- we are fudging the issue of redistribution of wealth to deliver policies that might ameliorate the surface of daily life, but are failing to reach deeper to the root causes of injustice;
- this leaves us standing as charged, that our 'cynicism often translates into complicity with the power we condemn' (Giroux, 2009, p 177);
- and some would even say that we have lost our clarity of purpose altogether!

Today, I want to concentrate on the divide that separates our theory from our practice. If we can address this, I feel that the rest will fall into place. For instance, by developing a critical living praxis, a unity of praxis, we develop theory in action and resist the notion that analysis is optional, or that every now and again we need to shut ourselves into a broom cupboard and theorise for a few minutes! Theory needs to be an integral part of critical practice so that we can explain why we are doing what we are doing at any stage of the process.

Recently, I have been reading Stuart Hall, who alerts us to another conjuncture, a point at which social, political, economic and ideological contradictions are condensed into a historical moment, presenting a crisis, but also an opportunity for change. During the rise of neoliberalism under Margaret Thatcher, Stuart Hall was one of the few political commentators who managed to keep up with what was happening, change was so immediate. I remember in an interview at the time that he said Thatcher had probably never even heard of the Gramscian concept of hegemony, but she sure knew how to do it!

Stuart Hall is a Gramscian thinker who identifies a historical moment as a point at which:

- society may move on to another version of the same system (Thatcher to Major);
- or a transformed version of the same system (Major to Blair);
- or relations can be radically transformed to create a new system.

I am suggesting that this is an opportunity, and if we manage to think fast enough and to seize it, we could create a situation where relations could be radically transformed for the better.

I now want to emphasise three points:

- Neoliberalism, or market fundamentalism, a fundamentally corrupt system, has come to be sold as global common sense. If we look at China, India and elsewhere, what we see are starving millions at the same time as the insatiable greed of privilege creating elitism. It is a system that rewards greed and ignores need.
- Class and other identities have been reconfigured under consumer capitalism.
- Our old ways of analysing are not keeping up with changing dominant hegemonies.

Stuart Hall says that effective interventions need to 'see' the forces of power critically. This involves 're-experiencing the ordinary as extraordinary' (Shor, 1992, p 122). As Freire attests, the stories of everyday life hold the answers to developing this approach. In order to do this, we must question everything, and when we see things critically, we begin to act critically. It's that well-known double act, *epistemology* and *ontology* – when we begin to see things differently, we act differently in the world.

In 2005, I watched a documentary on the story of Hurricane Katrina, and the consequences of the flood defences not being maintained to protect the mostly Black communities of New Orleans. Shocked, I witnessed dead bodies floating in the flood waters, as survivors stranded on rooftops appealed for help while the US carried on with business as usual, with President Bush failing to act on this national emergency. Henry Giroux challenges us for failing to critique this critical event acted out on the world stage; we failed to ask why this was happening before our very eyes.

The young man you see in Figure 7.2 (on p 135) is the image of the young man I saw featured in the documentary. I was reduced to tears listening to his story, how he was agonised by what was happening to his people, desperate to do something to help, when he noticed a yard full of yellow school buses lined up, and he thought, 'I can do something here, I know how to hotwire a bus!' So he leapt over the fence, and in a couple of seconds the engine was started. Off he went, ferrying the most vulnerable people of his community to safety, because all who could get out had left by that time. The people he transported were the very young, the very old, the disabled, mothers with children, all those who were in danger of drowning and starving and getting ill. He ferried them to the Dome, which was a temporary place of safety. I thought, 'What ingenuity, what a star, how could we reward something like that? There must be some medal we could pin on him to mark his sheer bravery and courage.' I was horrified, a few minutes later, to hear that he was incarcerated in jail for hotwiring a bus! If he had been somebody different, in some other location, would he have had the medal? Was it because of who he is and where he was that it became a punishment? Asking these questions we begin to touch the edges of the ways in which power discriminates.

Henry Giroux is right – we are not critiquing what is going on under our noses. He has helped us to understand how neoliberalism's emphasis on the centrality of producers and consumers within an ideology of the market gives rise to a politics of disposability. If you fall outside these key roles, those of generating profit, you fall off the radar and become disposable. This is what was acted out in New Orleans when the poor Black communities were seen as dispensable. It is a world in which the poor, the Black, the female, the young, the old, the sick and 'dis'abled are disposable players in the game of profit. By failing to be critical we accept the unacceptable contradictions we live by. My key point here is that we are allowing inhuman acts to be sold to us as common sense; we are not seeing, we are not challenging and we are not changing the contradictions we live by.

In order to get to grips with this, we must rewind history. If we think back to Thatcher, she did not act alone – she emerged at a moment in time in which neoliberalism, a little-known ideology, seized an opportunity. If anybody had suggested the idea a decade before, it would have been laughed out of existence. The very notion that we could develop a system in which the market rules the people, rather than the people ruling the market, would have been unthinkable. But it was a historic moment that offered an opportunity which was seized by Thatcher, Reagan, Pinochet, the IMF and the World Bank. It could not have been sold to the masses, however, without the invention of the powerful story of the 'welfare scrounger,' which has taken hold in public consciousness and has led to a hatred of the poor.

We need to get to grips with how dominant ideologies can so easily become a truth in public consciousness. In the 1980s, the story of free trade became very quickly one of profit assuming more importance than people and the planet, and stories that demonised the poor emphasised and legitimised that change. When we start to look at this rubbish about trickle-down theories, how it is important to make the rich richer to make the poor richer – tighten your belts, it will trickle down to you in time – we find, of course, that wealth does not trickle down, and that social inequalities just get wider. In the UK, when Margaret Thatcher came to power in 1979, only one in ten children was growing up in poverty, and by the time John Major handed over to the Blair government in 1997, child poverty had escalated to one in three. Despite Tony Blair's success in getting a cross-party consensus on the Child Poverty Act 2010, committing the British government to ending child poverty by 2020, it failed to achieve its mid-term targets, and child poverty is now predicted to increase dramatically by 2020.

Here is a contradiction for me: I am totally ashamed of living in the world's seventh richest country, where one in eight of our poor children don't get a hot meal, one in seven go to school without breakfast, 75,000 children are homeless, and yet 62 per cent of the UK's poorest children have got working parents. This is a very simple contradiction: why do I live in a rich country that doesn't feed its children? Poverty is a choice – it is a choice to make some people poor and others rich. Why are we making that choice? When I visited Norway, I was surprised at the feeling of inclusion and optimism, self-worth and pride that results when you live in a society where only one in twelve children grow up in poverty. However, as neoliberalism takes its toll, the pattern is one of increasing social divisions within countries and between countries, with some holding on to a strong element of acceptability, as in Norway. In Ireland, the statistic for child poverty is one in five.

We need to ask ourselves: whatever could be behind child poverty as a choice, not a necessity, as suggested by patterns of poverty emerging in rich countries? The story of poverty as a 'human failing' rather than a structural injustice is a powerful story to tell. It carries a message of human detritus, human waste and human disposability. Henry Giroux suggests that neoliberal societies have launched a war on youth, an assault against our children, and that this is indicative of a deep moral and political crisis. Young people are no longer 'where society invests its dreams, but where it hides its nightmares' (Giroux, 2013a). We see youth not as having problems, but as *being* the problem. Everyday conversations on the street reflect this – 'It's the youth of today that are the problem!' We hear it everywhere, another everyday contradiction.

So, to summarise my key points so far:

- Our lack of theory in community development has resulted in thoughtless, not critical, action.
- To practise empowerment, we need analyses of power; otherwise practice becomes tokenism.
- We have an eclectic theory base inspired by people such as Gramsci, Freire, and by feminism and anti-racism, but I suggest that this is no longer enough to keep up with the massive, unacceptable changes that we are witnessing in the world.
- We need thinking that helps us to analyse how neoliberalism undermines the essence of democracy by dehumanising some social groups as cheap lives, as dispensable, disposable and undesirable.

In pursuit of my last point, I have been inspired by Imogen Tyler's development of social abjection theory as a theory of power, subjugation and resistance. She takes neoliberalism beyond free market rule to present it as a form of social and cultural control in which state power, in the guise of a laissez-faire free market, becomes one of the most callous forms of social control we could come across. State power is constantly producing relations of Subject/Object in relations of power and disgust. To maintain power, it is essential for neoliberalism to have this abject Object as a disgusting object of derision, an unworthy form of human detritus. This image maintains power over the mass of people by turning public opinion against the poor, inciting fear and disgust. We have to be aware of the ways in which stigmatisation, through media representations, plays a key role in entrenching individual pathologies in public consciousness to create a hatred of the poor, blaming them for their own poverty and distracting attention from the structural discrimination that creates their reality. In Gramscian terms, this is dominant hegemony internalised as common sense, gaining public consent to govern for the market *against* the people.

To illuminate this point, one of the examples that Imogen Tyler offers is the way class politics is being reformulated in the caricature of the 'chav', reinforced by media stereotyping, both in the news and popular TV programmes, such as the Vicky Pollard character created by the comedian Matt Lucas. This image has taken hold to such an extent that it has had a massive impact and negative influence on young women in poverty by portraying them as 'feckless'. When we don't stop to question and think, we unwittingly reinforce stereotypes that have a huge impact on human lives.

Figure 9.1: Vicky Pollard, stereotyping 'fecklessness'

When I think back to the English riots of 2011, in my mind's eye I see David Cameron, on his reluctant return from holiday, summoned back because 'London's burning'. The riots quickly spread to other English cities, but didn't spread to Scotland, Wales or Ireland, North or South. Cameron had a look of Thatcher about him, thumping the table with grim determination, "This is criminality, pure and simple!" He was talking about gang membership, and called for punishment by imprisonment for the participants in the riots, with their families thrown out of their council housing. Not once did he ask whatever would cause our young people to behave like this.

The Archbishop of Canterbury at the time, Rowan Williams (it's important to look at who is speaking out, who are the dissenting voices), said that if something is not done to create decent lives for our young people, we can expect more riots. UNICEF suggested that this criminalisation of our children and young people was a likely breach of international law on children's rights, according to the UN Convention on the Rights of the Child 1989. *The Guardian*, in partnership with the LSE, conducted a survey into 'What prompted civil unrest?' (Lewis et al, 2011). They interviewed 270 participants from the major cities involved in the riots, and the results revealed that few of them had any involvement in gang membership, that the key factors were poverty, police attitudes, government policies and unemployment, all triggered by the police killing of Mark Duggan. At the same time as all this was going on, youth unemployment reached one million in the UK. We must set the evidence against the theory, and then develop the action.

In conclusion, we have to get critical. Neoliberalism is a corrupt system that privileges the already privileged. It creates a politics of disposability. The problem is the rich, *not* the poor: we have to lower the ceiling and *not* raise the floor. The future, as Wilkinson and Pickett emphasise in *The spirit level*, is community, *not* profit. We need theories of power in order to see critically, to awaken a sense of injustice and to act critically. Community development urgently needs a critical living praxis, a unity of theory and practice. I leave you with the suggestion that emancipatory action research could offer us a structure for developing theory in action, a critical living praxis with social justice and sustainability at its heart.

The spirit level

Wilkinson and Pickett (2010) made a huge impact on people's thinking when they published *The spirit level*, with the message that our quality of life is no longer dependent on further economic growth: it is about community and the way that we relate to each other. They argue that inequality is toxic, destroying trust, making people anxious and ill, and encouraging greed. They demonstrate how physical health, mental health, drug abuse, education, imprisonment, obesity, social mobility, trust and quality of community life, violence, teenage pregnancies and child wellbeing are much worse in unequal rich countries.

Wilkinson and Pickett emphasise the vital importance of social relationships to human health and wellbeing, and show that higher levels of income inequality damage the social fabric that contributes so much to healthy societies. They provide evidence from almost 150 studies that support this.

Their argument is that small government and market fundamentalism is the opposite of the truth. Inequality increases the need for big government, maintaining a public sector that provides for more police, more prisons, more health and social services to deal with the problems created by poverty. Ironically, the best way of achieving small government is to reduce inequality, and this could be done with low taxation if there were smaller gross earning differences.

Inequality is a threat to democracy. Greater inequality increases corruption in government and society. Trust, both in people and in government, is weakened and reduces the strength of community life. Poor people cannot afford decent housing as the rich divert resources to the consumption of luxuries.

As well as these more general effects of large income differences, there is now evidence that inequality played a central causal role in the financial crashes of 1929 and of 2008. These crashes both happened at the two peaks of inequality in the past hundred years after long periods of widening social divisions that led to rapid increases in debt. At the same time as the rich had escalating wealth, the less wealthy found it difficult to maintain their incomes. Rising house prices tempted people to invest in property. The bubble grew bigger and bigger, until it burst, with disastrous effects for the poorest.

Ironically, research shows that 90 per cent of Americans would prefer to live in a society like Sweden, where income differentials are more equal. British people, even though they hugely underestimate income differences, also think that income differences should be smaller. This suggests that more people want a just and fair world than is obvious in the media. Wilkinson and Pickett call for renewed action for equality based on this evidence, but suggest that because few people are aware of the scale of inequality and injustice, let alone the damage it does to everyone, education is the first port of call to change public consciousness.

Power of the powerless

Individualism, a key component of neoliberalism, is an idea that has promoted greed, created unsustainable inequalities, eroded trust, weakened community and threatened democracy. This disconnection from the whole has undermined a commitment to a common good and a healthy planet. Community development involves social change through collective action, so read this section on the 'power of the powerless' in this respect. Freire insisted that empowerment is not an individual experience; it is collective. The process of community development recognises the need to create the context for change on a personal and project level, but that the process must be extended into wider collective action for a social justice outcome. We cannot change the root causes of discrimination unless we act collectively!

The power of the powerless is the title of a discussion paper written in 1978 by Václav Havel, the Czech playwright and political dissident. He considers how punitive regimes can create dissidents of ordinary citizens, and looks at ideas for action by individuals linked by a common cause.

Powerlessness has to 'begin with an examination of the nature of power in the circumstances in which these powerless people operate' (Havel, 1978, quoted in Keane, 1985).

> ### Pause for thought ... the importance of ideas to action
>
> Zbygniew Bujak, a Solidarity activist, said that Havel's essay had a massive impact on collective action in the Ursus factory:
>
> > This essay reached us in 1979 at a point when we felt we were at the end of the road. Inspired by KOR [the Polish Workers' Defence Committee], we had been speaking on the shop floor, talking to people, participating in public meetings, trying to speak the truth about the factory, the country, and politics. There came a moment when people thought we were crazy. Why were we doing this? Why were we taking such risks? Not seeing any immediate and tangible results, we began to doubt the purposefulness of what we were doing. Shouldn't we be coming up with other methods, other ways? Then came the essay by Havel. Reading it gave us the theoretical underpinnings for our activity. It maintained our spirits; we did not give up, and a year later – in August 1980 – it became clear that the party apparatus and the factory management were afraid of us. We mattered. And the rank and file saw us as leaders of the movement. When I look at the victories of Solidarity, and of Charter 77, I see in them an astonishing fulfillment of the prophecies and knowledge contained in Havel's essay (1978).
>
> (Zbygniew Bujak, quoted on Vaclav Havel's website, http://www.vaclavhavel.cz/)

After the launch of Charter 77, a human rights petition from Czechoslovakian writers and intellectuals to their communist government, *The power of the powerless* was published. Similar to Freire and Gramsci, Havel was put under continuous surveillance, weekly interrogation, and then imprisoned from 1979 until February 1983. As with Freire and Gramsci, we must ask ourselves why encouraging people to think for themselves weakens power, yet deepens democracy.

The Occupy movement

The Occupy movement is an ongoing international action against global social and economic inequalities. It is part of the global justice movement, and bears testament to the power of 'transformation by Twitter'! Social media has changed the nature of collective action, demonstrating its immediacy and its collective strength. The Occupy slogan became 'We are the 99%' to expose neoliberal systems that unjustly reward the richest one per cent at the expense of the rest, creating a global super-rich.

Inspired by the Arab Spring, Occupy started in Kuala Lumpur in July 2011. However, the first Occupy protest widely covered by the world's media was Occupy Wall Street in New York on 17 September 2011. Within three weeks, Occupy protests had taken place in over 95 cities across 82 countries, and in the US, occupied 600 communities. By 1 December, there were 2,686 Occupy communities worldwide. Occupy Edinburgh was even given official sanction

Figure 9.2: The Occupy movement slogan

WE
ARE THE
99%
THAT WII NO LONGER TOLERATE
the GREED and CORRUPTION of the
1%

by the city council. The movement was described as a 'democratic awakening' by Cornel West, activist and Princeton University professor, in the *Occupied Wall Street Journal* on 18 November 2011:

> We the people of the global Occupy movement embody and enact a deep democratic awakening with genuine joy and fierce determination. Our movement – leaderless and leaderful – is a soulful expression of a moral outrage at the ugly corporate greed that pushes our society and world to the brink of catastrophe. We are aware that our actions have inaugurated a radical enlightenment in a moment of undeniable distrust and disgust with oligarchic economies, corrupt politicians, arbitrary rule of law and corporate media weapons of mass distraction. And we intend to sustain our momentum by nurturing our bonds of trust, fortifying our bodies, hearts and minds and sticking together through hell or high water in order to create a better world through a deep democratic revolution.
>
> We refuse to be mere echoes of the vicious lies that support an illegitimate status quo. Our deep democratic awakening takes the form of we everyday people raising our individual and collective voices to tell the painful truths about unjust systems and unfair structures that yield unnecessary social misery. (West, 2011)

Cornel West can be seen, in Gramscian terms, as a *traditional intellectual*, a catalyst for critical consciousness and action for change.

Figure 9.3: The Occupy movement outside St Paul's, London

Source: Marcus Lindstrom

Occupy St Paul's, one of the high-profile Occupy sites, was eventually evicted in February 2012, but not before the Executive Director of Financial Stability at the Bank of England stated that the protesters were right to criticise bankers and politicians, to persuade them 'to behave in a more moral way'.

The Occupy movement is ongoing and active. Natalie Nougayrède, in *The Guardian Weekly*, on Tuesday, 16 December 2014, talks about 2014 as a year when democratic values were fought for and sometimes lost, as a year where the question of *people power versus state hard power* became ever more prominent. Her message is that once people want change, it becomes much harder for politicians to sell the same old stories. Civil societies are standing up to the establishment and demanding accountability, so the process is likely to continue in 2015, as pro-democracy and anti-corruption movements make more use of social media to raise awareness, focusing on a new political conversation that is 'in tune' with a grassroots approach.

In the wake of the English riots in 2011, when the Archbishop of Canterbury warned us to either give our children hope or expect more riots, there were reports about the high levels of anger and despair in young people. A YouGov poll conducted for the Prince's Trust in 2014 found that one in 10 young people in Britain feel they have nothing to live for, which is often expressed as self-loathing and panic attacks over fear for the future. Long-term unemployed young people are over twice as likely to believe they have nothing to live for. On a global scale, it is the younger generation that is bearing the full brunt of the fall-out of the 2008 economic crash and the crisis of world capitalism (Hyland, 2014).

National Community Activists Network

The National Community Activists Network (NatCAN) (http://nationalcan. ning.com) plays a crucial part in electronically providing a public space for creating critical dissent dialogue. It was originally started as a North West England free online interactive forum, which has gone national, even international, connecting local/regional groups, such as Bren Cook's UCLAN Freire Institute Facilitator Programme, to anyone involved in the business of trying to bring about social change. There is no constitution; there are no funding constraints and no distance problems in connecting people. As with the Occupy movement, in an age of privatisation of public spaces and distance limitations on face-to-face dialogue, the concept of critical public spaces is moving into virtual reality, exploring the internet and social media's role in new ways of organising collectively.

Joe Taylor, an activist in NatCAN, plays a key role in keeping community development critical by posting new ideas and events on the NatCAN website. He often offers visitors to the website a précis of new books, inviting them to discuss the relevance of the ideas to action by joining a webinar. This gives community workers the opportunity to come together in critical debate for action and reflection in virtual reality. On 25 October 2014, he posted, 'If I had to pick just one book that every activist should read it would be this book from Naomi Klein. [Read my extracts] and consider getting the book then trying your best to persuade as many people as you can to do the same.' He was talking about Naomi Klein's *This changes everything: Capitalism vs The Climate*. Here is an introduction to some of her key points. They weave together social justice and environmental justice in ways that help to make sense of the interconnection between fairness and sustainability.

> Faced with a crisis that threatens our survival as a species, our entire culture is continuing to do the very thing that caused the crisis, only with an extra dose of elbow grease behind it.... Living with this kind of cognitive dissonance is simply part of being alive in this jarring moment in history, when a crisis we have been studiously ignoring is hitting us in the face – and yet we are doubling down on the stuff that is causing the crisis in the first place.... Climate change has never received the crisis treatment from our leaders, despite the fact that it carries the risk of destroying lives on a vastly greater scale than collapsed banks or collapsed buildings. But we need not be spectators in all this: politicians aren't the only one with the power to declare a crisis. Mass movements of regular people can declare one too.... Slavery wasn't a crisis for British and American elites until abolitionism turned it into one. Racial discrimination wasn't a crisis until the civil rights movement turned it into one. Sex discrimination wasn't a crisis until feminism turned it into one. Apartheid wasn't a crisis until the anti-apartheid movement turned it into one. In the very same way, if

enough of us stop looking away and decide that climate change is a crisis worthy of Marshall Plan levels of response, then it will become one, and the political class will have to respond, both by making resources available and by bending the free market rules that have proven so pliable when elite interests are in peril. ... (Klein, 2014, p 2)

As part of the project of getting our emissions down to the levels many scientists recommend, we once again have the chance to advance policies that dramatically improve lives, close the gap between rich and poor, create huge numbers of good jobs, and reinvigorate democracy from the ground up.... (Klein, 2014, p 10)

For any of this to change, a worldview will need to rise to the fore that sees nature, other nations, and our own neighbours not as adversaries, but rather as partners in a grand project of mutual reinvention.... (Klein, 2014, p 23)

The overriding principle must be to address the twin crises of inequality and climate change at the same time. Put another way, only mass social movements can save us now. (Klein, 2014, p 406)

Pause for thought...

Visit the NatCAN website and explore the possibility of using it as public space for creating critical dissent dialogue.

Reflect on the ideas in the above extract from Naomi Klein's book. What makes sense in your own experience and your practice? How do you see the links between social justice and environmental justice? What implications does this have for your practice?

Create a dialogue group or join a webinar on NatCAN to take these ideas deeper as part of an evolving critical praxis.

The right to dissent

In 1984, the Thatcher government, putting its neoliberal project into action, declared war on Britain's unions, taking on the National Union of Mineworkers (NUM), the strongest union in the country. Government announcements of pit closures threatened not only one of Britain's largest industries, but also communities built around the pitheads to serve the interest of the industry for generations. The justification was that coal mining was no longer economic, yet evidence later emerged that the Thatcher government and its intelligence had plotted behind closed doors to destroy the NUM as part of a much bigger secret war against organised labour and political dissent, to dismantle any blocks to the profit-making imperative of neoliberalism.

Against the might of the state, 160,000 coal miners spent the next year in a struggle that changed the course of history. The Miners' Strike attracted support from all over the world, but it was not enough to counter the impact of state hegemonic control at its best. The women of the mining communities took immediate action, to the shock of Margaret Thatcher, who had expected that she could appeal to them to force the miners back to work. Starting off as Miners' Wives, they rose up in support of their families and communities, threatened by starvation tactics. Initially they set up soup kitchens to feed families whose benefits had been cut. Although many of these women had never been outside their mining communities, their outrage at the threat of the government's attack on their families, and their strong, tight-knit culture, gave them the confidence to rise up and give public talks all over the country and abroad, organised as Women Against Pit Closures. 'Never the same again' was their famous quote. Alliances across difference emerged, and at many demonstrations and picket lines coachloads of supporters would swell the numbers. This was the heyday of new social movements, and women, gay and lesbian groups, greens and others stood together, marching the streets in support of the miners, banners raised in solidarity, from 'Liverpool Labour Councillors Support the Miners' to 'Lesbians and Gays Against Pit Closures' and 'The Black Solidarity Group'. Yet the Thatcher government, determined to smash the NUM and the trade union movement as a whole, rolled out the might of the state machine. Hegemony in action: the power of persuasion was asserted through the media, gaining consent by convincing the public at large that the miners were 'the enemy within', undermining the moral fabric of society, threatening democracy. At the same time, riot police trained in violent tactics, using their powers of coercion, brutally attacked miners on picket lines.

The 1984–85 Miners' Strike is seen as one of the greatest examples of collective action in recent history. The British trade union movement was a beacon of hope to workers around the world. Seamus Milne published *The enemy within* in 1994, exposing Margaret Thatcher and her government as the 'real enemy within', out to destroy freedom and democracy by employing the secret services of the British state to go to astonishing lengths to destroy the NUM's power. The Miners' Strike had an enormous impact on British culture: the country, battered by the force of harsh neoliberal policies, was divided by the stories told by this powerful dominant hegemony. When I was in Nicaragua in 1985, we were taken to meet a senior army officer involved in defending the country's borders to support their participatory democracy against attacks supported by the US. To my surprise, he told us that his impoverished country had, in solidarity, sent money to support the British miners' struggle, and then asked, "How has their cause been used to deepen democracy for the people?".

Theory in action 9: Political dissent, collective action and deepening democracy

Issue

Collective action is the stage of community development that leads to a social justice outcome. Deepening democracy through critique and dissent are necessary components of analysing hegemonic power and what action is needed to bring about transformative change. We are living in times of advanced individualism in which power has actively dismantled critique, dissent and collective protest in order to give free rein to profit.

Evidence

Deepen your understanding of collective action, alliance and the power of hegemony by watching *Still the Enemy Within*, 2014 (directed by Owen Gower). It is a documentary that gives voice to miners involved in the struggle set against archive material of the Miners' Strike 1984–85. A powerful testament of the cost to families and communities who took on the full might of the state for a year of their lives, it offers a retrospective analysis. Personal stories and political critiques give insight into one of British history's biggest political struggles against dominant hegemony, looking at the past to understand the present, in order to do something about the future.

Analysis

Critique the section on the Battle of Orgreave, in which Margaret Thatcher refers to 'the rule of mob versus rule of law', with attention to the concept of 'criminality' and how it is used. 'They are breaking the law and have got to be prevented' versus 'Not one single miner was found guilty of anything'.

On alliances: listen to the interview with the representative of 'Lesbians and Gays Support the Miners', paying particular attention to the power of alliance between those united in struggle.

On solidarity and collective action: listen to the section on the Trades Union Congress (TUC) refusal to negotiate a 24-hour general strike, paying attention to the key fractures to collective action.

Towards the end of the film, listen to the Nottinghamshire miner who says, "We should have listened to Arthur." Find evidence of why he says that. What are some of the facts that support his testimony?

At the end of the film, the consequences of government action are highlighted. In 2014, official evidence was released that revealed the truth about the government's tactics against the miners. Think about this evidence: how does it influence the way you see the Miners' Strike?

Action

In the film, listen to the miners who say, "Even though the state's against you, you can fight back", "We might have lost the battle, but we haven't lost the war", "If we'd won, this would have definitely been a better world for everybody", and the woman from Women Against Pit Closures who says: "Other parts of the country didn't realise that the police and the government were breaking the law". Discuss in your dialogue group how this is relevant to practice. How does this add to a theoretical toolkit for your *critical praxis*? How does it help you to plan collective action in your own practice?

Staying critical

Critical living praxis involves not only a unity of thinking and doing, but keeping the ideas relevant to the changing political context in order to inform action that is capable of change. Education is fundamental to democracy, and a just society needs citizens who are critical, self-reflective, knowledgeable, discerning and courageous enough to speak truth to power and to act for change. Freirean critical pedagogy is a process of co-creating new knowledge from lived experience as active participants in deepening democracy. Today we are faced with a much bigger democratic challenge, as global markets govern not only people but also nation states. In this sense, the global context is now the platform for democracy, meeting our responsibility for the plight of others everywhere, recognising the interdependence and interconnectedness of people and the planet. This calls for new understanding of power, of local–global connections, and new ways of organising collective action sufficiently powerful to counter dominant global profit-making interests. Theory, in this respect, is not only an ability to analyse and understand the current global crises of social justice and sustainability, but also the ability to imagine and to create an intervention in a world that is careering out of control. More critical knowledge imagines more effective forms of intervention. Gramsci's insight into the role of organic and traditional intellectuals is one we have to claim in relation to knowledge creation, respecting that everybody is an intellectual with the ability to be self-critical, to connect knowledge to the world in a critical way, and to act as part of a bigger struggle for democracy and justice (Giroux, 2013b). At this current historical conjuncture, we need to nurture a culture of questioning in which critique generates hope, critical consciousness generates passion, and imagination forges action for justice and democracy.

Zibechi (2010, p 11) identifies that 'societies in movement expose social fault lines, which are uncovered as society shifts away from its previous location'. This creates democratic spaces within which to create critical dissent dialogue and build counternarratives for justice, bringing the margins of life alive as 'epistemological moments' reveal new possibilities.

Here is a final word from Paulo Freire:

> [T]he more radical the person is, the more fully he or she enters into reality so that, knowing it better, he or she can transform it. This individual is not afraid to confront, to listen, to see the world unveiled. This person is not afraid to meet the people or to enter into a dialogue with them. This person does not consider himself or herself the proprietor of history or of all people, or the liberator of the oppressed; but he or she does commit himself or herself, within history, to fight at their side. (Freire, 1972, p 2)

But my concluding challenge comes from Naomi Klein:

> "History knocked on your door, did you answer?" That's a good question, for all of us. (Klein, 2015, p 466)

Painel Paulo Freire, detalhe, by Luiz Carlos Cappellano, published under the Creative Commons Attribution-Share Alike 3.0 Unported licence.

References

Abdallah, S., Michaelson, J., Shah, S., Stoll, L. and Marks, N. (2012) *The Happy Planet Index: 2012 report*, London: New Economics Foundation.

Alinsky, S (1969) *Reveille for radicals*, New York: Vintage Press.

Alinsky, S (1972) *Rules for radicals*, New York: Vintage Press.

Allman, P. and Wallis, J. (1997) 'Commentary: Paulo Freire and the future of the radical tradition', *Studies in the Education of Adults*, vol 29, pp 113-20.

Anthias, F. and Yuval-Davis, N. (1992) *Racialised boundaries; Race, nation, gender, colour and class and the anti-racist struggle*, London: Routledge.

Belenky, M., Clinchy, B., Goldberger, N. and Tarule, B. (eds) (1986) *Women's ways of knowing*, New York: Basic Books.

Belenky, M., Clinchy, B., Goldberger, N. and Tarule, J. (eds) (1997) *Women's ways of knowing: The development of self, voice and mind* (2nd edn), New York: Basic Books.

Bhavani, R., Mirza, H.S. and Meetoo, V. (2005) *Tackling the roots of racism*, Bristol: Policy Press.

Blewitt, J. (2008) *Community, empowerment and sustainable development*, Totnes: Green Books.

Boal, A. (2008) *Theatre of the oppressed* (new edn), London: Pluto.

Bowers, C.A. and Apffel-Marglin, F. (eds) (2004) *Re-thinking Freire: Globalization and the environmental crisis*, Mahwah, NJ: Lawrence Erlbaum Associates.

Brookfield, S. and Holst, J. (2011) *Radicalised learning: Adult education for a just world*, San Francisco, CA: John Wiley & Sons.

Brown, G. (2000) 'Our children are our future', Speech by Gordon Brown, Chancellor of the Exchequer, to Child Poverty Action Group conference, 15 May, London.

Burns, D. (2007) *Systemic action research: A strategy for whole systems change*, Bristol: Policy Press.

Cahill, C., Moore, I.R. and Threatts, T. (2008) 'Different eyes/open eyes', in J. Cammarota and M. Fine (eds) *Revolutionizing education: Youth participatory action research in motion*, New York: Routledge, pp 89-124.

Calouste Gulbenkian Foundation (1968) *Community work and social change: A report on training*, London: Longman.

Cameron, D. (2011) Debate on public disorder, House of Commons, 11 August (www.publications.parliament.uk/pa/cm201011/cmhansrd/cm110811/debtext/110811-0001.htm).

Chomsky, N. (2013) 'Pedagogy of the oppressed: Noam Chomsky, Howard Gardner and Bruno della Chiesa Askwith Forum' (www.chomsky.info/audionvideo.htm).

Chomsky, N. (2015) 'Noam Chomsky on Scottish independence', National Community Activists Network (http://nationalcan.ning.com/video/noam-chomsky-on-scottish-independence).

Commission on Social Justice (1994) *Social justice: Strategies for national renewal*, London: Verso.

Coote, A. (2015) *People, planet, power: Towards a new social settlement* (www. neweconomics.org).

Craig, G. (2008) 'The limits of compromise? Social justice, "race" and multiculturalism', in G. Craig, T. Burchardt and D. Gordon (eds) *Social justice and public policy: Seeking fairness in diverse societies*, Bristol: Policy Press, pp 231-50.

Craig, G., Derricourt, N. and Loney, M. (eds) (1982) *Community work and the state: Towards a radical approach*, London: Routledge & Kegan Paul.

Craig, G., Atkin, K., Chattoo, S. and Flynn, R. (2012) *Understanding 'race' and ethnicity: Theory, history, policy, practice*, Bristol: Policy Press.

Dale, J. (2011) 'Economic justice and the sustainable global society', Quakers in Britain, 24 September (www.quaker.org.uk/transcript-presentation-jonathan-dale).

Danaher, G., Schirato, T. and Webb, J. (2000) *Understanding Foucault*, London: Sage.

Darder, A (2002) *Reinventing Paulo Freire: A pedagogy of love*, Boulder CO: Westview.

Darder, A. (2009) 'Teaching as an act of love: reflections on Paulo Freire and his contributions to or lives and our work', in A. Darder, M.P. Boltodano and R.D. Torres (eds) *The critical pedagogy reader* (2nd edn), Abingdon: Routledge, pp 567-78.

Darder, A., Baltodano, M.P. and Torres, R.D. (eds) (2009) *The critical pedagogy reader* (2nd edn), Abingdon: Routledge.

Davidson, A. (1977) *Antonio Gramsci: Towards an intellectual biography*, London: Merlin Press.

Davison, S. (2011) 'What Antonio Gramsci offers to social democracy', Policy Network, 10 October (www.policy-network.net/pno_detailaspx?ID=4064&title=+What+Antonio+Gramsci+offers+to+social+democracy).

de Beauvoir, S. (1949) *Le deuxieme sexe* [*The second sex*] (trs C. Borde and S. Malovany-Chevalier), Paris: Gallimard.

Deacon, B. and Yeates, N. (2011) 'Radicalising social policy in the 21st century: a global approach', in A. Walker. A. Sinfield and C. Walker, *Fighting poverty, inequality and injustice: A manifesto inspired by Peter Townsend*, Bristol: Policy Press, pp 257-74.

Dixson, A.D., Rousseau, C.K. and Donnor, J.K. (eds) (2005) *Critical race theory in education: All God's children got a song*, Abingdon: Routledge.

Dorling, D. (2007) 'A think-piece for the Commission on Integration and Cohesion', June, Wetherby: HMSO.

Duncan Smith, I. (2013) Speech by the Rt Hon Iain Duncan Smith MP, Kids Company, 31 January (www.gov.uk/government/speeches/kids-company).

Dworkin, A. (1981) *Pornography: Men possessing women*, London: The Women's Press Ltd.

Dworkin, A. (1987) *Intercourse*, New York: Basic Books.

Fanon, F. (2004) *Wretched of the earth*, London: Penguin.

Fanon, F. (2008) *Black skin, White masks*, London: Pluto Press.

Fenn, C. and Owen, P. (2011) 'Rioters in their own words', *The Guardian*, 5 December.

Fine, M. (2008) 'An epilogue of sorts', in J. Cammarota and M. Fine (eds) *Revolutionizing education: Youth participatory action research in motion*, New York: Routledge, pp 213-34.

Fisher, W.F. and Ponniah, T. (2003) *Another world is possible: Popular alternatives to globalization at the World Social Forum*, London: Zed Books.

Forgacs, D. (ed) (1988) *A Gramsci reader*, London: Lawrence & Wishart.

Foucault, M. (1980) *Power/knowledge: Selected interviews and other writings*, Brighton: Harvester Wheatsheaf.

Foucault, M. (2008) *The birth of biopolitics*, New York: Palgrave Macmillan.

Freire, N. (2014) Keynote to 'Paulo Freire and Transformative Education: changing lives and transforming communities' Conference, University of Central Lancashire, April.

Freire, N. and Macedo, D. (eds) (1998) *The Paulo Freire reader*, New York: Continuum.

Freire, N. and de Oliveira, W. (2014) *Pedagogy of solidarity*, Walnut Creek, CA: Left Coast Press.

Freire, P (1965) *Education: The practice of freedom*, Danbury CT: Writers and Readers.

Freire, P. (1972) *Pedagogy of the oppressed*, Harmondsworth: Penguin.

Freire, P. (1985) *Politics of education: Culture, power and liberation*, London: Macmillan.

Freire, P. (1993) *Pedagogy of the city* (trs D. Macedo), New York: Continuum.

Freire, P. (1997) *Pedagogy of the heart*, New York: Continuum.

Freire, P. (2001) *Pedagogy of freedom: Ethics, democracy and civic courage*, Oxford and Lanham, MD: Rowman & Littlefield.

Freire, P. (2005) *Education for critical consciousness*, London: Continuum.

Freire, P (2005a) *Pedagogy of indignation*, Boulder CO: Paradigm Publishers.

Freire, P. and Macedo, D.P. (1995) 'A dialogue: culture, language, and race', *Harvard Educational Review*, vol 65, no 3, pp 377-402.

Friedan, B. (1963) *The feminine mystique*, New York: W.W. Norton & Co.

Gadotti, M. (1994) *Reading Paulo Freire: His life and work*, New York: State University of New York Press.

Gamble, D.N. and Weil, M.O. (1997) 'Sustainable development: the challenge for community development', *Community Development Journal*, vol 32, no 3, July, pp 210-22.

George, S. (1999) 'A short history of neo-liberalism: twenty years of elite economics and emerging opportunities for structural change', Conference on 'Economic sovereignty in a globalising world', Bangkok, 24-26 March.

Gillborn, D. (2008) *Racism and education: Coincidence or conspiracy*, Abingdon: Routledge.

Giroux, H. (2006a) *Stormy weather: Katrina and the politics of disposability*, Boulder, CO: Paradigm Publishers.

Giroux, H. (2006b) 'Katrina and the politics of disposability', *In These Times,* 14 September (www.inthesetimes.com/article/2822).

Giroux, H. (2009) *Youth in a suspect society: Democracy of disposability*, NY: Palgrave Macmillan.

Giroux, H. (2013a) *America's education deficit and the war on youth*, New York: Monthly Review Press.

Giroux, H. (2013b) *On critical pedagogy*, New York: Bloomsbury.

Giroux, H., Lankshear, C., McLaren, P. and Peters, M. (1996) *Counternarratives: Culture studies and critical pedagogies in postmodern spaces*, New York and London: Routledge.

Gough, I., Abdullah, S., Johnson, V., Ryan-Collins, J. and Smith, C. (2011) *The distribution of total greenhouse gas emissions by households in the UK, and some implications for social policy*, London: Centre for Analysis of Social Exclusion, London School of Economics and Political Science.

Graham, M. (2007) *Black issues in social work and social care*, Bristol: Policy Press.

Gramsci, A. (1971) *Selections from the prison notebooks of Antonio Gramsci*, New York: International Publishers.

Gramsci, A. and Togliatti, P. (1919) 'Antonio Gramsci', *L'Ordine Nuovo*, 21 June, vol 1, no 7.

Gregg, P., Waldfogel, J. and Washbrook, E. (2005) *Expenditure patterns post-welfare reform in the UK: Are low-income families starting to catch up?*, CASEpaper, London: Centre for Analysis of Social Exclusion, London School of Economics and Political Science.

Gunn, A (1978) *Habitat: Human settlements in an urban age*, Oxford: Pergamon.

Habermas, J. (1989) *The structural transformation of the public sphere: An inquiry into a category of bourgeois society*, Cambridge: Polity Press.

Harkness, S., Gregg, P. and Macmillan, L. (2012) *Poverty, the role of institutions, behaviours and culture*, York: Joseph Rowntree Foundation.

Havel, V. (1978) *The power of the powerless* (translated by Paul Wilson), London: Hutchinson (http://vaclavhavel.cz/showtrans.php?cat=eseje&val=2_aj_eseje.html&typ=HTML).

Hill, D. (ed) (2000) *Education, education, education: Capitalism, socialism and 'The Third Way'*, London: Cassell.

Hill Collins, P. (1990) *Black feminist thought: Knowledge, consciousness, and the politics of empowerment*, Boston, MA: Unwin Hyman.

HM Government (2012) *Measuring child poverty: A consultation on better measures of child poverty*, November, London: The Stationery Office (https://www.gov.uk/government/uploads/system/uploads/attachment_data/file/228829/8483.pdf).

Holman, B. (2012) 'Why I rejected my MBE', *The Guardian*, 4 June.

Holst, J. (2006) 'Paulo Freire in Chile, 1964-1969: *Pedagogy of the oppressed* in its sociopolitical economic context', *Harvard Educational Review*, vol 76, no 2, Summer, pp 243-70.

hooks, b. (1989) *Talking back: Thinking feminist, thinking black*, Boston, MA: South End Press.

hooks, b. (1993) 'bell hooks speaking about Paulo Freire – the man, his work', in P. McLaren and P. Leonard (eds) *Paulo Freire: A critical encounter*, London: Routledge, pp 146-54.

hooks, b. (2015) *Yearning: Race, gender and cultural politics*, London: Routledge.

Hope, A. and Timmel, S. (1999) *Training for transformation: A handbook for community workers*, Book 4, London: ITDG Publishing.

Hope, A. and Timmel, S. with Hodzi, C (1984) *Training for transformation: A handbook for community workers*, Books 1-3, Gweru, Zimbabwe: Mambo Press.

Horton, M and Freire, P (1990) *We make the road by walking: Conversations on education and social change*, Philadelphia: Temple University Press.

Hyland, J. (2014) 'Surveys of British youth find growing anger and despair', World Socialist Web Site, 8 January (www.wsws.org/en/articles/2014/01/08/yout-j08.html).

InvestmentWatch (2013) 'The richest 300 people on earth have as much wealth as the poorest 3 billion', 21 July (http://investmentwatchblog.com/the-richest-300-people-on-earth-have-as-much-wealth-as-the-poorest-3-billion).

Irwin, J. (2012) *Paulo Freire's philosophy of education: Origins, developments, impacts and legacies*, London: Continuum.

Jones, O. (2011) *Chavs: The demonization of the working class*, London: Verso.

Keane, J. (ed) (1985) *The power of the powerless: Citizens against the state in Central-Eastern Europe* (translated by Paul Wilson), London: Hutchinson.

Kemmis, S. (2006) 'Participatory action research and the public sphere', *Educational Action Research*, vol 14, no 4, pp 459-76.

Kemmis, S. (2010) 'What is to be done? The place of action research', *Educational Action Research*, vol 18, no 10, pp 417-27.

Killeen, D. (2008) *Is poverty in the UK a denial of people's human rights?*, York: Joseph Rowntree Foundation.

Klein, N. (2015) *This changes everything: Capitalism vs The Climate*, London: Allen Lane.

Kothari, U. (2001) 'Power, knowledge and social control in participatory development', in B. Cooke and U. Kothari (eds) *Participation: The new tyranny*, London: Zed Books, pp 139-52.

Ladson-Billings, G. and Tate, IV, W.F. (2006) 'Toward a critical race theory of education', in H. Lauder, P. Brown, J. Dillabough and A.H. Halsey (eds) *Education, globalization and social change*, Oxford: Oxford University Press, pp 570-85.

Lansley, S. (2013) 'Poverty minus a pound: how the poverty consensus unravelled', *Poverty: Journal of the Child Poverty Action Group*, issue 145, Summer, pp 14-17.

Lawlor, E., Spratt, S., Shaheen, F. and Beitler, D. (2011) *Why the rich are getting richer: The determinants of economic inequality*, London: New Economics Foundation.

Lawrence, P. (2012) '"Race", education and children's policy', in G. Craig, K. Atkin, S. Chattoo and R. Flynn (eds) (2012) *Understanding 'race' and ethnicity: Theory, history, policy, practice*, Bristol: Policy Press, pp 151-66.

Layard, R. (2005) *Happiness: Lessons from a new science*, London: Penguin.

Layard, R. and Dunn, J. (2009) *A good childhood: Searching for values in a competitive age*, London: Penguin.

Learning for Democracy Group (2008) *Learning for democracy: Ten propositions and ten proposals* (www.ict-21.ch/l4d/mod/file/download.php?file_guid=484487).

Ledwith, M. (2011) *Community development: A critical approach*, Bristol: Policy Press.

Lewis, P., Newburn, T. and Roberts, D. (2011) *Reading the riots: Investigating England's summer of disorder*, London: *The Guardian*/London School of Economics and Political Science.

Mackie, R. (1980) 'Contributions to the thought of Paulo Freire', in R. Mackie (ed) *Literacy and revolution: The pedagogy of Paulo Freire*, London: Pluto Press, pp 93-119.

Macrine, S.L. (ed) (2009) *Critical pedagogy in uncertain times: Hope and possibilities*, New York: Palgrave Macmillan.

McCormack, C. (2009) *The wee yellow butterfly*, Glendaruel: Argyll.

McIntosh, P. (2004) 'White privilege: unpacking the invisible knapsack', in M. Andersen and P. Hill-Collins (eds) *Race, class and gender: An anthology*, Belmont, CA: Wadsworth Publishing.

McLaren, P. (2009) 'Critical pedagogy: a look at the major concepts', in A. Darder, M.P. Baltodano and R.D. Torres (eds) *The critical pedagogy reader* (2nd edn), Abingdon: Routledge, pp 61-83.

McLaren, P. and Leonard, P. (1993) *Paulo Freire: A critical encounter*, London: Routledge.

McNiff, J. (2012) 'Travels round identity: transforming cultures of learned colonisation', *Educational Action Research*, vol 20, no 1, pp 129-46.

Marshall, J. (2001) 'Self-reflective inquiry practices', in P. Reason and H. Bradbury (eds) *Handbook of action research*, London: Sage Publications, pp 433-99.

Martin-Baró, I. (1994) 'The role of the psychologist', in A. Aron and S. Corne (eds) *Writings for a liberation psychology*, Cambridge, MA: Harvard University Press.

Mayo, P. (2004) *Liberating praxis: Freire's legacy for radical education and politics*, Westport, CT: Praeger.

Mayo, P. (2013) *Echoes from Freire for a critically engaged pedagogy*, New York: Bloomsbury.

Milne, S (1994) *The enemy within*, London: Verso

Monroe, J. (2015) '"Breadline Britain", I live in the seventh richest country in the world', *The Huffington Post*, 23 March (www.huffingtonpost.co.uk/jack-monroe/breadline-britain-seventh-richest-country-in-the-world_b_3435314.html).

Morris, C.B. (2008) 'Paulo Freire: community-based arts education', *Journal of Thought*, Spring–Summer.

Murphy, M. (2012) *The Happy Planet Index: 2012 report: A global index of sustainable well-being*, London: NEF (www.happyplanetindex.org)

Nastic, D. (2013) 'Child wellbeing in the UK', *Poverty: Journal of the Child Poverty Action Group*, issue 145, Summer, London: Child Poverty Action Group, pp 9-13.

NEF (New Economics Foundation) (2004) *A well-being manifesto for a flourishing society* (available at www.neweconomics.org/programmes/well-being).

NEF (2015) *Responses to austerity: How groups across the UK are adapting, challenging and imagining alternatives* (www.new economics.org)

Pizzey, E. (1979) *Scream quietly or the neighbours will hear*, Harmondsworth: Penguin.

Popple, K. (1995) *Analysing community work: Its theory and practice*, Buckingham: Open University Press.

Popple, K. (2013) 'The impact of neoliberal economic and social policies: the role of community developement', Keynote to Principles, Policies and Perspectives conference, National University of Ireland, Maynooth, 14 November.

Pratt-Clarke, M.A.E. (2010) *Critical race, feminism and education: A social justice model*, New York: Palgrave Macmillan.

Reason, P. and Bradbury, H. (eds) (2001) *Handbook of action research: Participative inquiry and practice*, London: Sage Publications.

Reason, P. and Rowan, J. (1981) *Human inquiry: A sourcebook of new paradigm research*, New York: Wiley.

Revel, J. and Negri, T. (2011) *The common in revolt, Negri in English*, 14 August, (antonionegriinenglish.wordpress.com/2012/01/30/the-common-in-revolt/).

Ridge, T. (2004) 'Putting children first: addressing the needs and concerns of children who are poor', in P. Dornan (ed) *Ending child poverty by 2020: The first five years*, London: Child Poverty Action Group, pp 4–11.

Rikowski, G. and McLaren, P. (1999) 'Postmodernism in educational theory', in D. Hill, P. McLaren, M. Cole and G. Rikowski (eds) *Postmodernism in educational theory: Education and the politics of human resistance*, London: The Tuffnell Press, pp 1–9.

Riordan, S (2008) 'NGOs: the sine qua non of adapting to climate change in Africa', in J. Blewitt (ed) *Community, empowerment and sustainable development*, Totnes: Green Books, pp 33–58.

Roderick, I. with Jones, N. (2008) 'The converging world', in J. Blewitt (ed) *Community, empowerment and sustainable development*, Totnes: Green Books, pp 17–32.

Rowan, J. (1981) 'Dialectical paradigm for research', in P. Reason and J. Rowan (eds) *Human inquiry: A sourcebook for new paradigm research*, Chichester: Wiley, pp 93–112.

Rowbotham, S. (1973) *Hidden from history: 300 years of women's oppression and the fight against it*, London: Pluto Press.

Royal Society, The (2012) *People and the planet: Summary and recommendations*, April, London: The Royal Society.

Rutter, M. and Madge, N. (1976) *Cycles of disadvantage: A review of research*, London: Heinemann.

Serrant Green, L. (2004) 'Black Caribbean men, sexual decisions and silences', Unpublished PhD, Nottingham: University of Nottingham.

Shaw, M. (2004) *Community work: Policy, politics and practice*, Hull and Edinburgh: Universities of Hull and Edinburgh.

Shor, I. (1992) *Empowering education: Critical teaching for social change*, London and Chicago, IL: University of Chicago Press.

Shor, I. (2000) 'Why education is politics', in I. Shor and C. Pari (eds) *Education is politics: Critical teaching across differences, postsecondary*, Portsmouth NH: Heinemann.

Shor, I. and Freire, P. (1987) *A pedagogy for liberation: Dialogues on transforming education*, London: Bergin and Garvey.

Tandon, R. (2008) 'Participation, citizenship and democracy: reflections on 25 years of PRIA', *Community Development Journal*, vol 43, no 3, pp 284-96.

Taylor, P. (1993) *The texts of Paulo Freire*, Buckingham: Open University Press.

Thomas, D. (1983) *The making of community work*, London: George Allen & Unwin.

Thomas, M. (2015) *100 acts of minor dissent*, London: September Publishing.

Thompson, N. (2006) *Anti-discriminatory practice* (4th edn), Basingstoke: Palgrave Macmillan.

Torres, C.A. (1993) 'From the *Pedagogy of the oppressed* to a luta continua', in P. McLaren and P. Leonard (eds) *Paulo Freire: A critical encounter*, London: Routledge, pp 119-45.

Townsend, P. (1979) *Poverty in the United Kingdom*, London: Allen Lane.

Townsend, P. (1986) 'Foreword: "Democracy for the poor"', in M. McCarthy, *Campaigning for the poor: CPAG and the politics of welfare*, London: Croom Helm.

Townsend, P. (1995) 'Poverty: Home and away', *Poverty*, no 91, Summer.

Townsend, P. (2009) *Building decent societies: Rethinking the role of social security in state building*, Geneva: International Labour Organization/Palgrave Macmillan.

Townsend, P. and Abel-Smith, B. (1965) *The poor and the poorest*, London: G.Bell & Sons.

Toynbee, P. and Walker, D. (2015) *Cameron's coup: How the Tories took Britain to the brink*, London: Guardian Faber Publishing.

Toynbee, P. and Walker, D. (2015a) 'Cameron's five-year legacy: has he finished what Thatcher started?', in *The Guardian*, 28 January.

Tyler, I. (2013) *Revolting subjects: Social abjection and resistance in neoliberal Britain*, London: Zed.

UNICEF (2007) *Child poverty in perspective: An overview of child well-being in rich countries*, Innocenti Report Card 7 (www.unicef.org.uk).

UNICEF (2013) *Child well-being in rich countries: A comparative overview*, Innocenti Report Card 11, Florence: UNICEF Office of Research.

Walker, A., Sinfield, A. and Walker, C. (eds) (2011) *Fighting poverty, inequality and injustice*, Bristol: Policy Press.

Weiler, K. (1994) 'Freire and a feminist pedagogy of difference', in P. McLaren and C. Lankshear (eds) *Politics of liberation: Paths from Freire*, London: Routledge.

West, C. (2011) 'A love supreme', *The Occupied Wall Street Journal*, 18 November (http://occupiedmedia.us/2011/11/a-love-supreme/).

Wilkinson, R. and Pickett, K. (2010) *The spirit level: Why equality is better for everyone*, Harmondsworth: Penguin.

Williams, Z. (2012) 'The Saturday interview: Stuart Hall', *The Guardian*, 11 February.

Williamson, M. (2011) 'Getting our priorities right', Action for Happiness, 12 April (www.actionforhappiness.org/news/getting-our-priorities-right).

Wink, J (2010) *Critical pedagogy: Notes from the real world* (4th edn), New Jersey: Pearson Education.

Wintour, P. (2015) 'Government to scrap child poverty target before tax credits cut', *The Guardian*, 1 July.

Wollstonecraft, M. (1792) *A vindication of the rights of women*, Boston, MA: Thomas and Andrews.

Yeates, N. and Deacon, B. (2011) 'Radicalising social policy in the 21st century: a global approach', in A. Walker. A. Sinfield and C. Walker, *Fighting poverty, inequality and injustice: A Manifesto Inspired by Peter Townsend*, Bristol, Policy Press, pp 257-74.

Young, A. (1990) *Femininity in dissent*, London: Routledge.

Younghusband, E. (1959) *Report of the working party on social workers in the local authority health and welfare services*, London: HMSO.

Zibechi, R. (2010) *Dispersing power: Social movements as anti-state forces*, Oakland, CA: AK Press.

Index

Note: Page numbers in **bold** refer to exercises (theory in action). Page numbers in *italics* indicate figures and page numbers ending in *g* refer to terms in the glossary.

Printed and bound by CPI Group (UK) Ltd, Croydon, CR0 4YY

09/06/2025

14685900-0001